Monsters & Beasts

An Image Archive for Artists & Designers

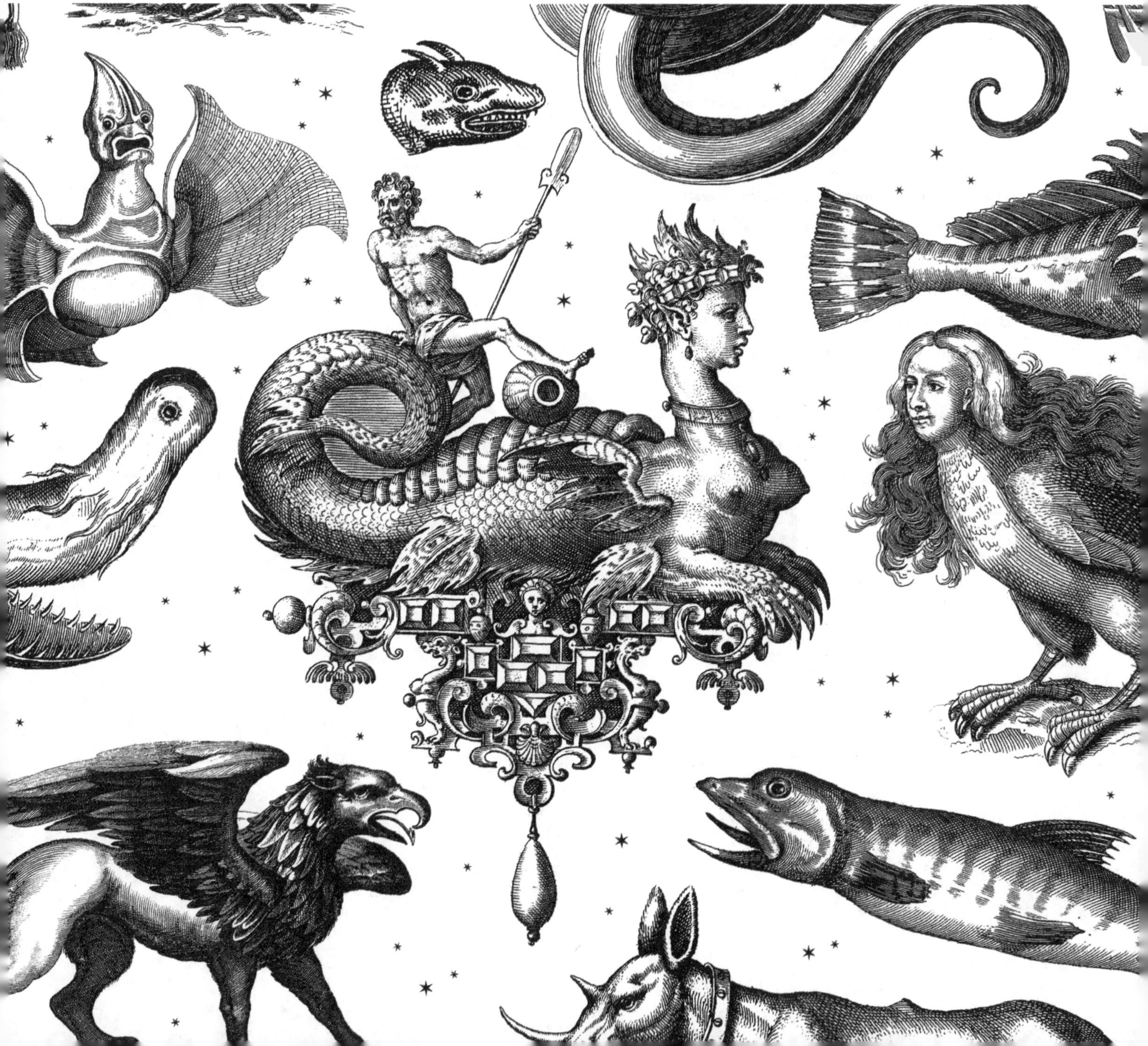

Introduction

This title is one of our most exciting and bizarre releases to date. We have created a comprehensive and diverse pictorial archive of beasts and monster illustrations for the practical use of artists and designers, or to be appreciated by curious minds.

This title features hundreds of exquisitely crafted 17th and 18th-century etchings and engravings of monsters and beasts. This pictorial archive features serpents, animal mutations, sea monsters, dragons, griffins, chimeras, bizarre human mutations and abnormalities, extraordinary fanciful animals and much more.

With the aid of digital image editing technology, we have been able to restore incredibly rare 17th-century artwork into high-resolution images that are now suitable for use in graphic design projects, and many other creative applications.

We hope you enjoy this resource.

MONSTERS AND BEASTS

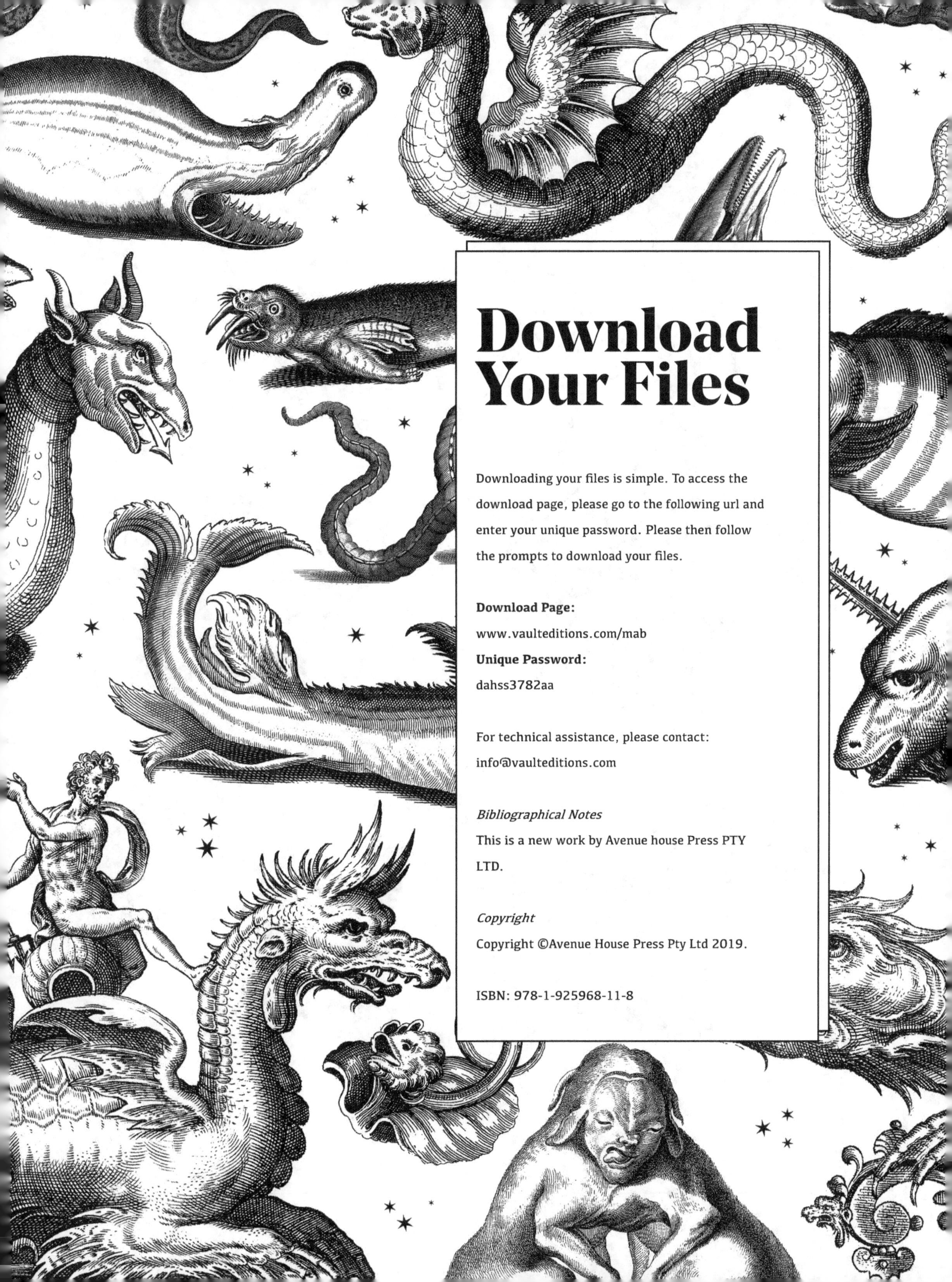

Download Your Files

Downloading your files is simple. To access the download page, please go to the following url and enter your unique password. Please then follow the prompts to download your files.

Download Page:

www.vaulteditions.com/mab

Unique Password:

dahss3782aa

For technical assistance, please contact:

info@vaulteditions.com

Bibliographical Notes

This is a new work by Avenue house Press PTY LTD.

Copyright

Copyright ©Avenue House Press Pty Ltd 2019.

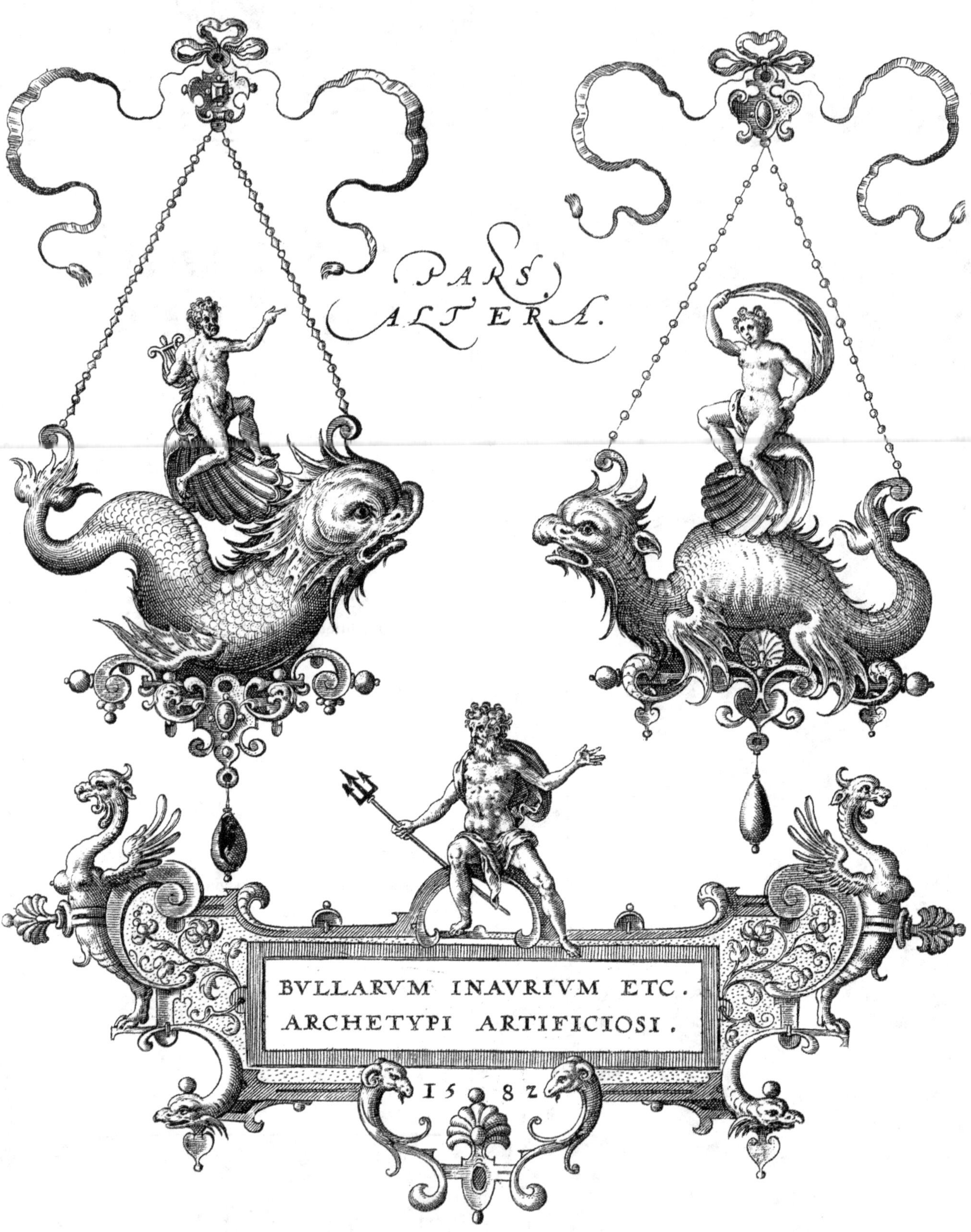
PARS.
ALTERA.

BVLLARVM INAVRIVM ETC.
ARCHETYPI ARTIFICIOSI.

1582

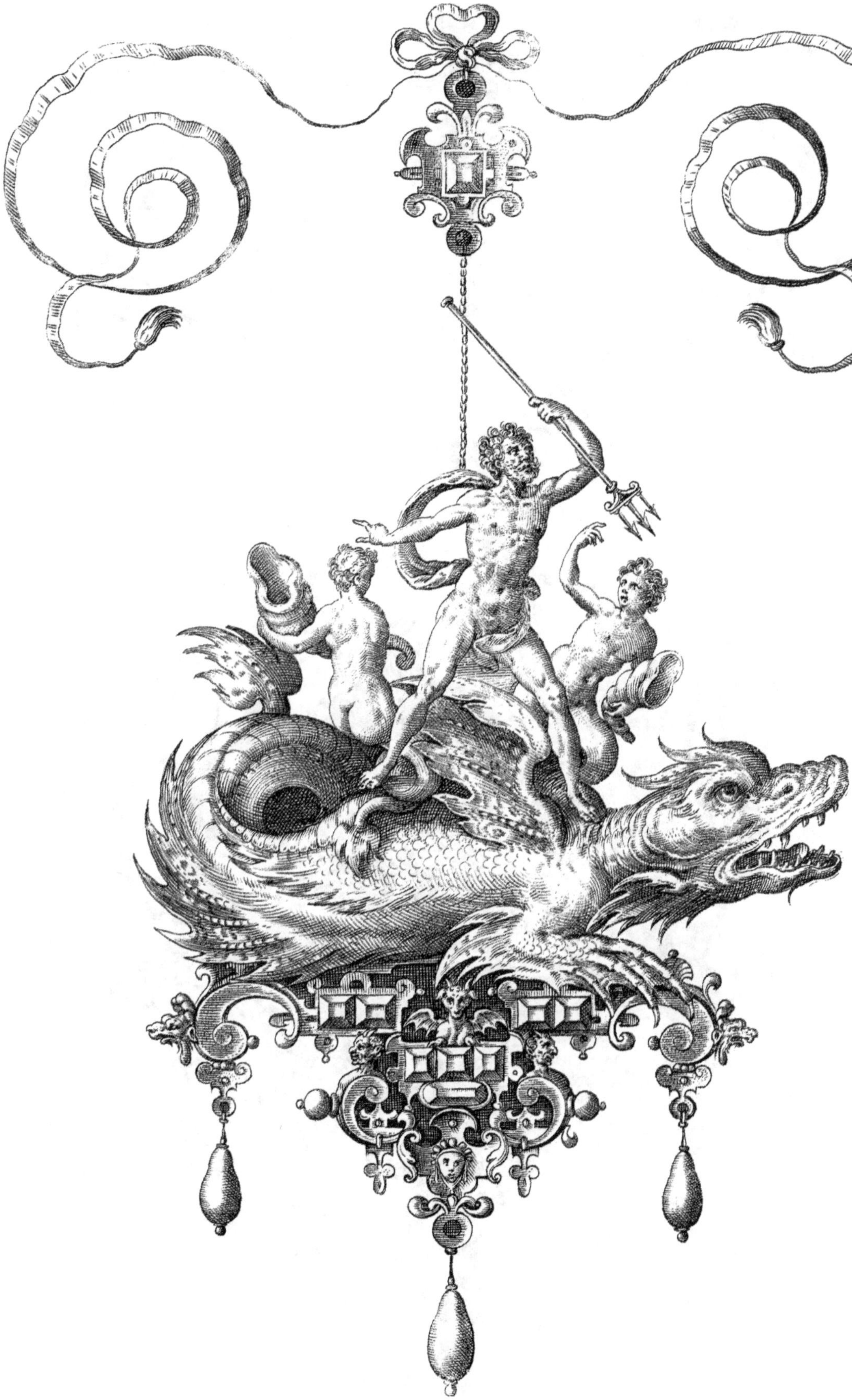

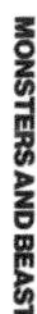

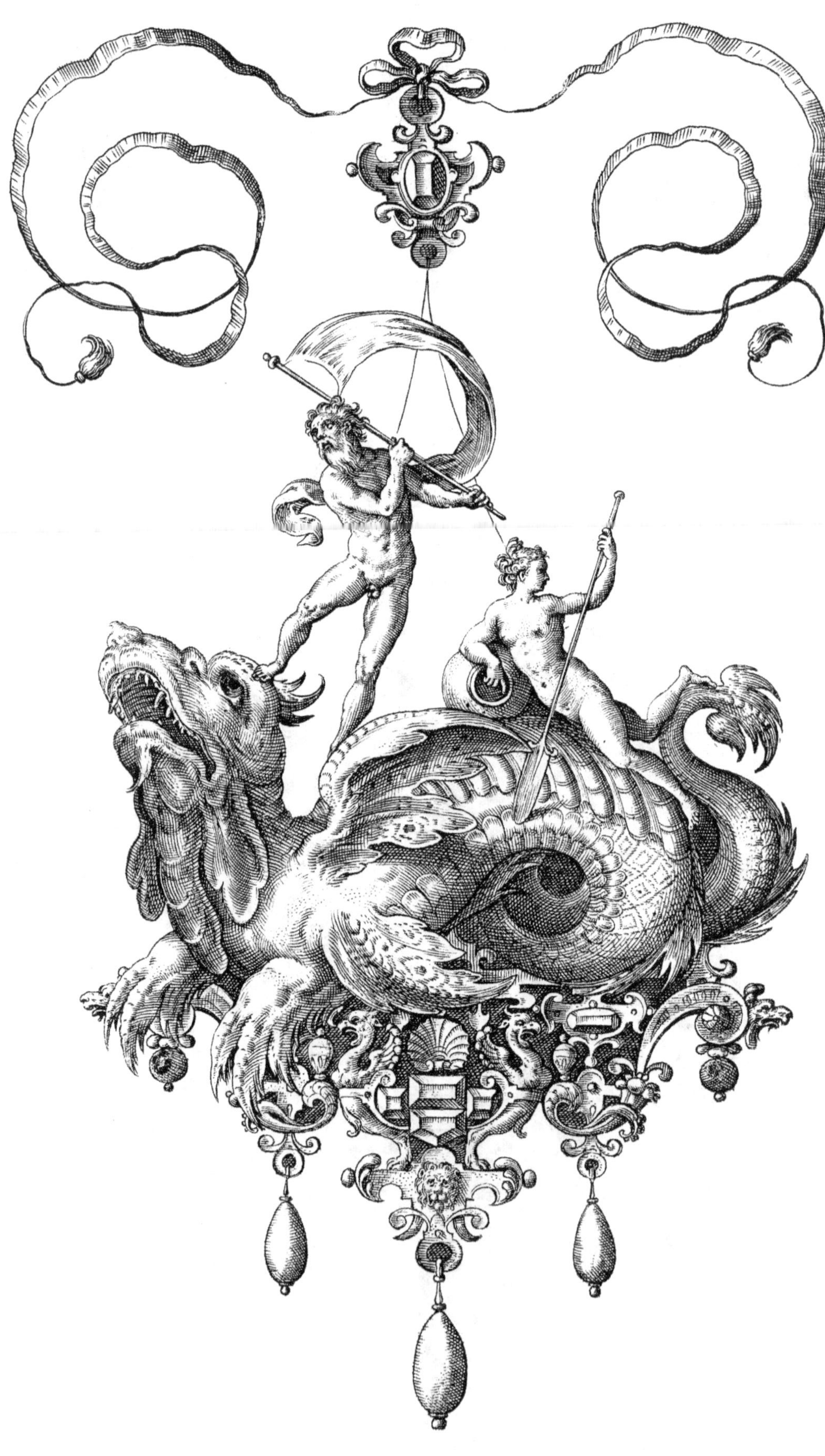

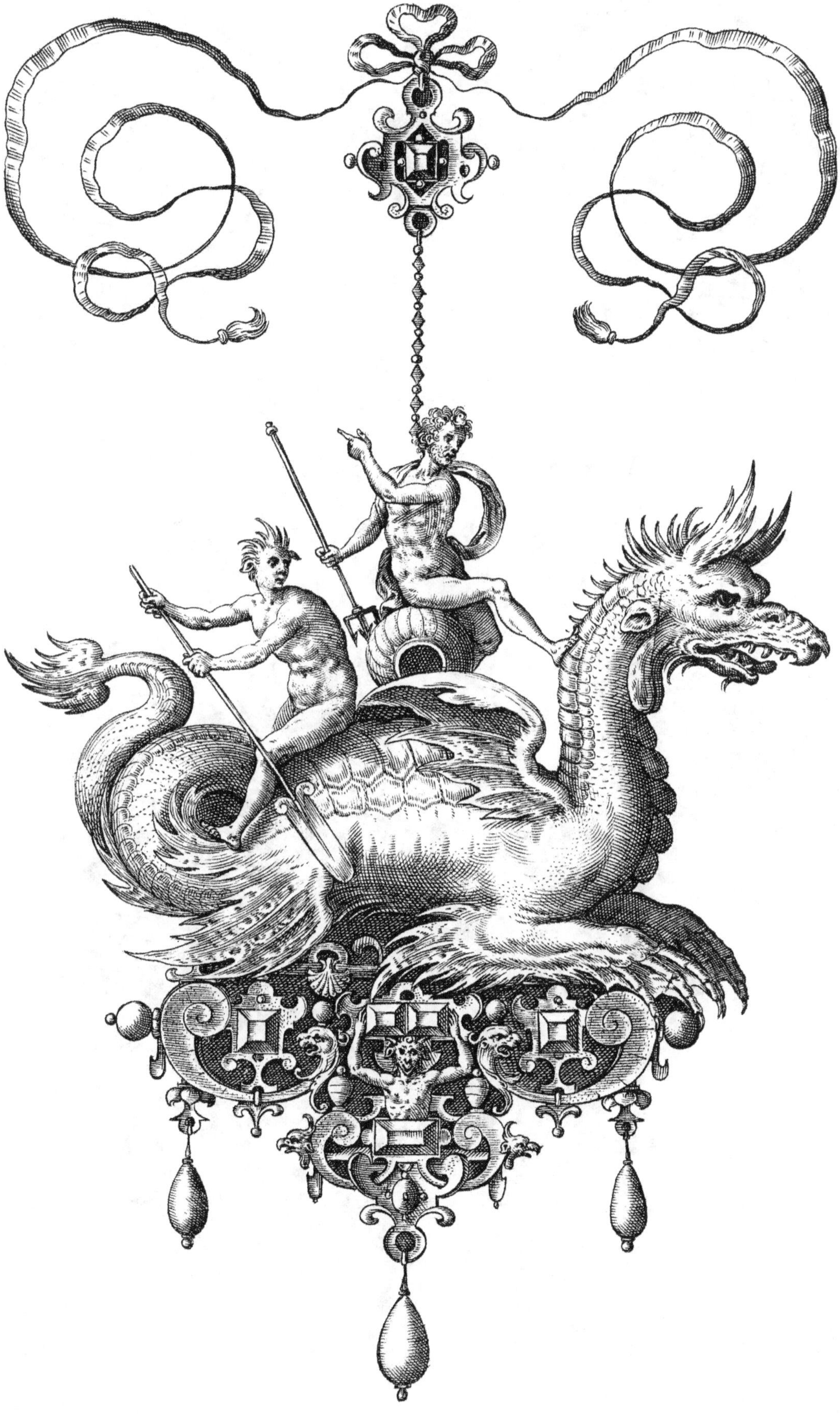

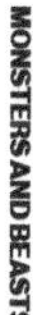
MONSTERS AND BEASTS

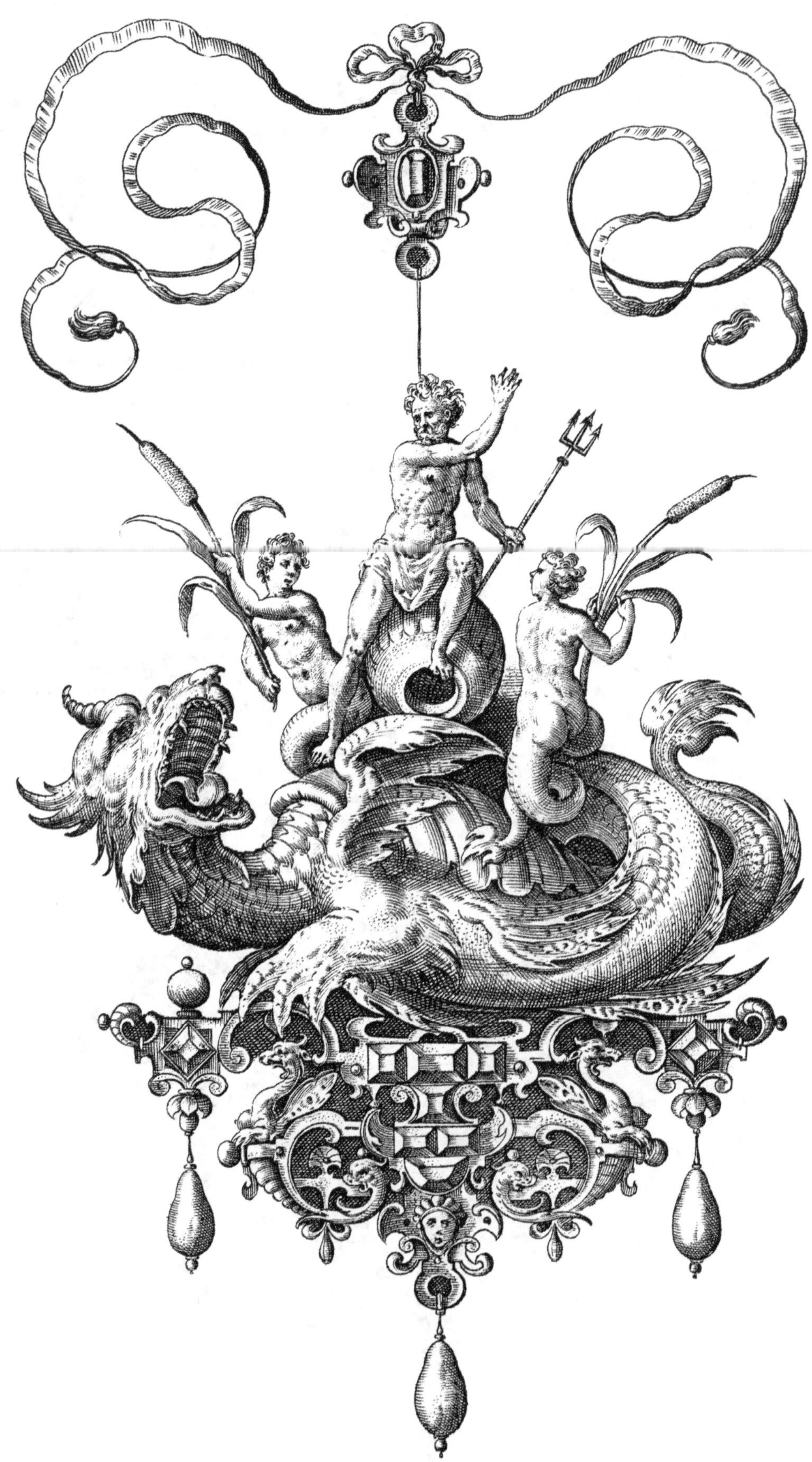

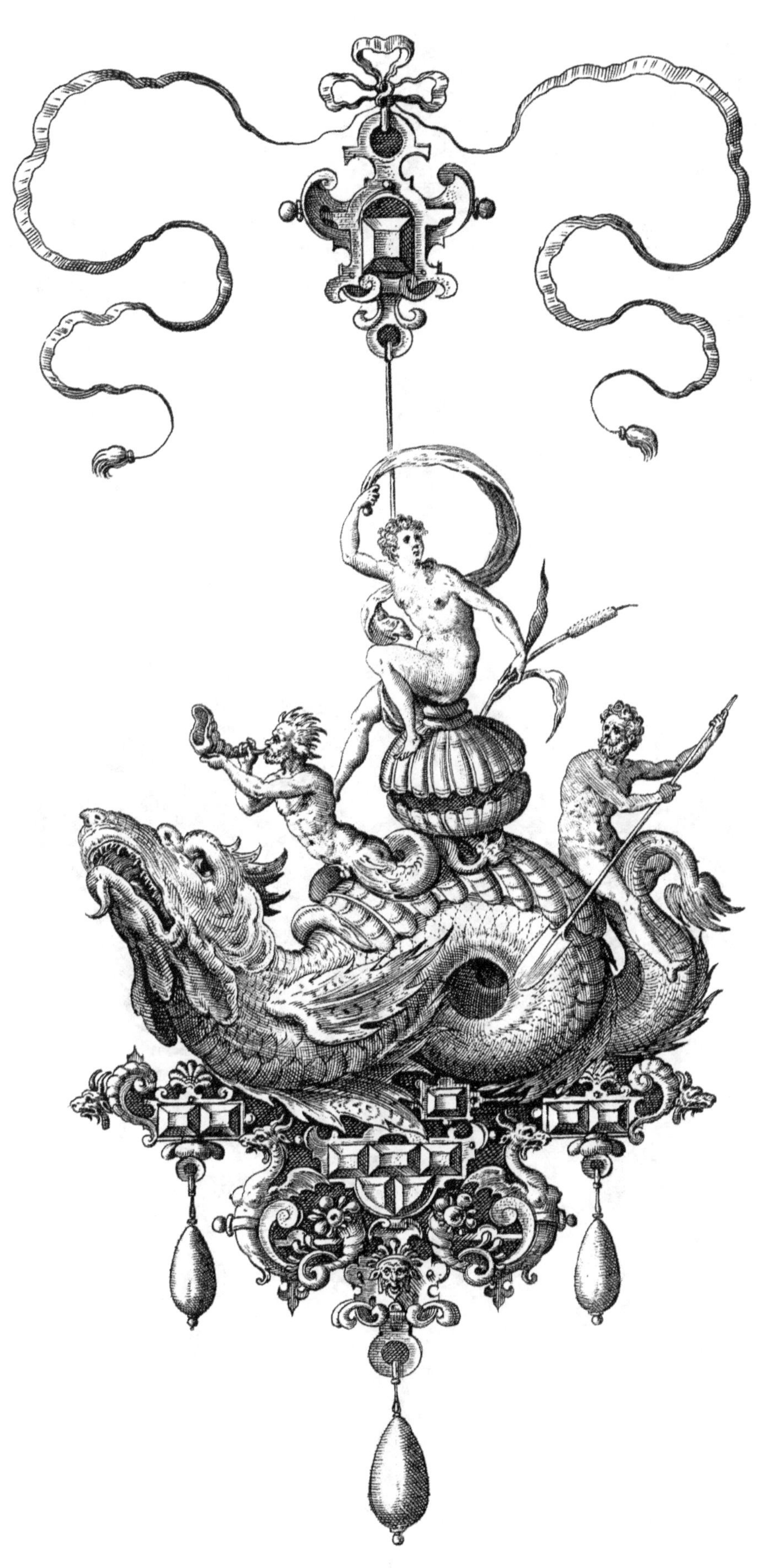

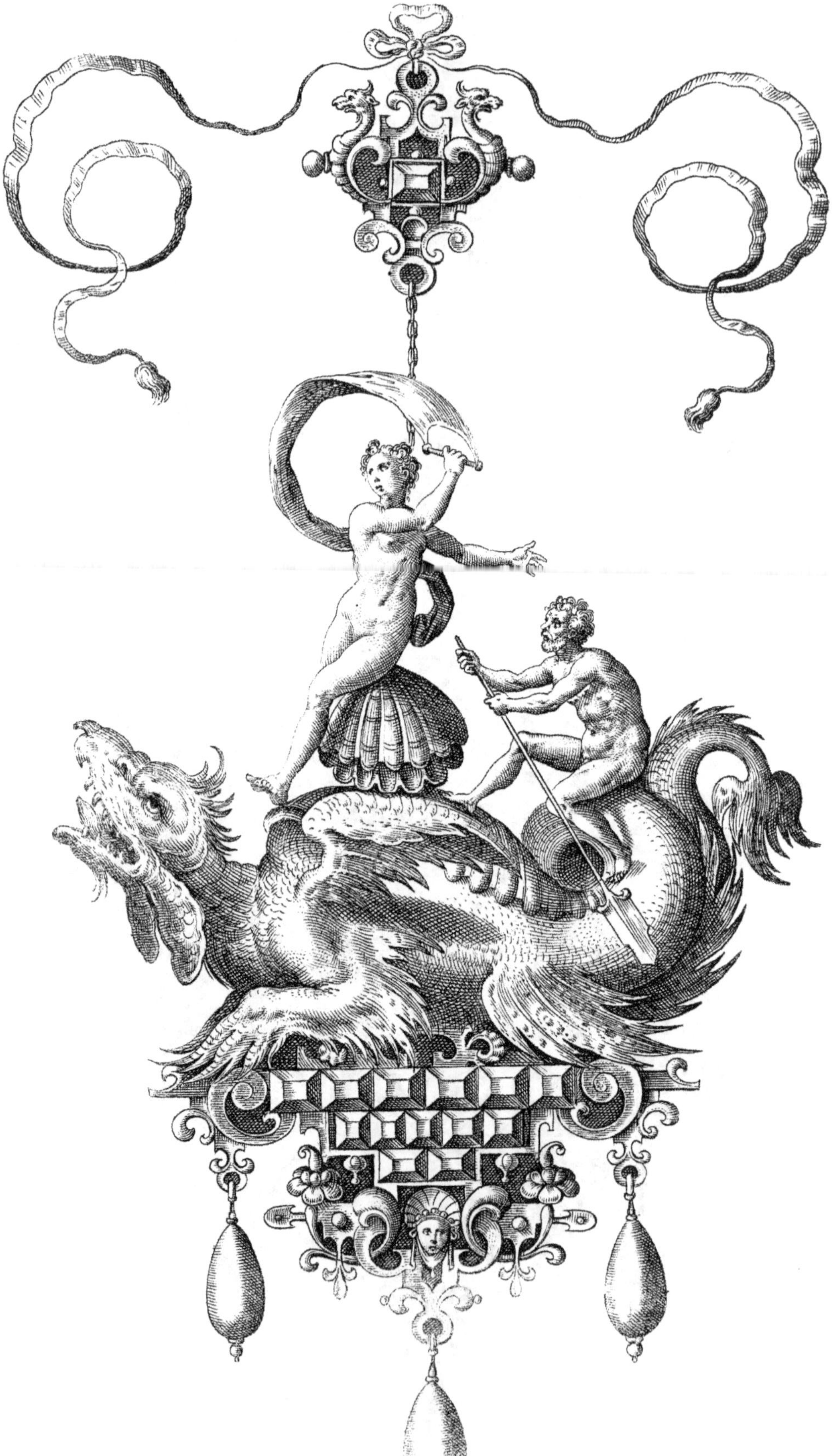

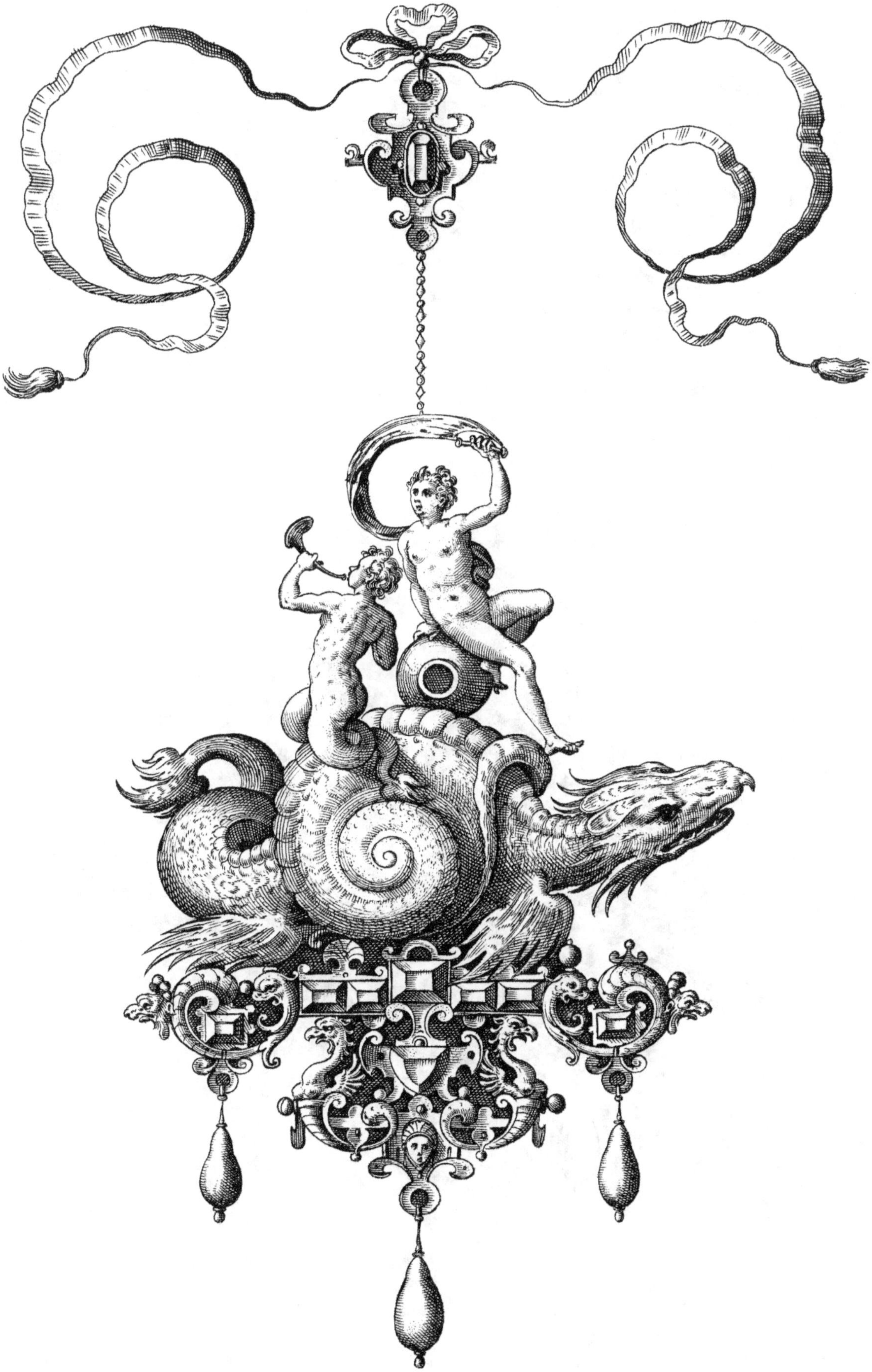

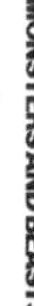
MONSTERS AND BEASTS

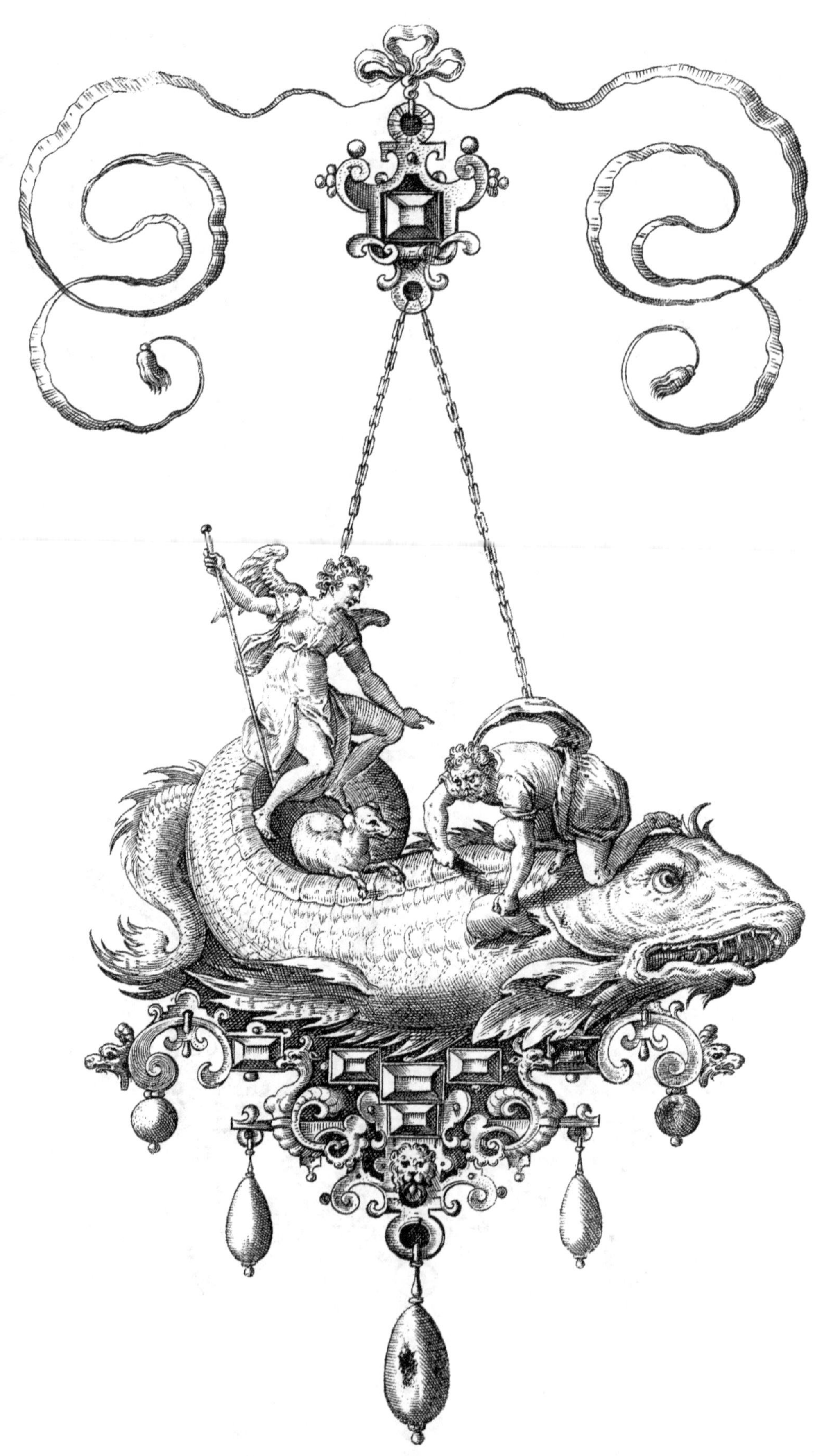

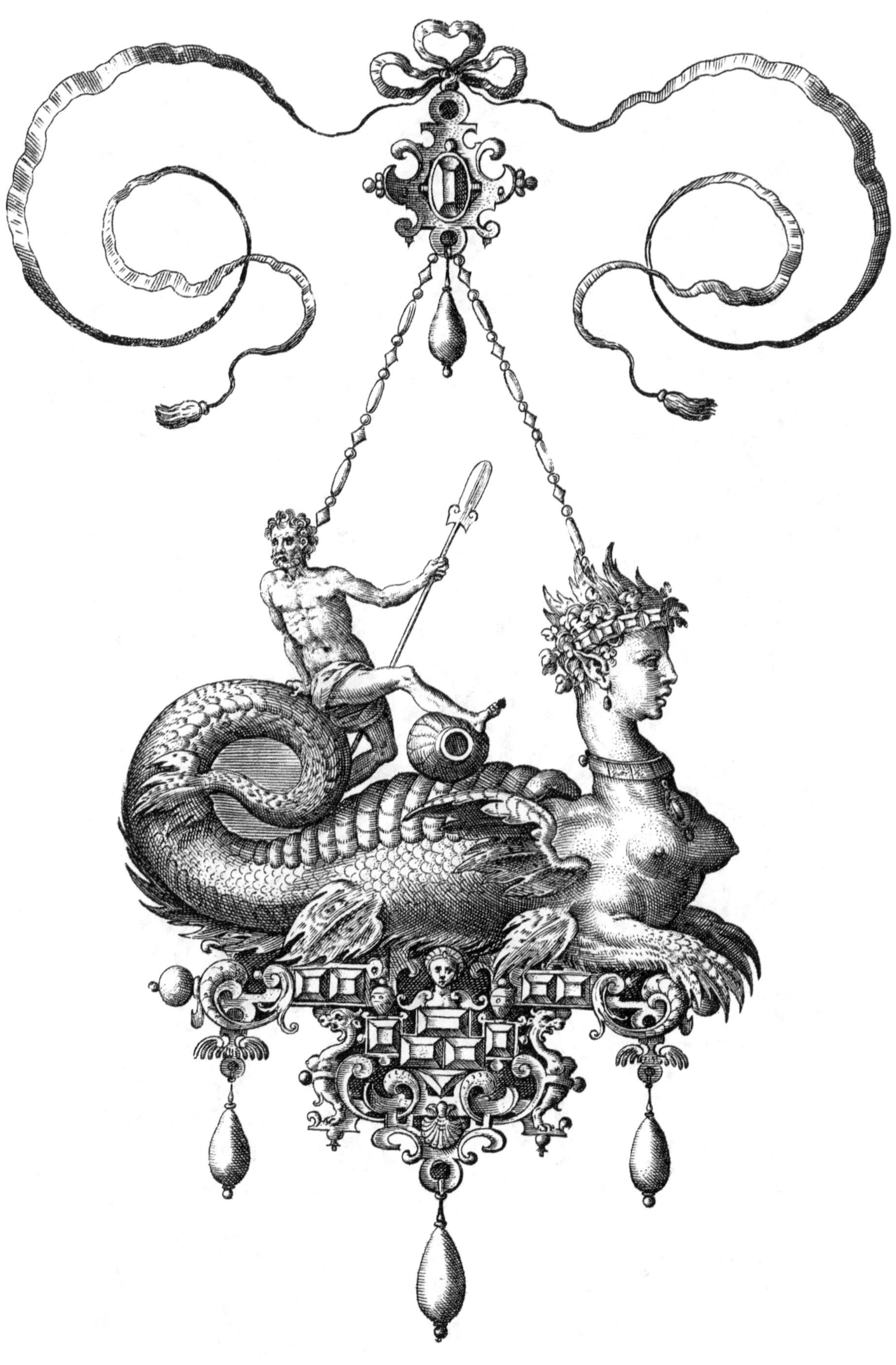

A11

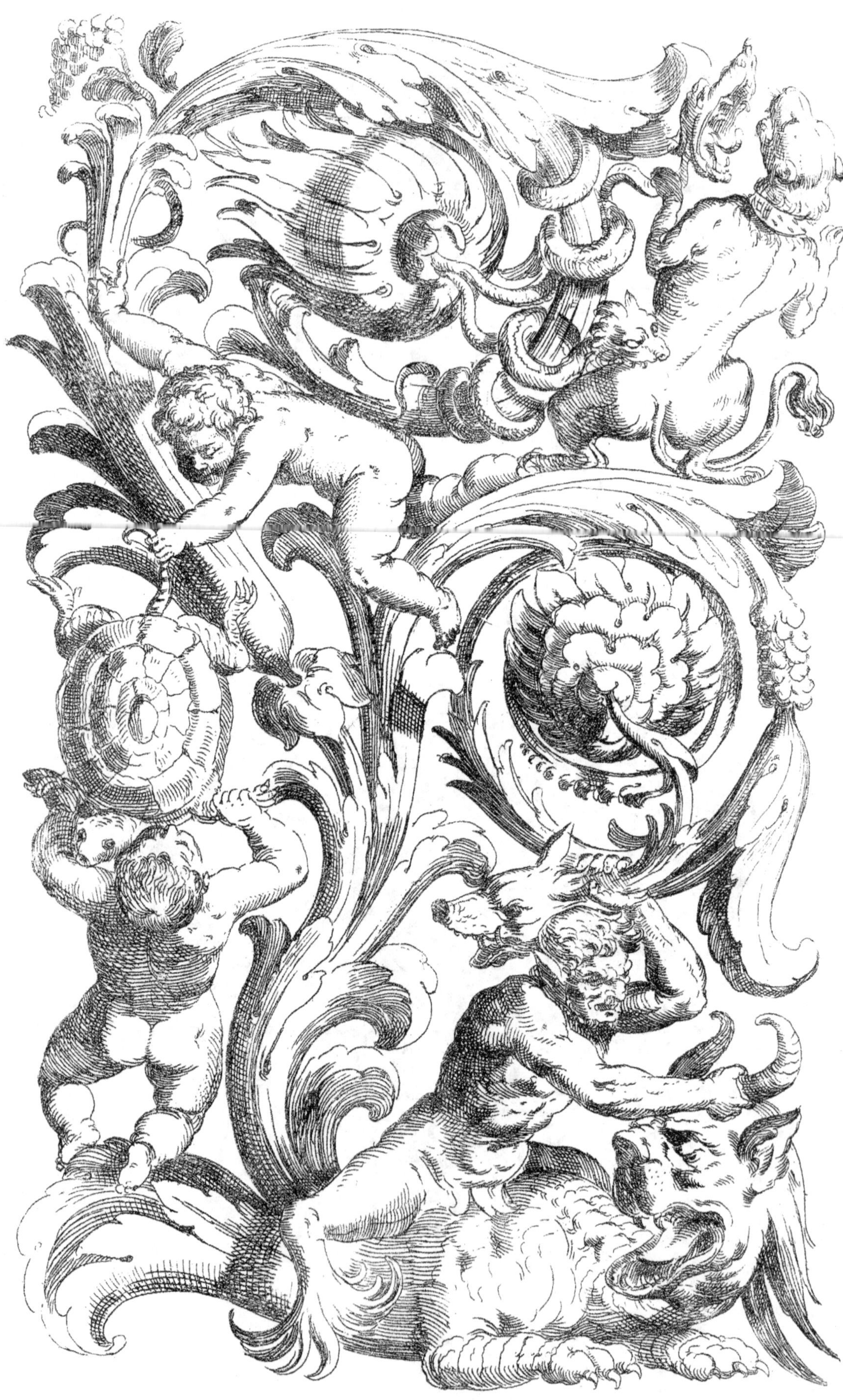

A12

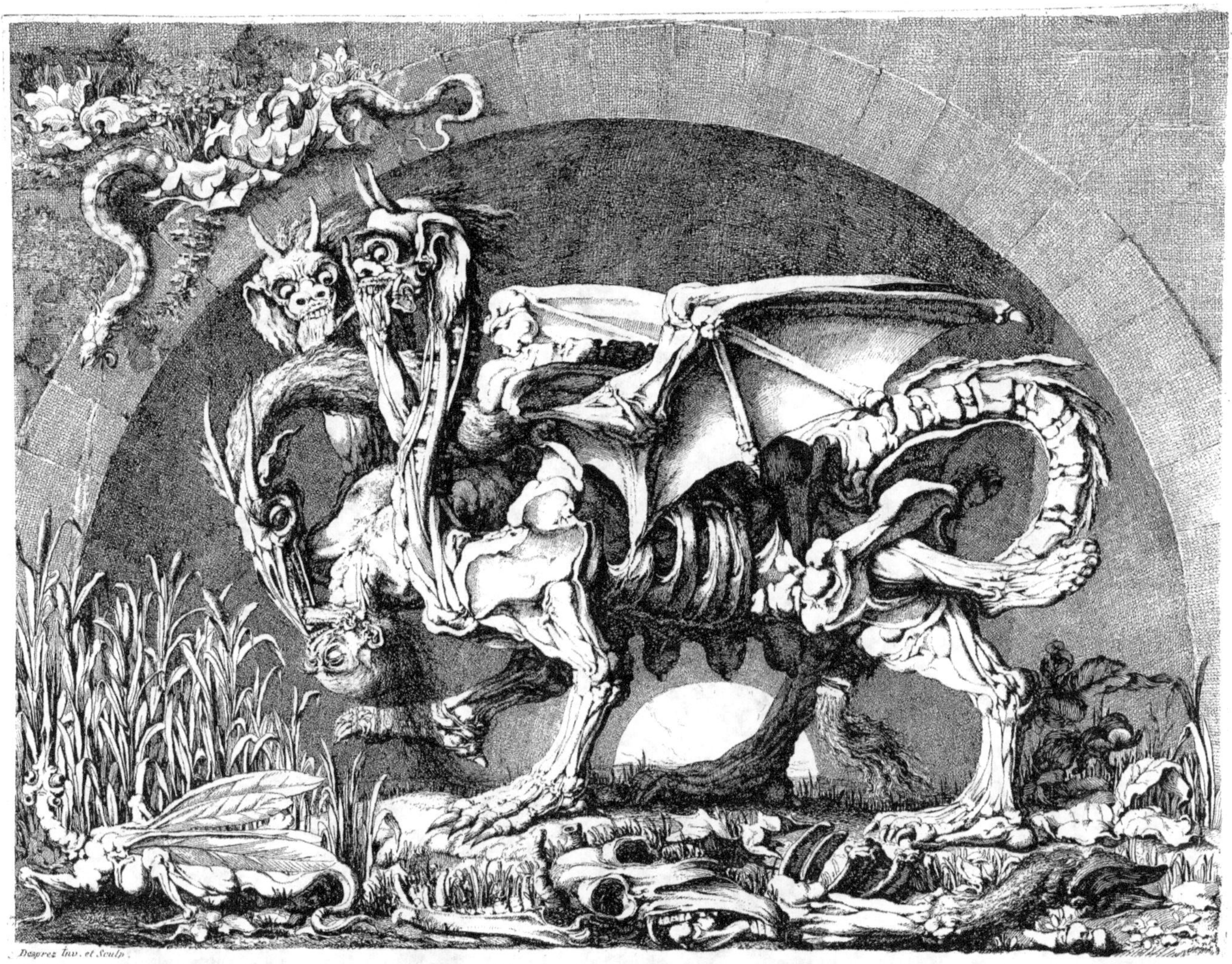

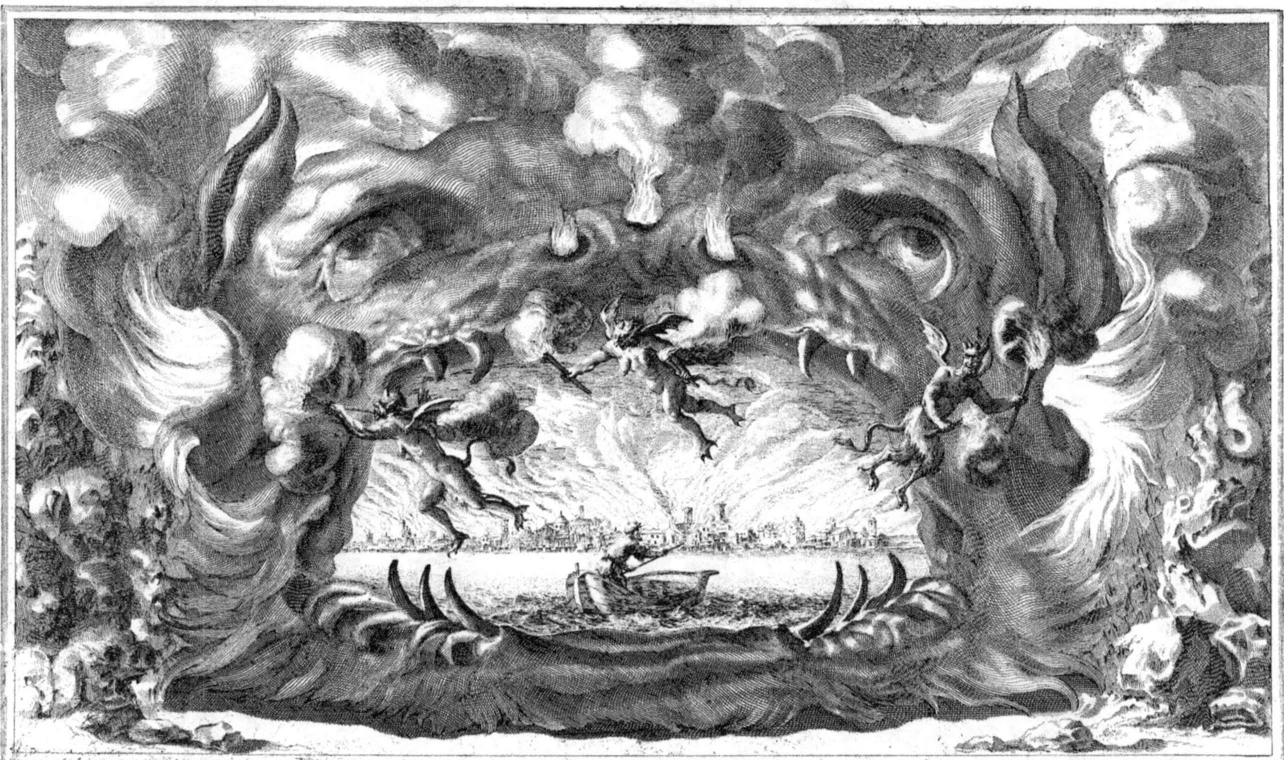

A13

A14

A15

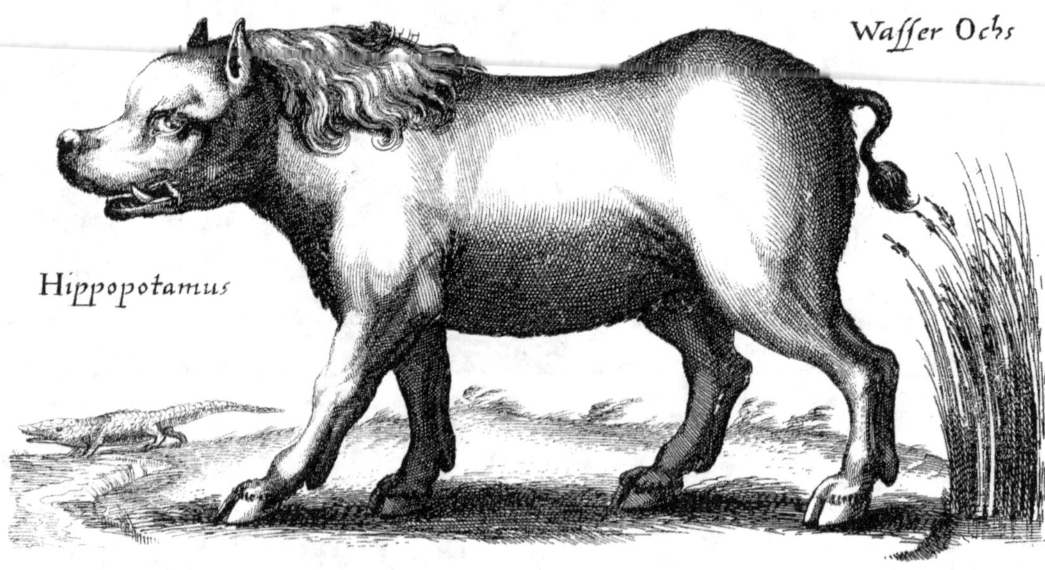

A16

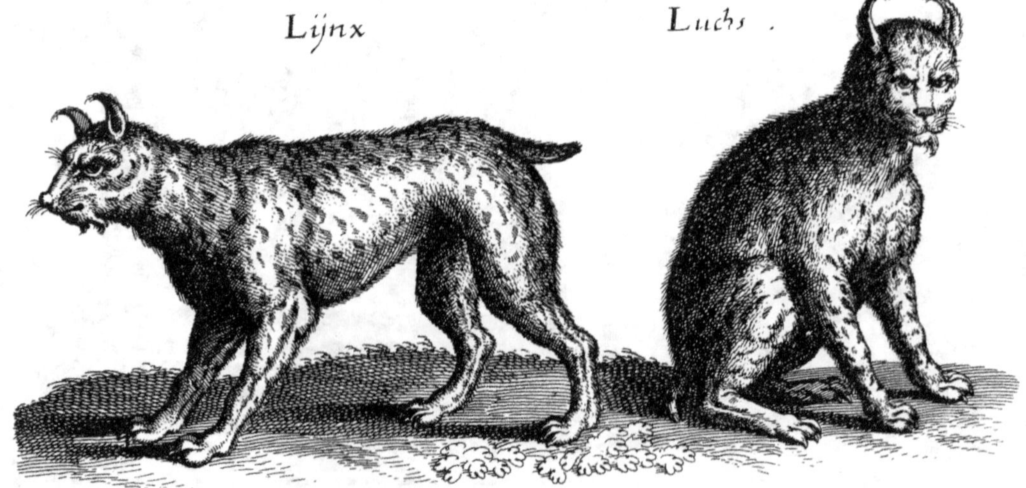

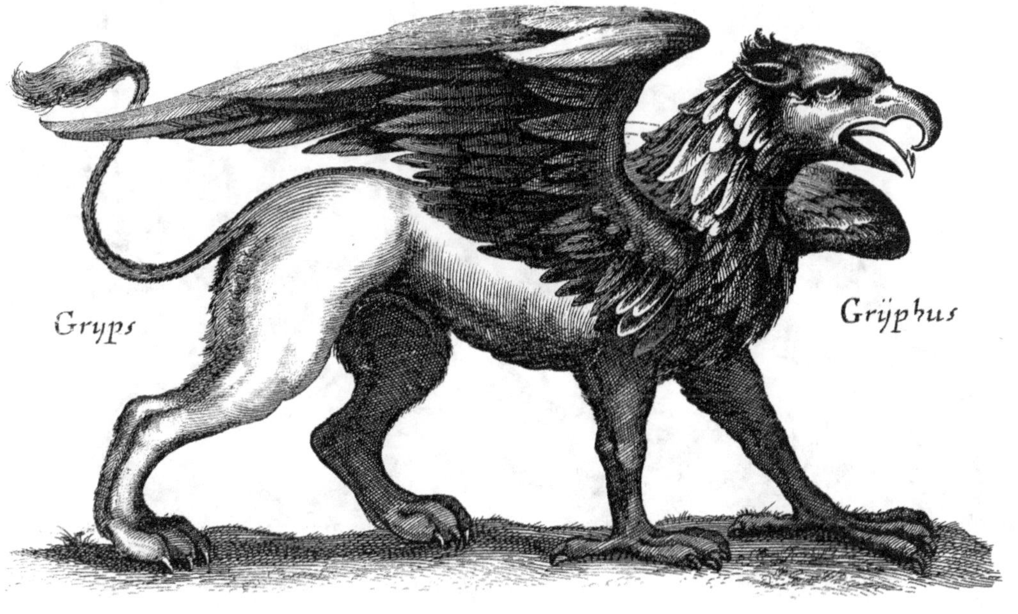

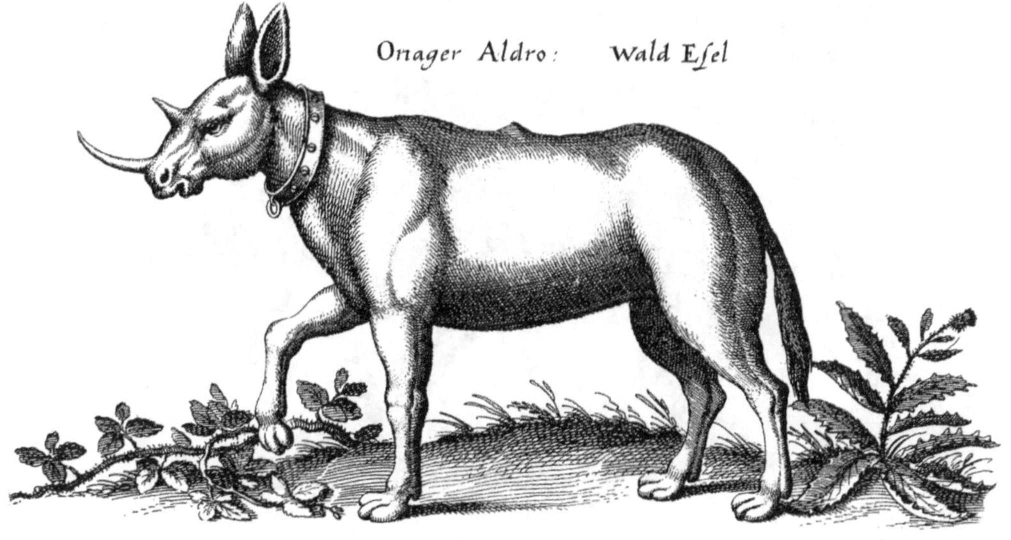

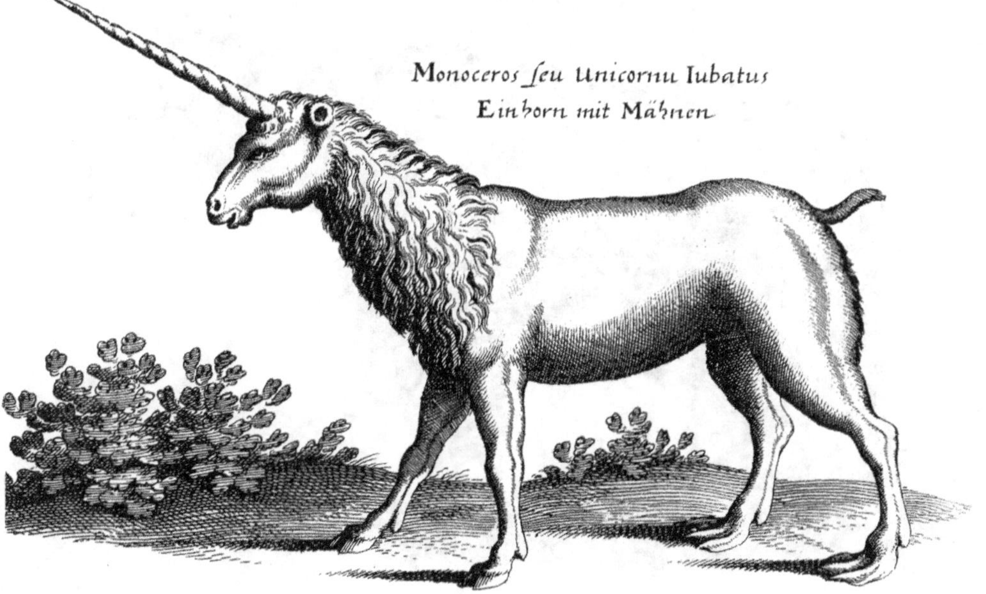

MONSTERS AND BEASTS

A20

Alce Mas.

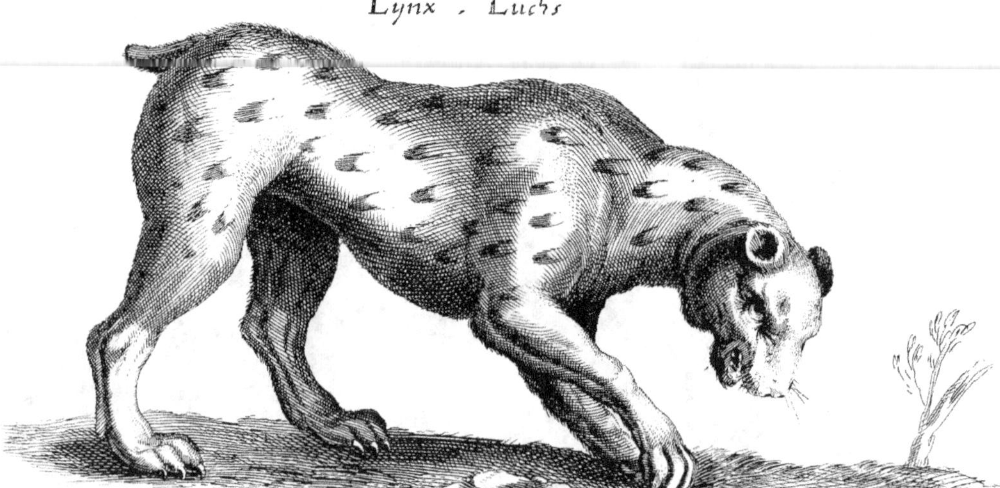

A21

Lÿnx . Luchs

A22

Tigris Geſneri

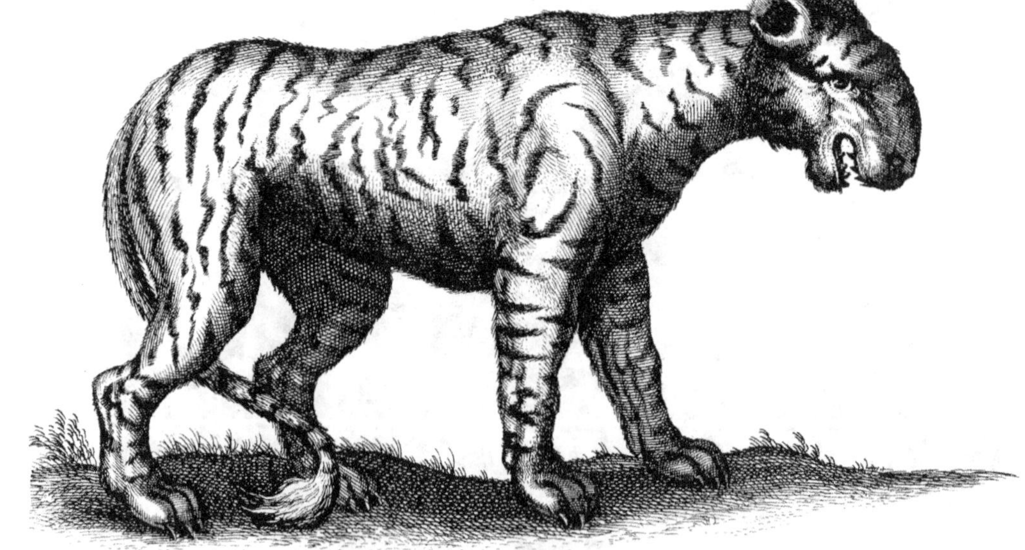

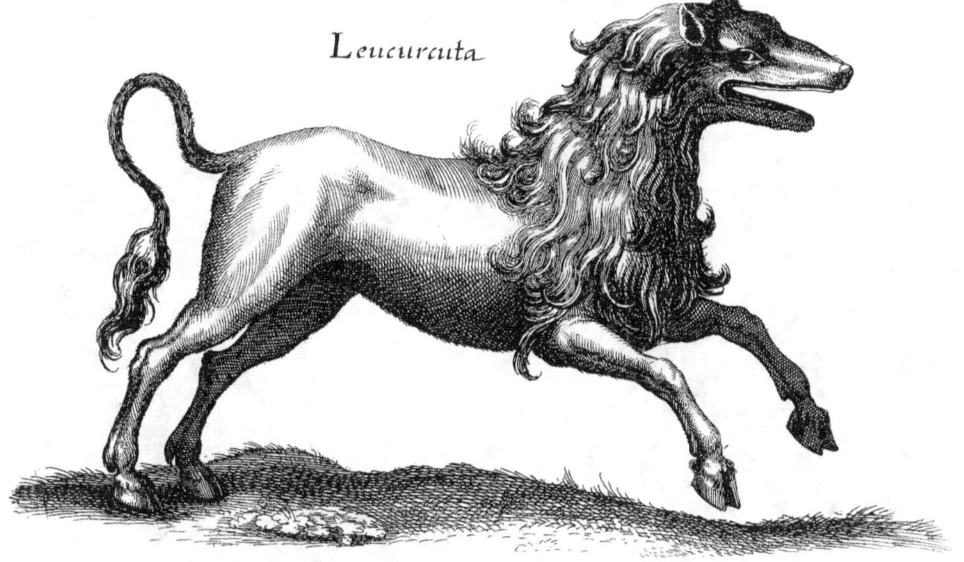

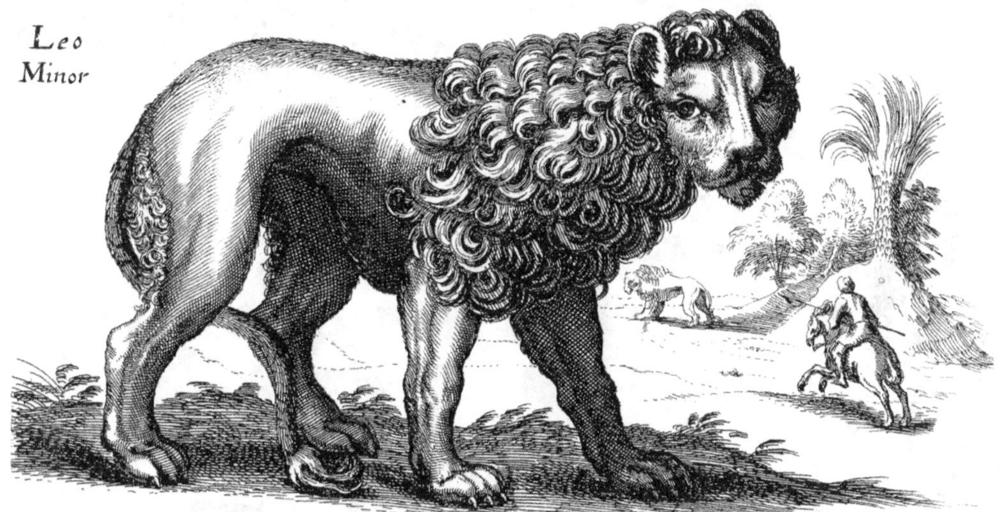

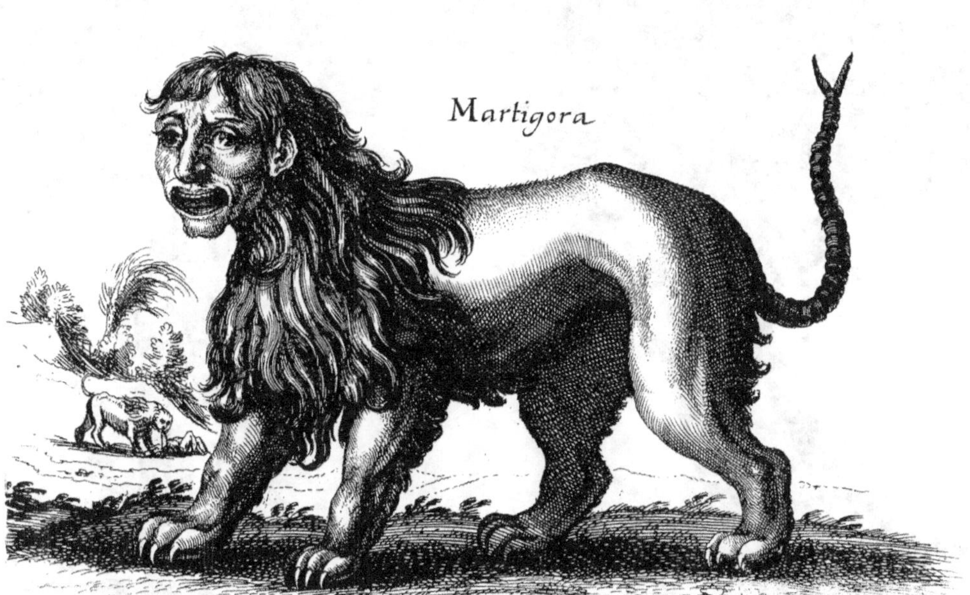

MONSTERS AND BEASTS

A26

A27

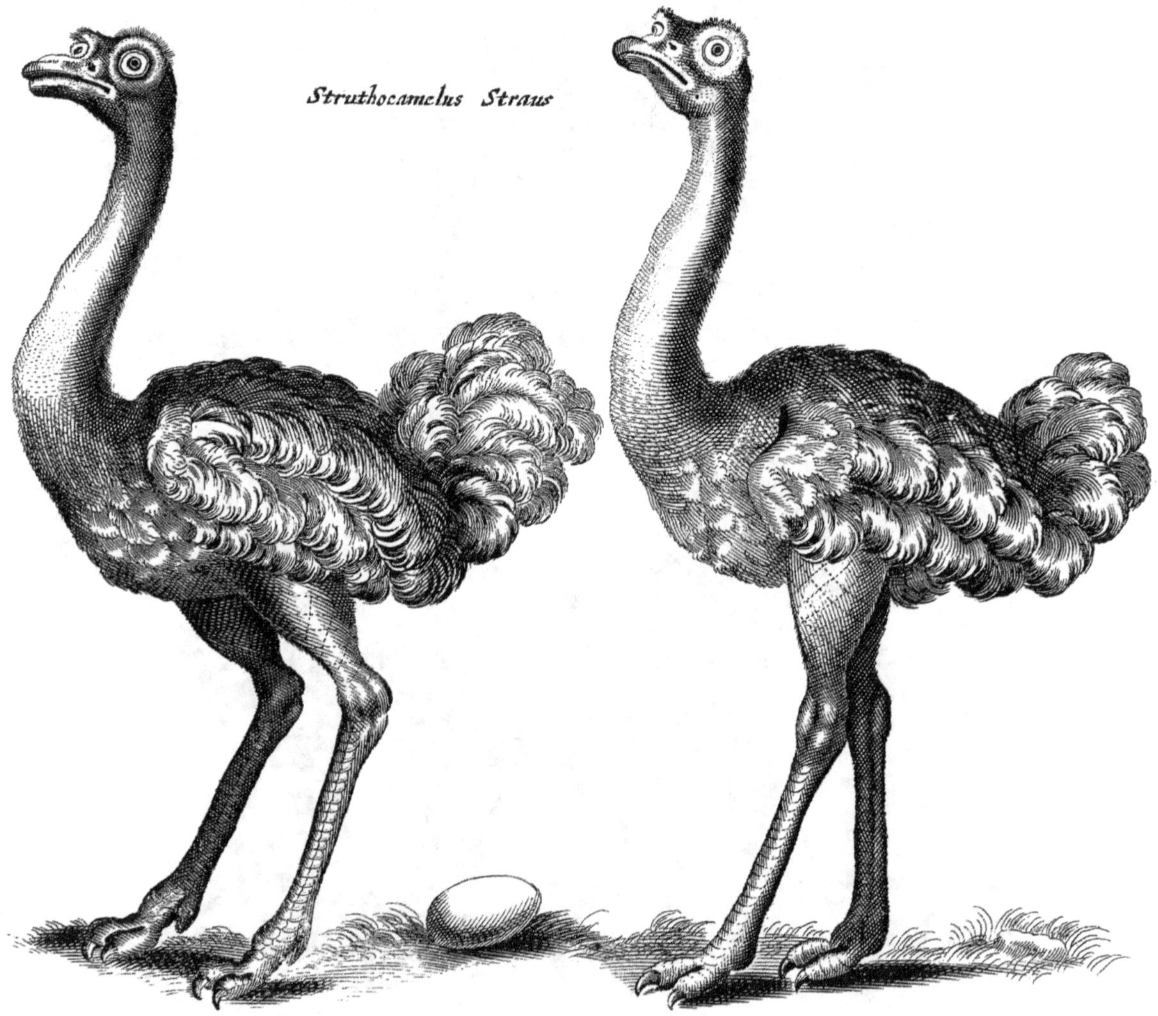

A28

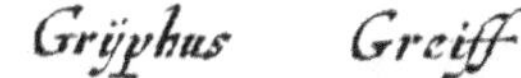

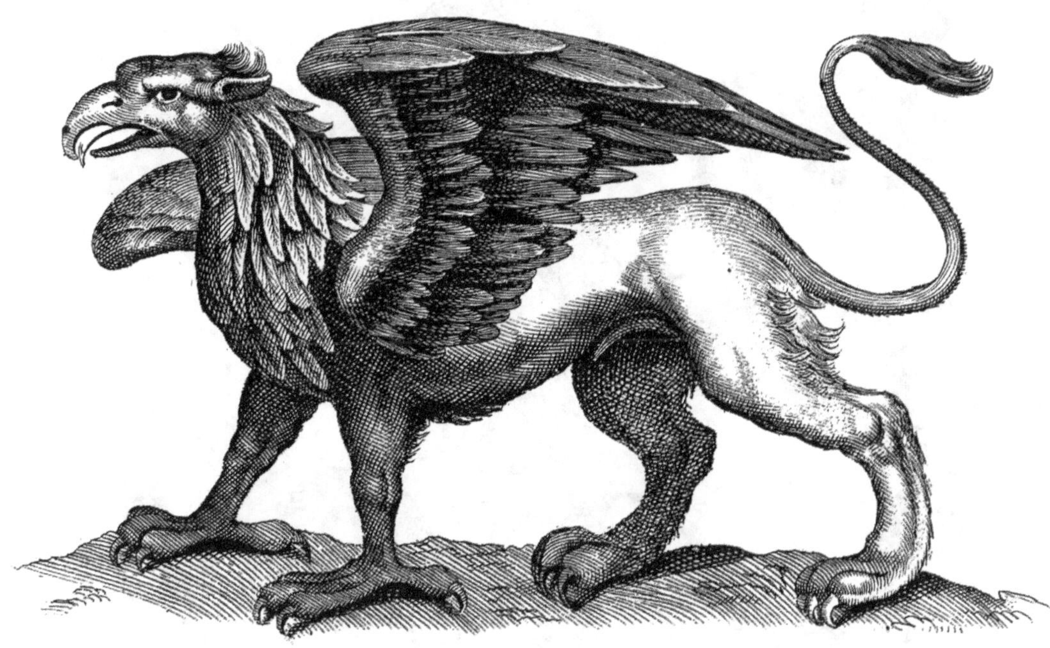

A29

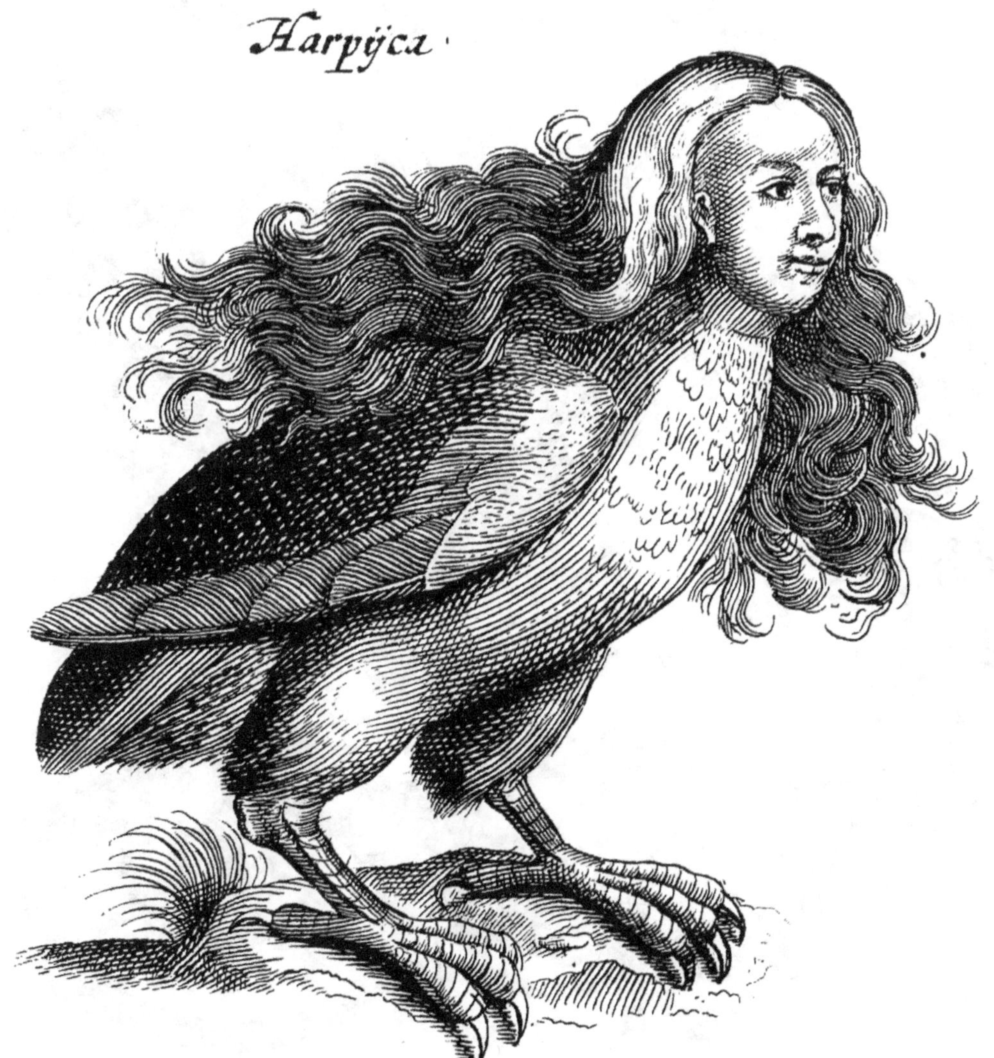

A30

Ouum galli putatum Aldro
Ouum galli natum Regii anno 1628 Aldro
Draco Apicios Greuini
Aldro.

A31

Hydra Septiceps Ges. Aldro.
Hydra Septiceps :
Aldro.

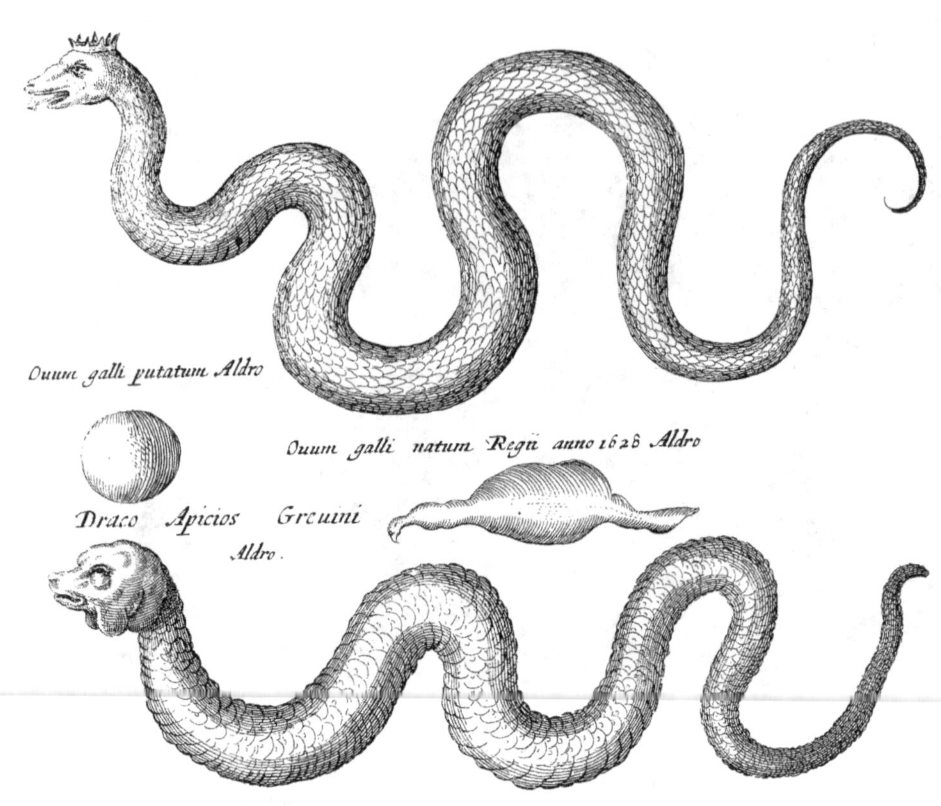

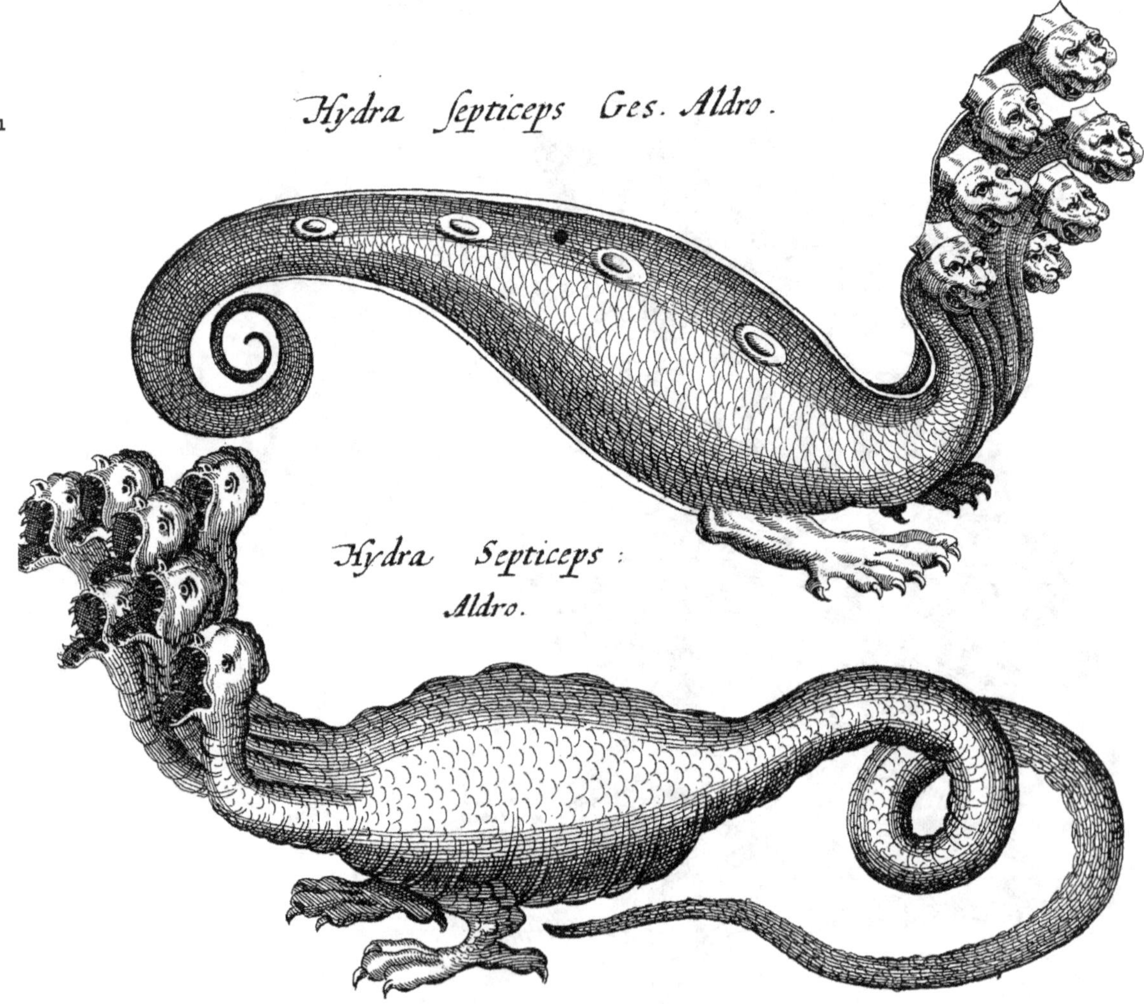

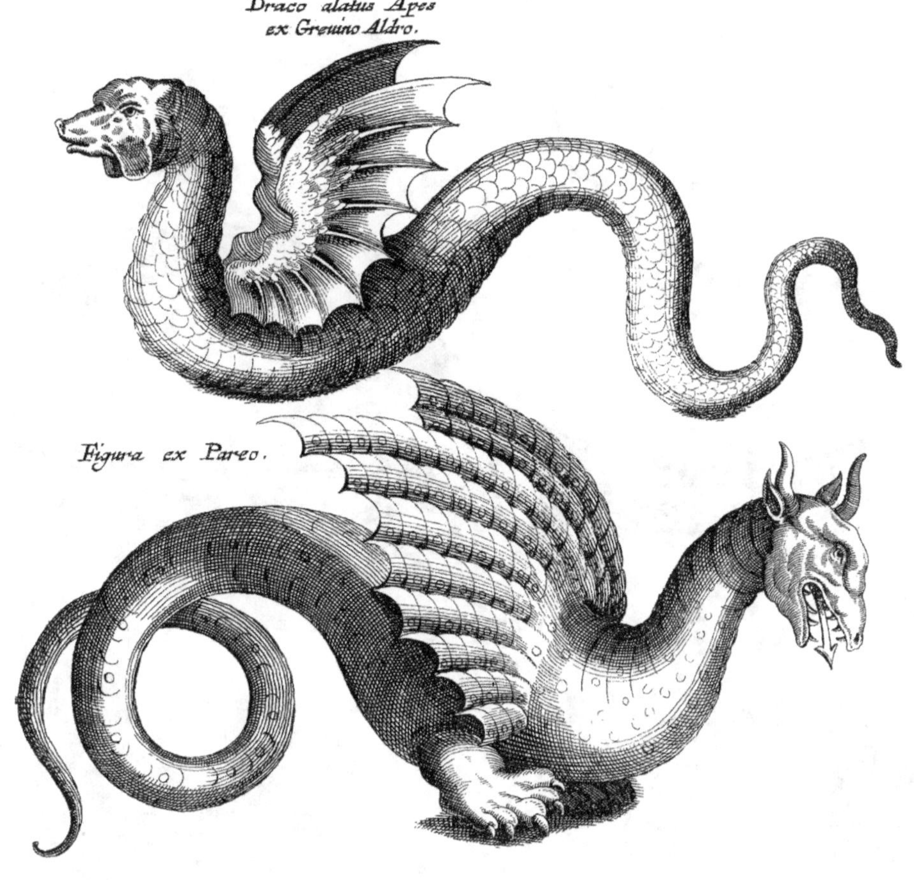

Draco alter ex Raia   *exsicata concinnatus*
                                                                   Aldro

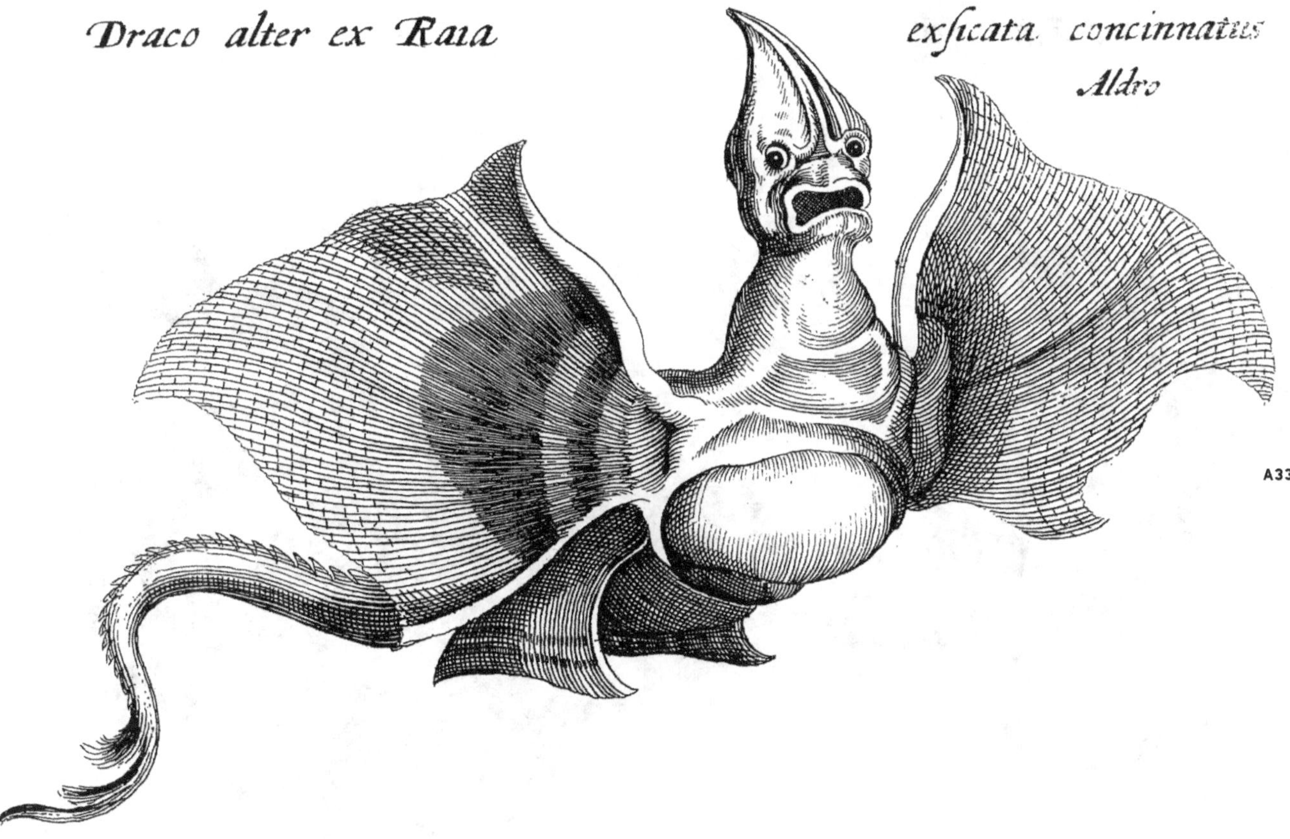

A34

Basiliscus in solitudine Africæ vivens
Aldro.

iscus ex Raia

effictus proné et supiné pictus
Aldro.

A35

Draco bipes apteros captus in
Agro Bononiensi.

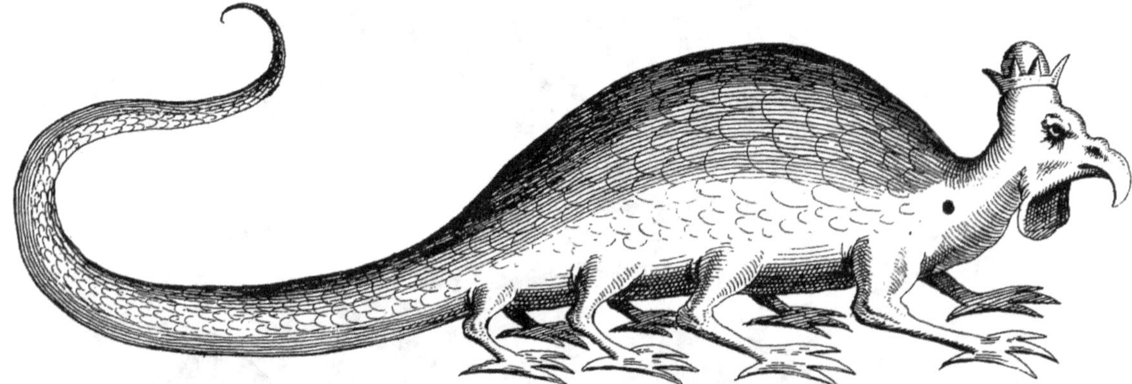

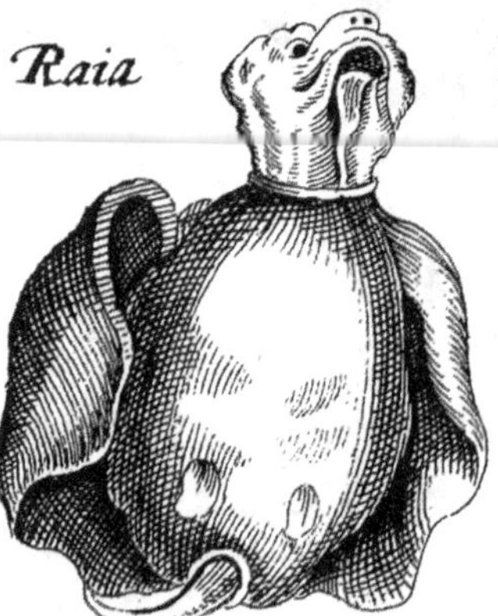

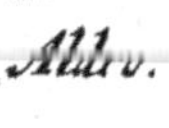

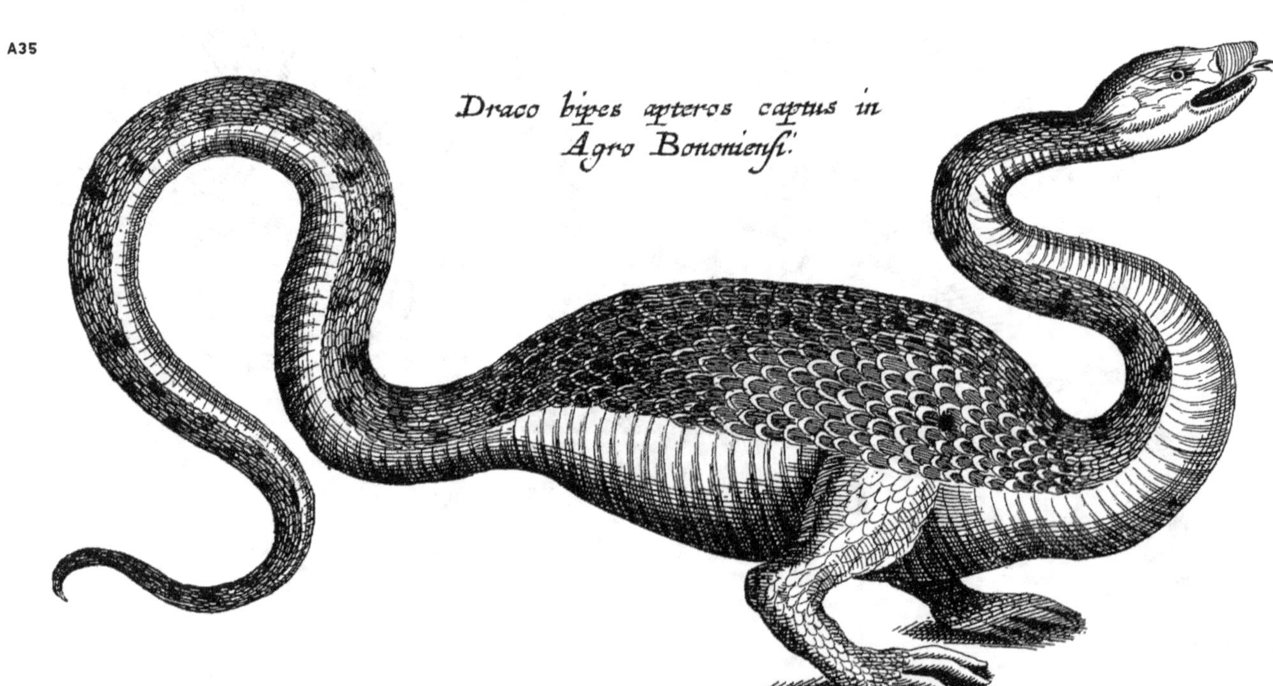

A36

Draco ex Raia effictus
Aldrou.

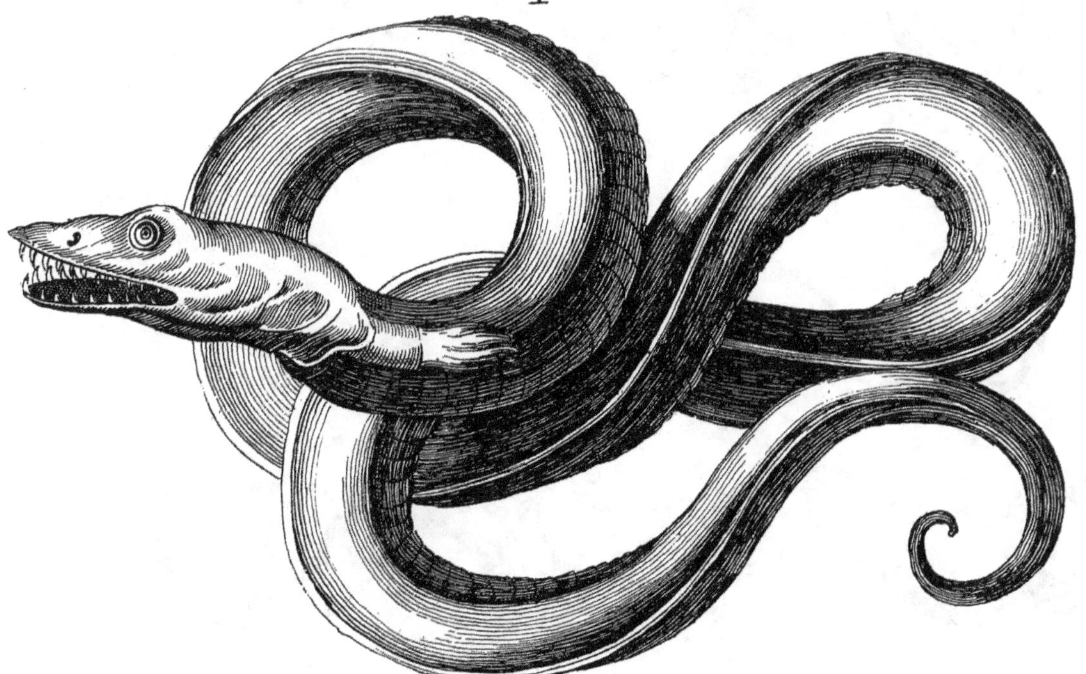

Draco Æthiopicus .

A37

Serpens　Marinus .

A38

Cerastes Greuini Aldrou. Gehörnichte Schlangh

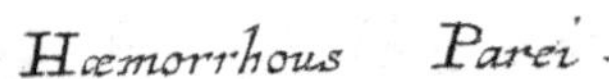

Cerastes ex Libya Aldrou.

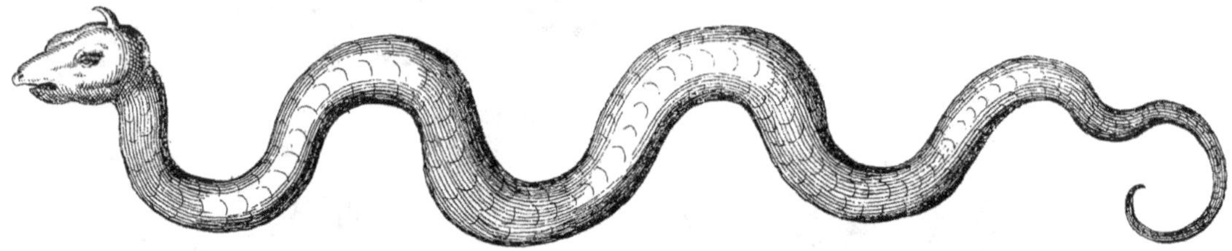

Hæmorrhous   Parei.

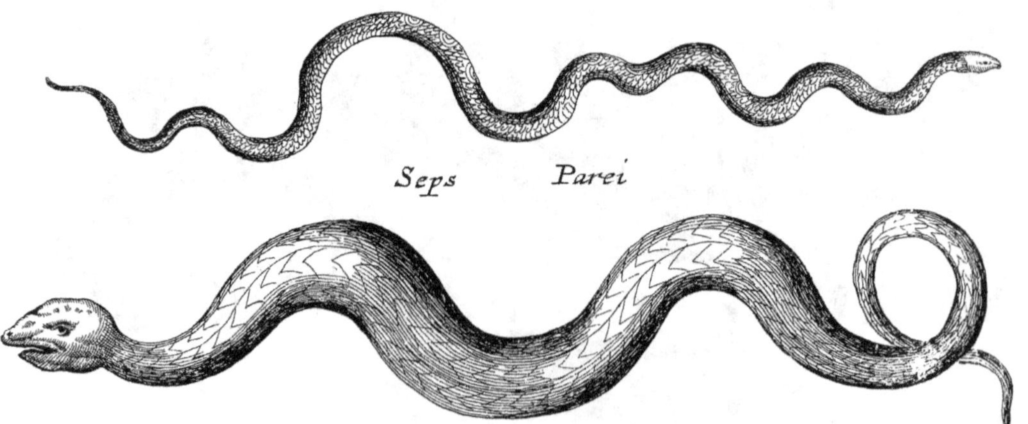

Seps   Parei

Serpens Marinus Mari Noruegico familiaris Aldr.

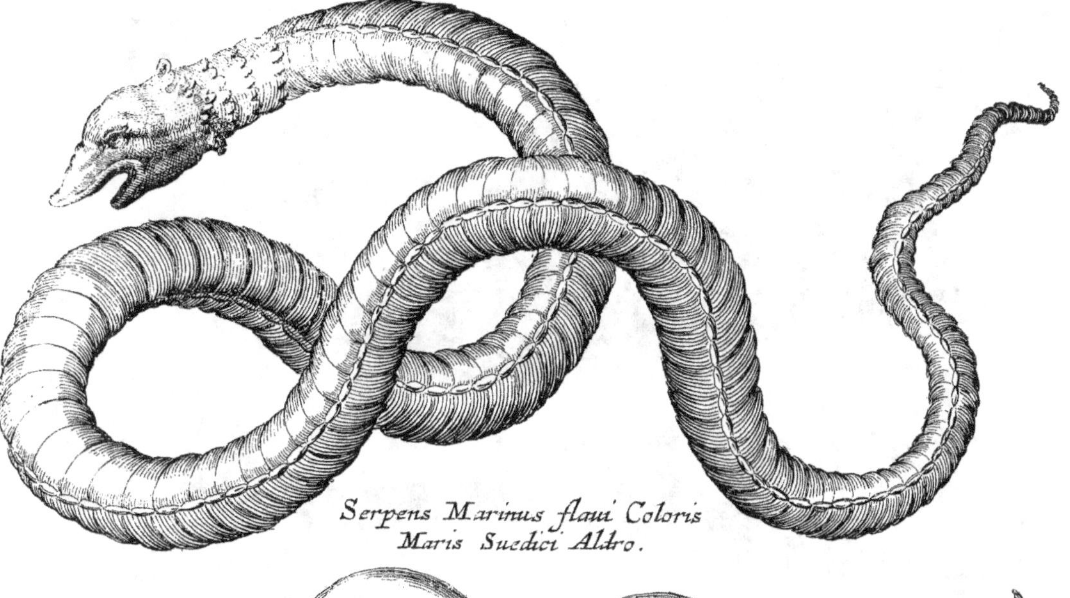

*Serpens Marinus flaui Coloris
Maris Suedici Aldro.*

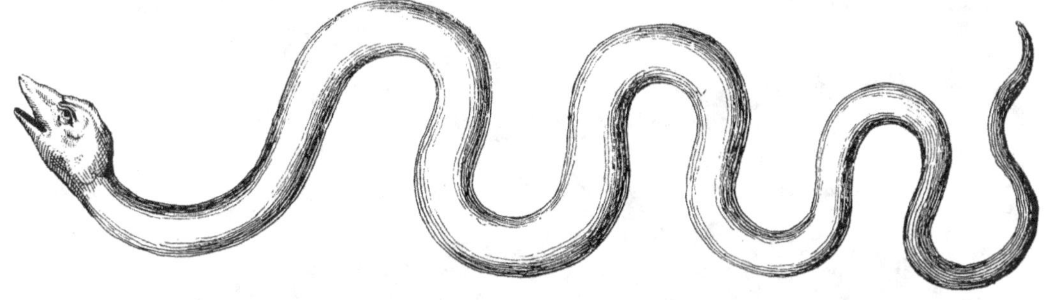

*Scolopendra Marina.
Aldro.*

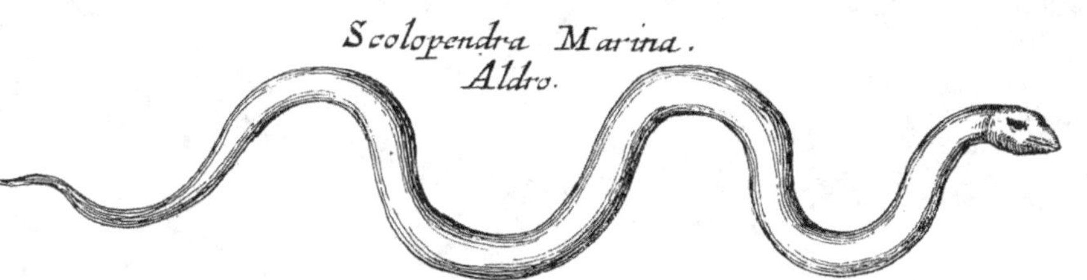

Scolopendra Marina amethystini Coloris Aldr

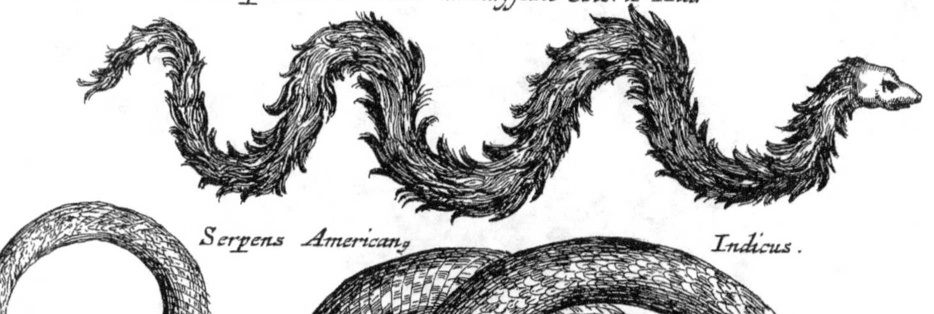

Serpens Americanus   *Indicus.*

A41

MONSTERS AND BEASTS

Tab. XLIII
Utilis Piscis serram ad inſtar
Piſcis habens
Delphinus prior
Delphin
Delphinus Alter
Delphin
Antiq
Metal
Antiq
Metal
Delphinus
Delphin
Fæmina
Weiblein
Delphinus alius
Ein ander art Delphin

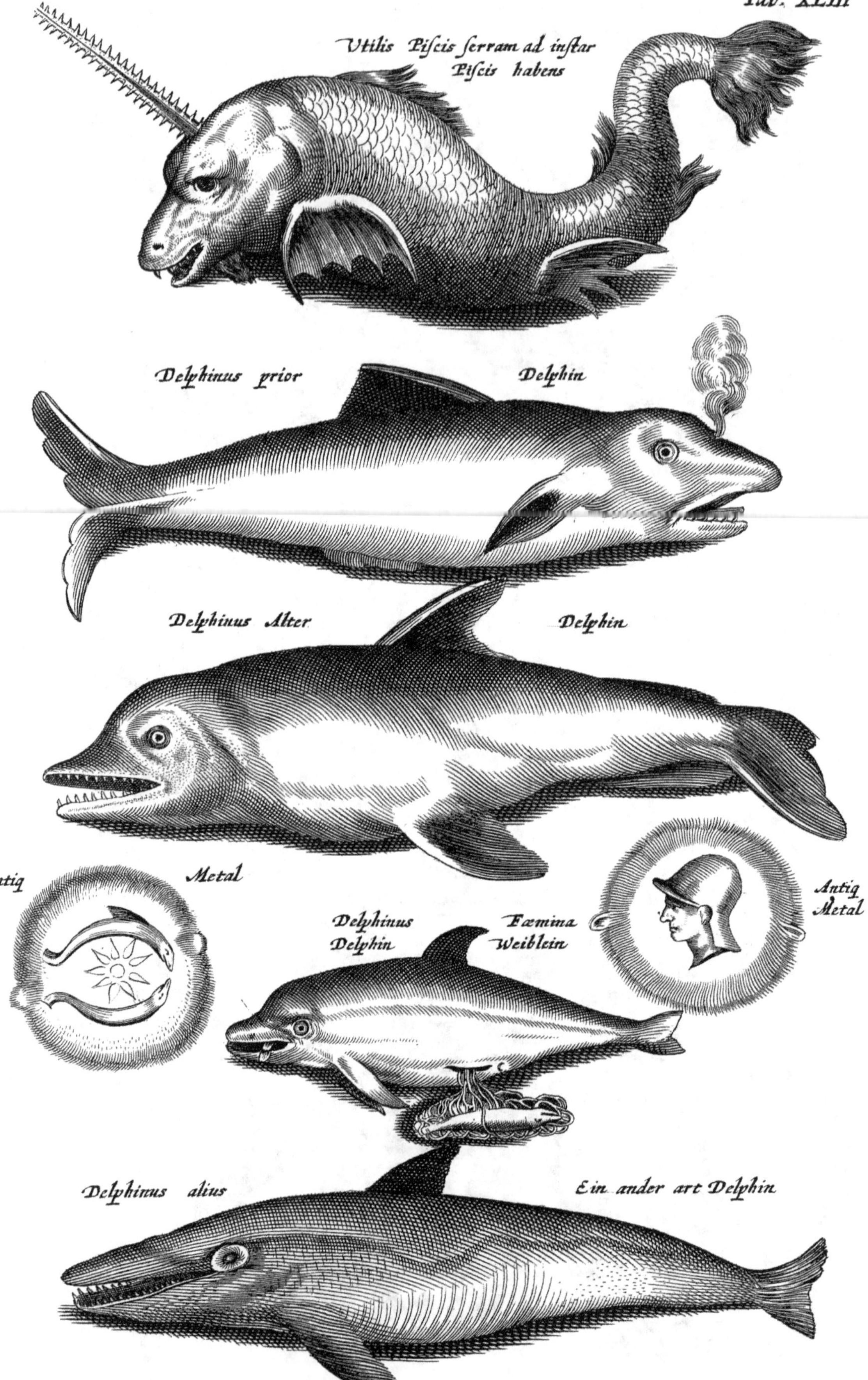

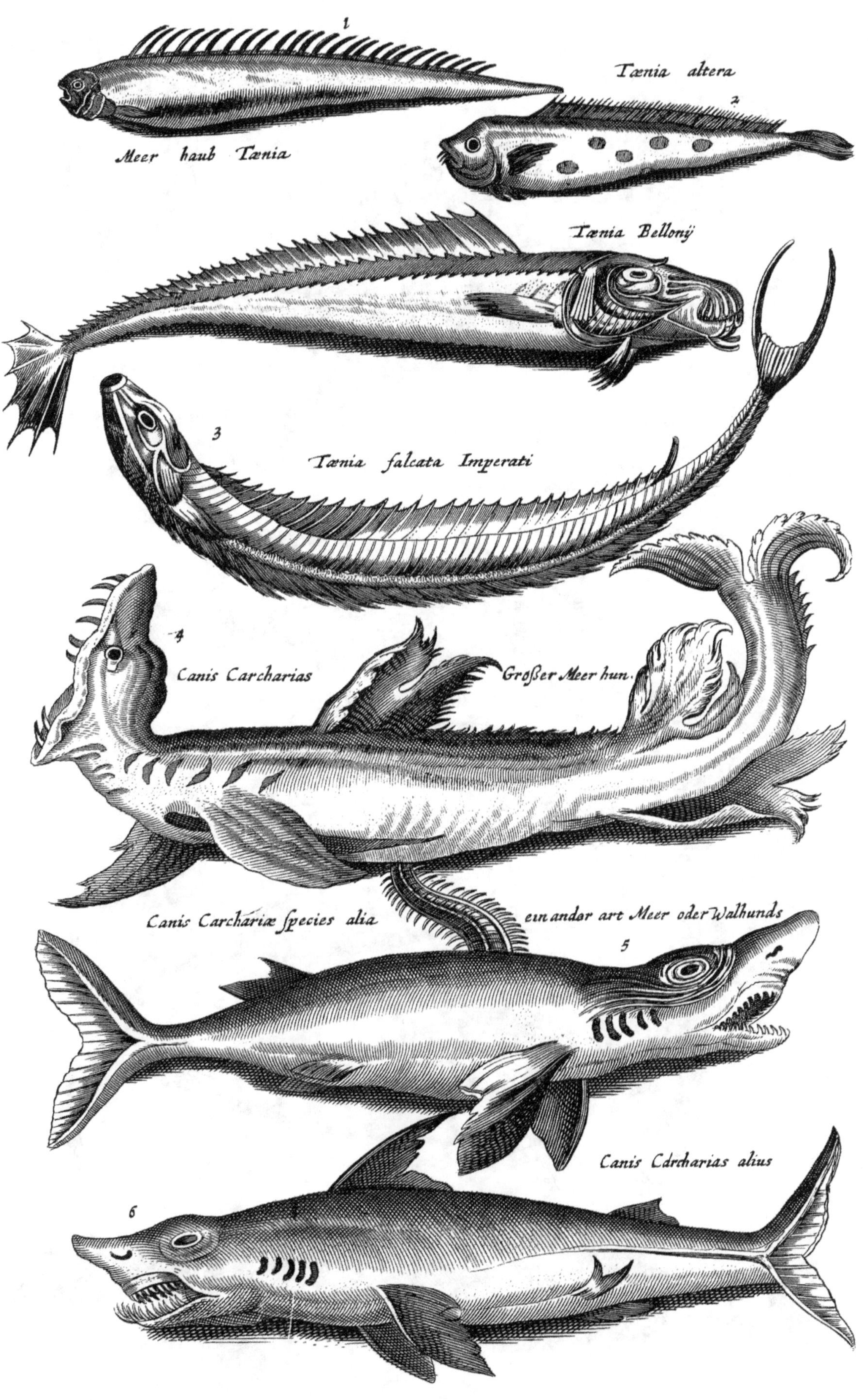
1
Tænia altera
Meer haub Tænia
Tænia Bellonÿ
3
Tænia falcata Imperati
4
Canis Carcharias
Großer Meer hun.
Canis Carchariæ species alia
ein ander art Meer oder Walhunds
5
Canis Carcharias alius
6

A43

Tab. VII

Mandibula Canis marini
des meer hunds gebis.

Canis Carchariæ
dentium feries
Meer hund gebis

*Galeus
Centrina dittus*   *Sawhund*

Vulpecula Marina   *Fuchs Hund Meer fuchs*

*Altus Galeus feu Contrina
Sauhund ander aert*

Simia Marina   *Meer Aff.*

Simia Marina Danica

Zigana   Meerschlegel   Meerwag

Zigæna feu   Libella altera

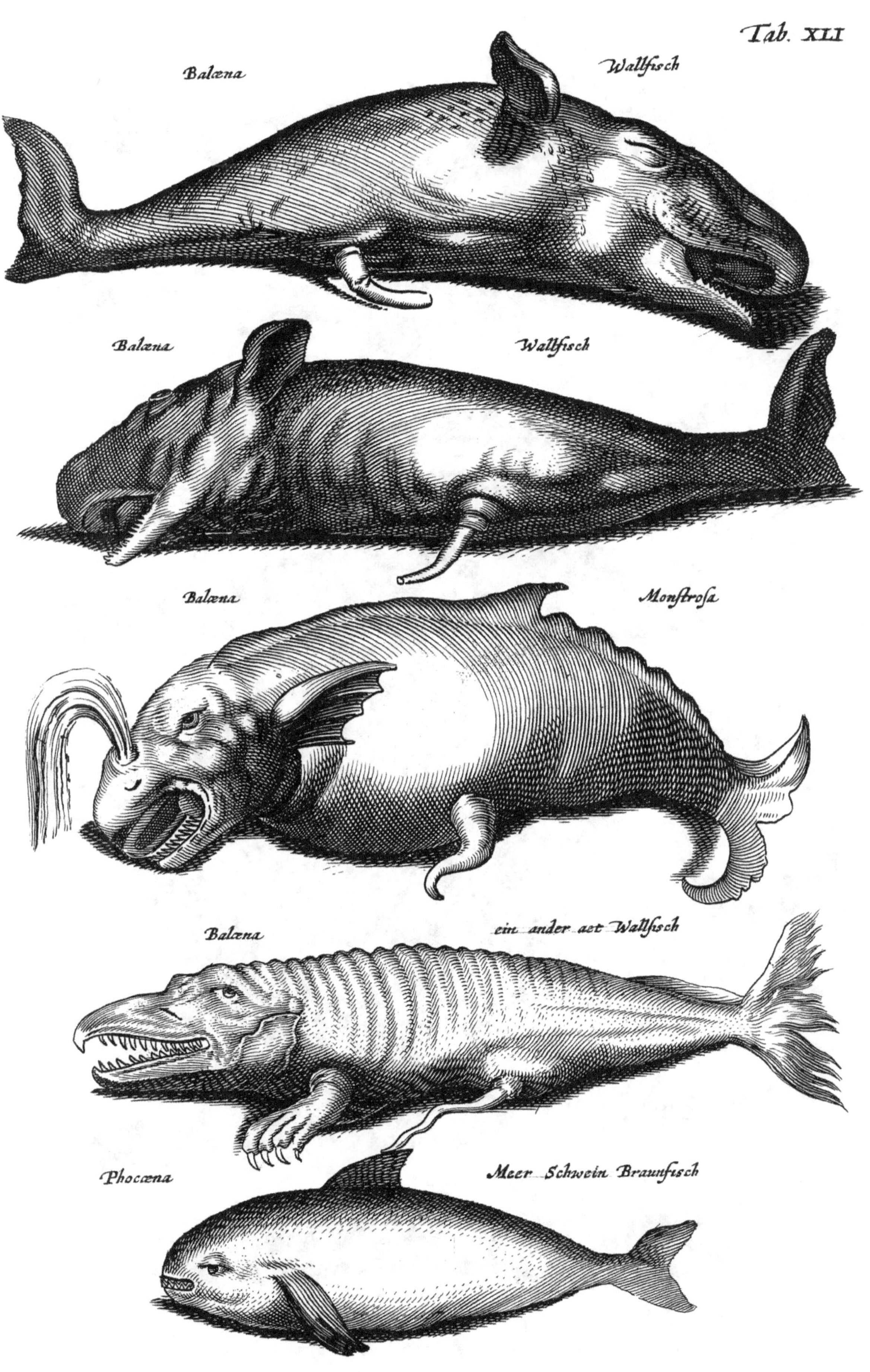
Balæna
Wallfisch
Balæna
Wallfisch
Balæna
Monstrosa
Balæna
ein ander art Wallfisch
Phocæna
Meer Schwein Braunfisch

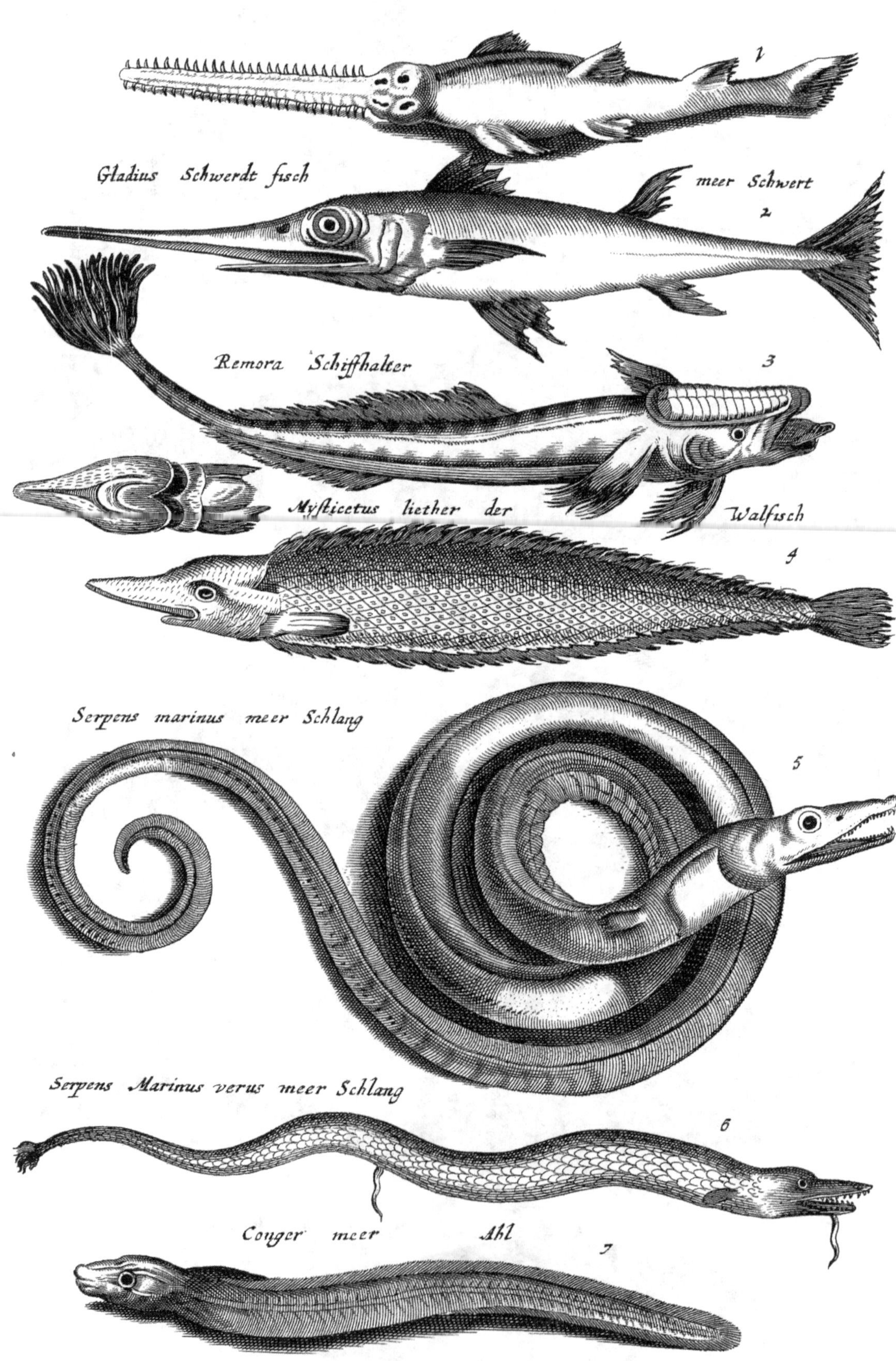
Gladius Schwerdt fisch
meer Schwert
Remora Schiffhalter
Mysticetus liether der
Walfisch
Serpens marinus meer Schlang
Serpens Marinus verus meer Schlang
Couger meer Ahl
1
2
3
4
5
6
7

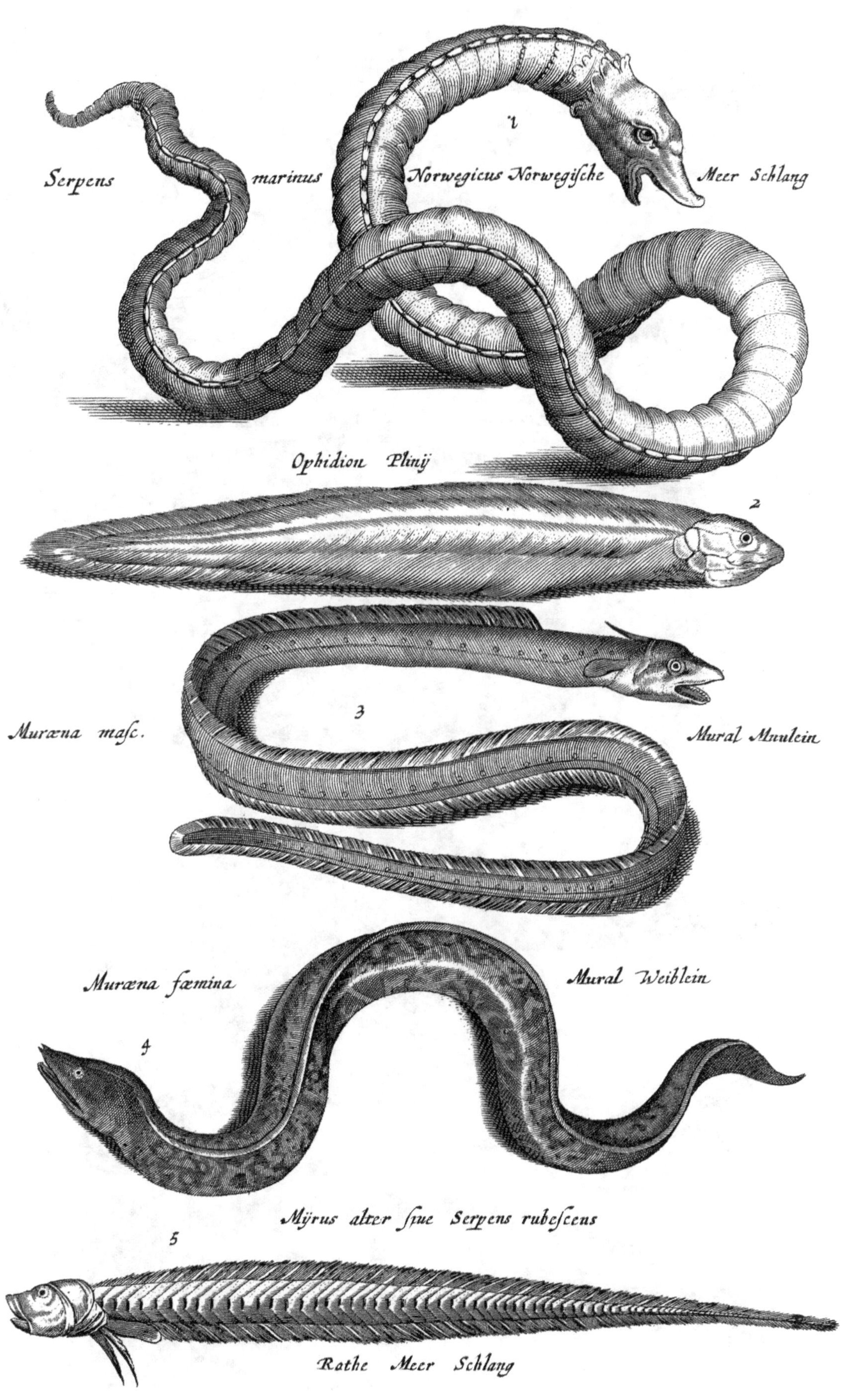
Serpens marinus Norwegicus Norwegische Meer Schlang
1
Ophidion Plinij
2
Muræna masc.
Mural Mnulein
3
Muræna fæmina
Mural Weiblein
4
Mijrus alter sue Serpens rubescens
5
Rathe Meer Schlang

A47

Aculeatus marinus Major
Tab. XLVII
1
Lupus Marinus
Schonfeldij
2
Lijcostonius
Balthucus
3
Sioxpius Marinus
4
Midom Supunis
5
Spirinchus
6
Siluri vera affigios
7

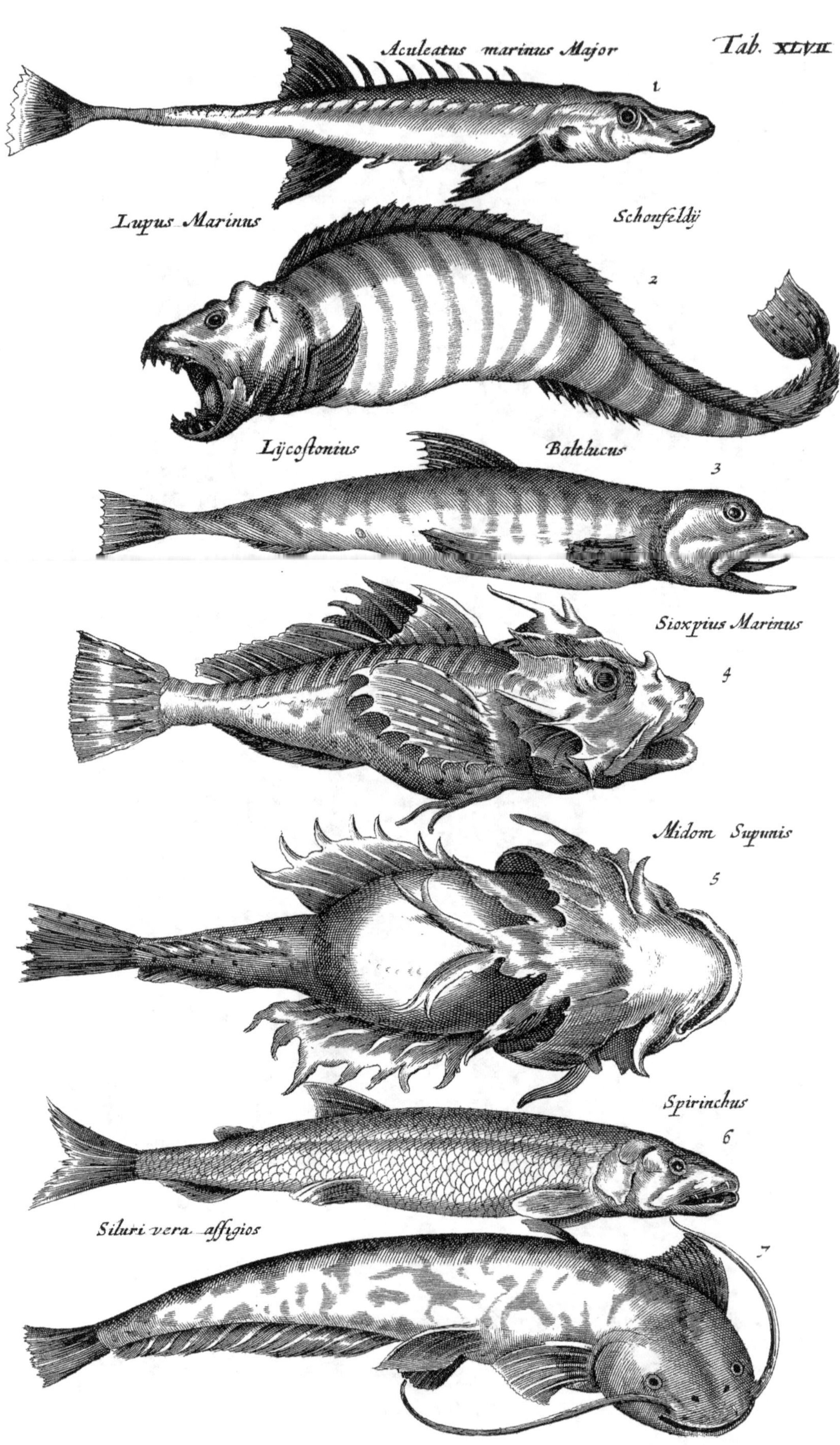

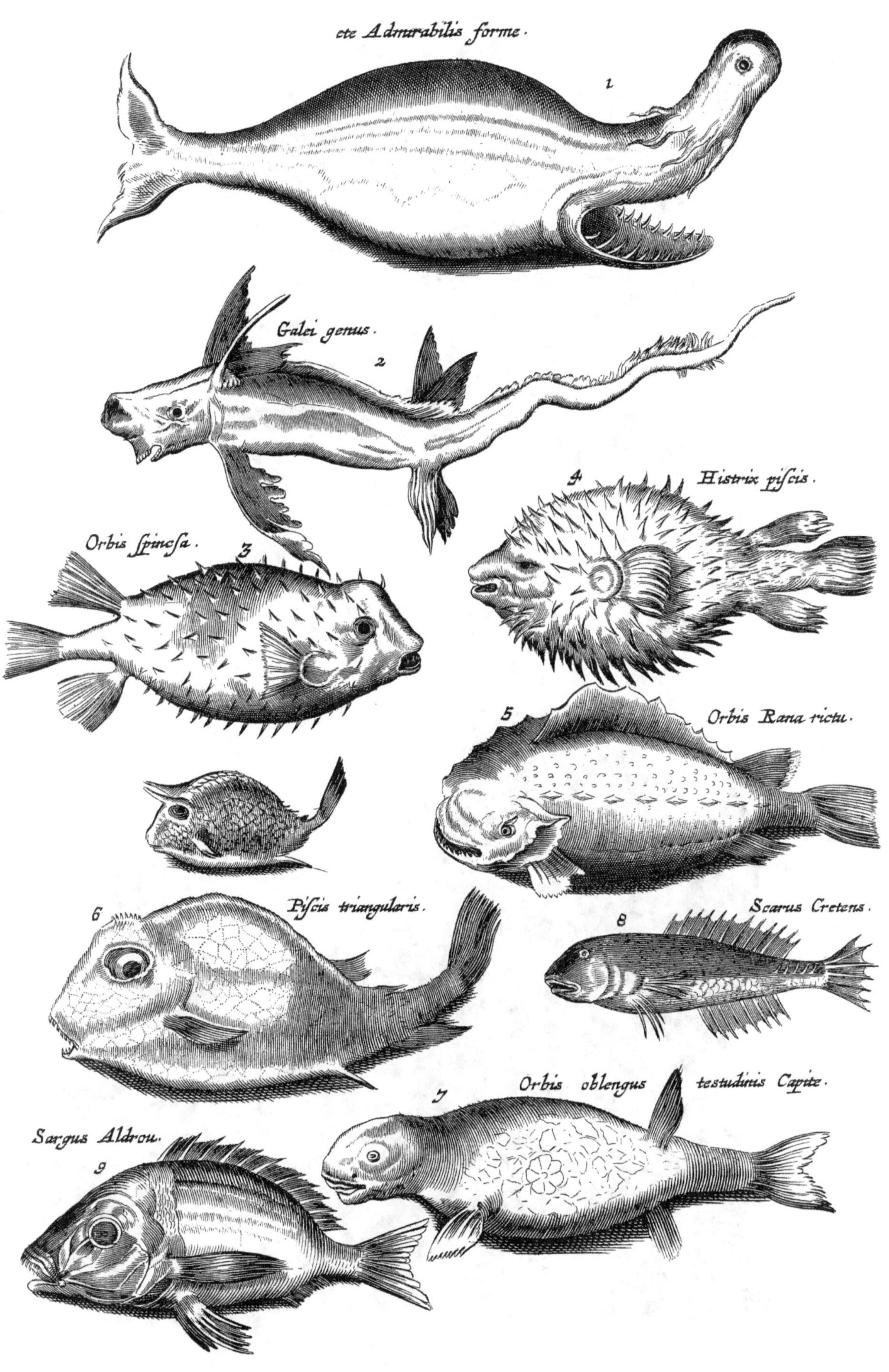

cte Admirabilis forme.
1
Galei genus.
2
Histrix piscis.
4
Orbis spinosa.
3
Orbis Rana rictu.
5
Piscis triangularis.
Scarus Cretens.
8
6
Orbis oblengus testudinis Capite.
7
Sargus Aldrou.
9

A49

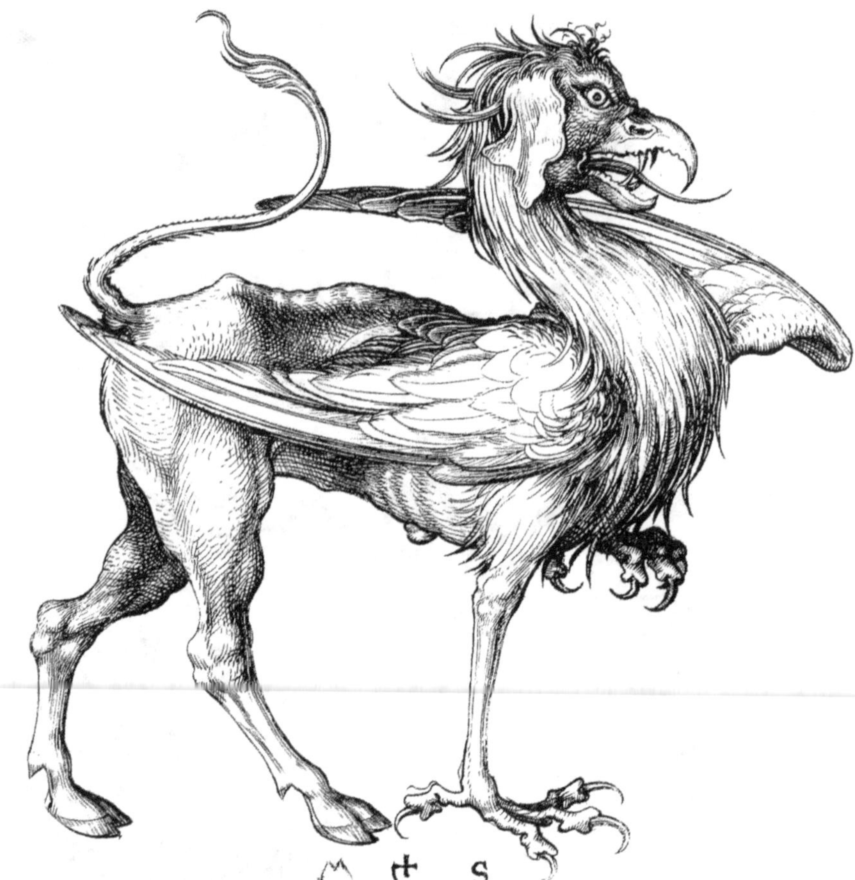

A50

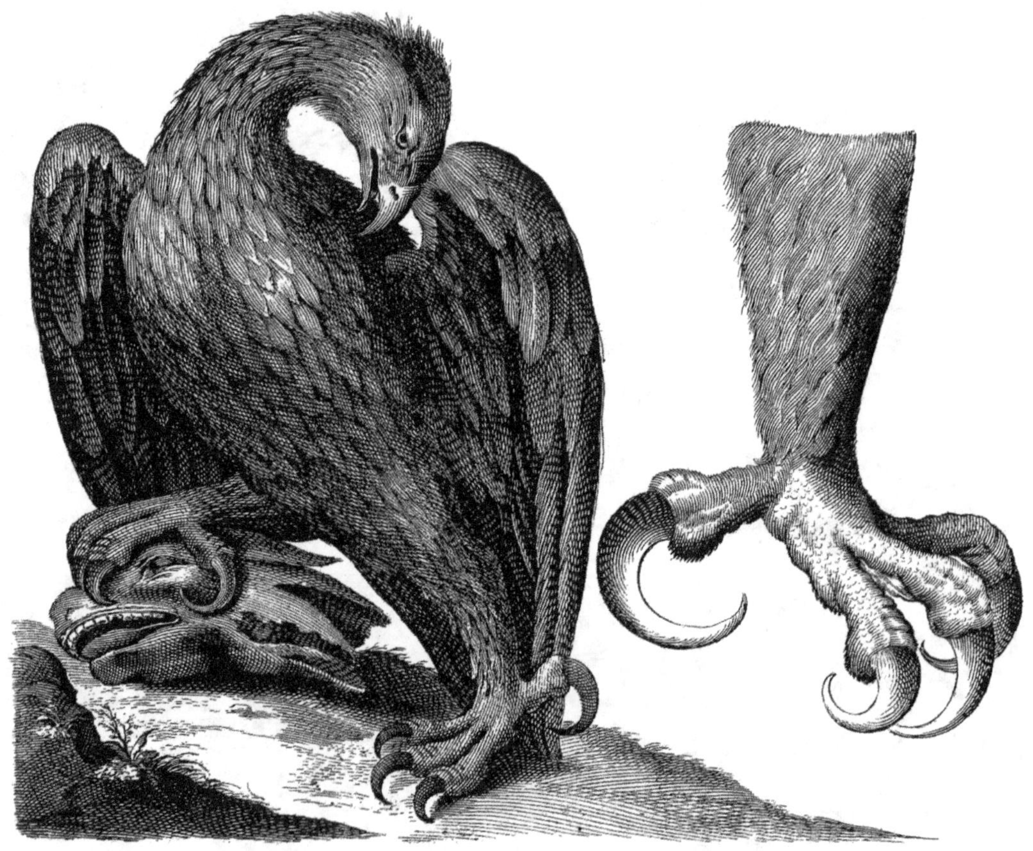

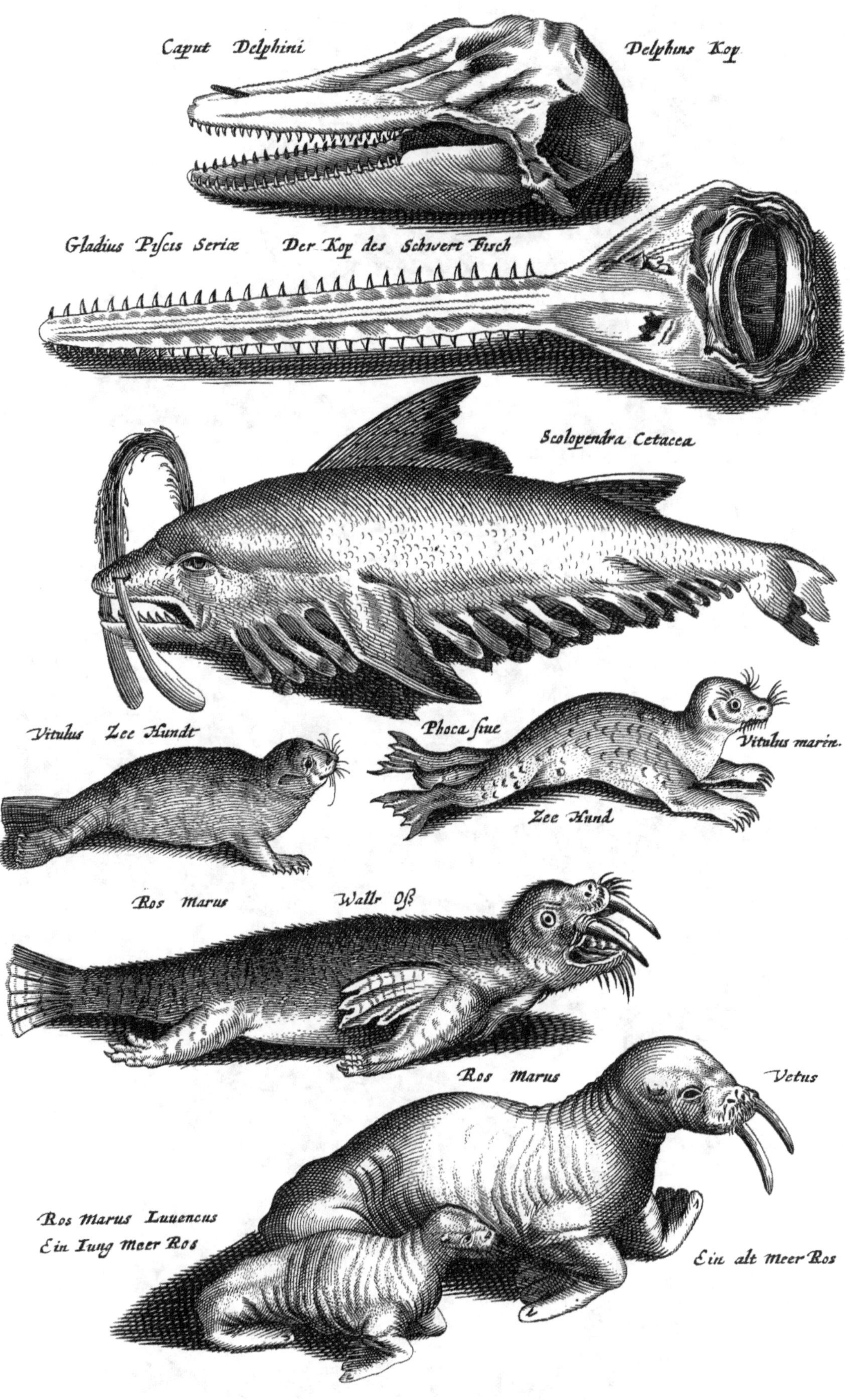
Caput Delphini
Delphins Kop
Gladius Piscis Seriæ
Der Kop des Schwert Fisch
Scolopendra Cetacea
Vitulus Zee Hundt
Phoca siue
Vitulus marin.
Zee Hund
Ros Marus
Wallr Oß
Ros Marus
Vetus
Ros Marus Luuencus
Ein Iung Meer Ros
Ein alt Meer Ros

A52

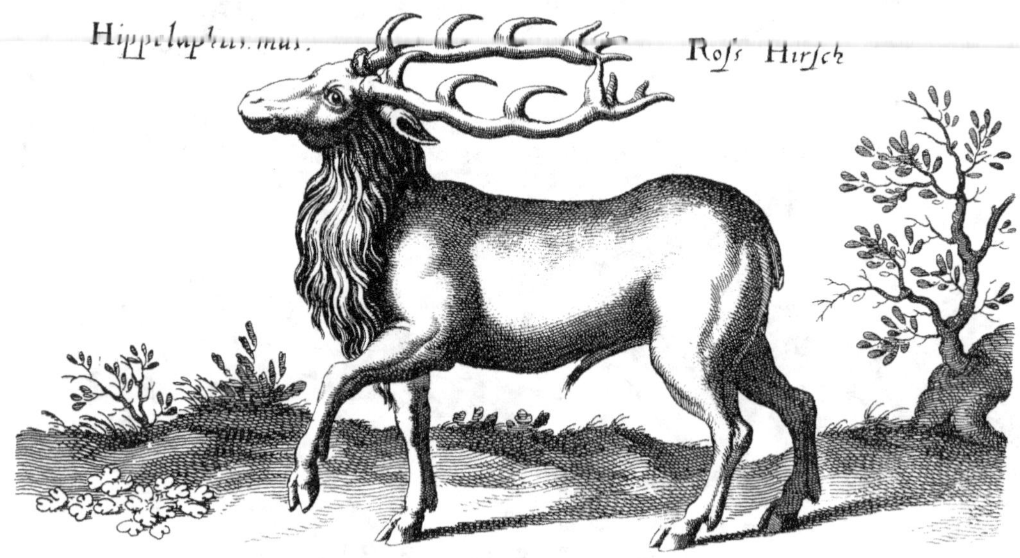

A53

A54

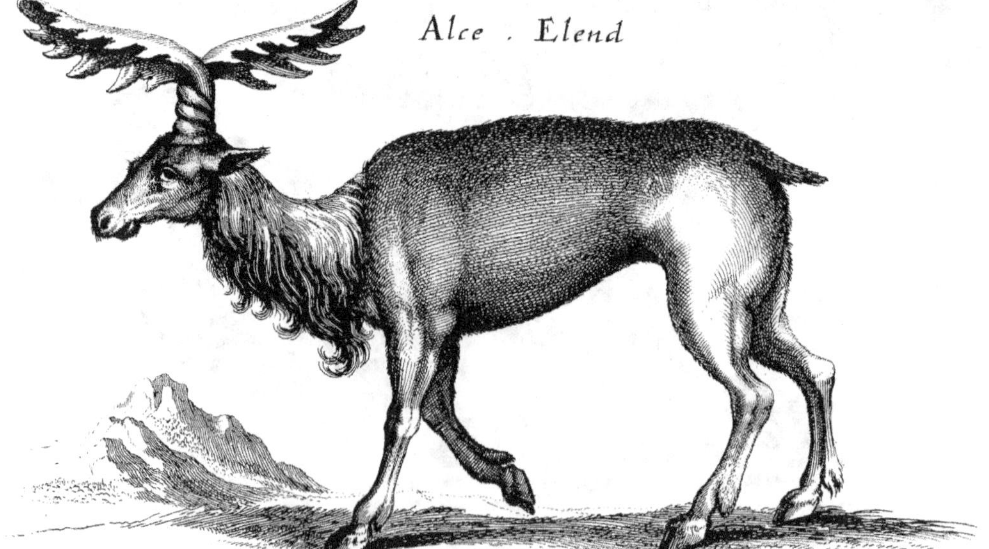

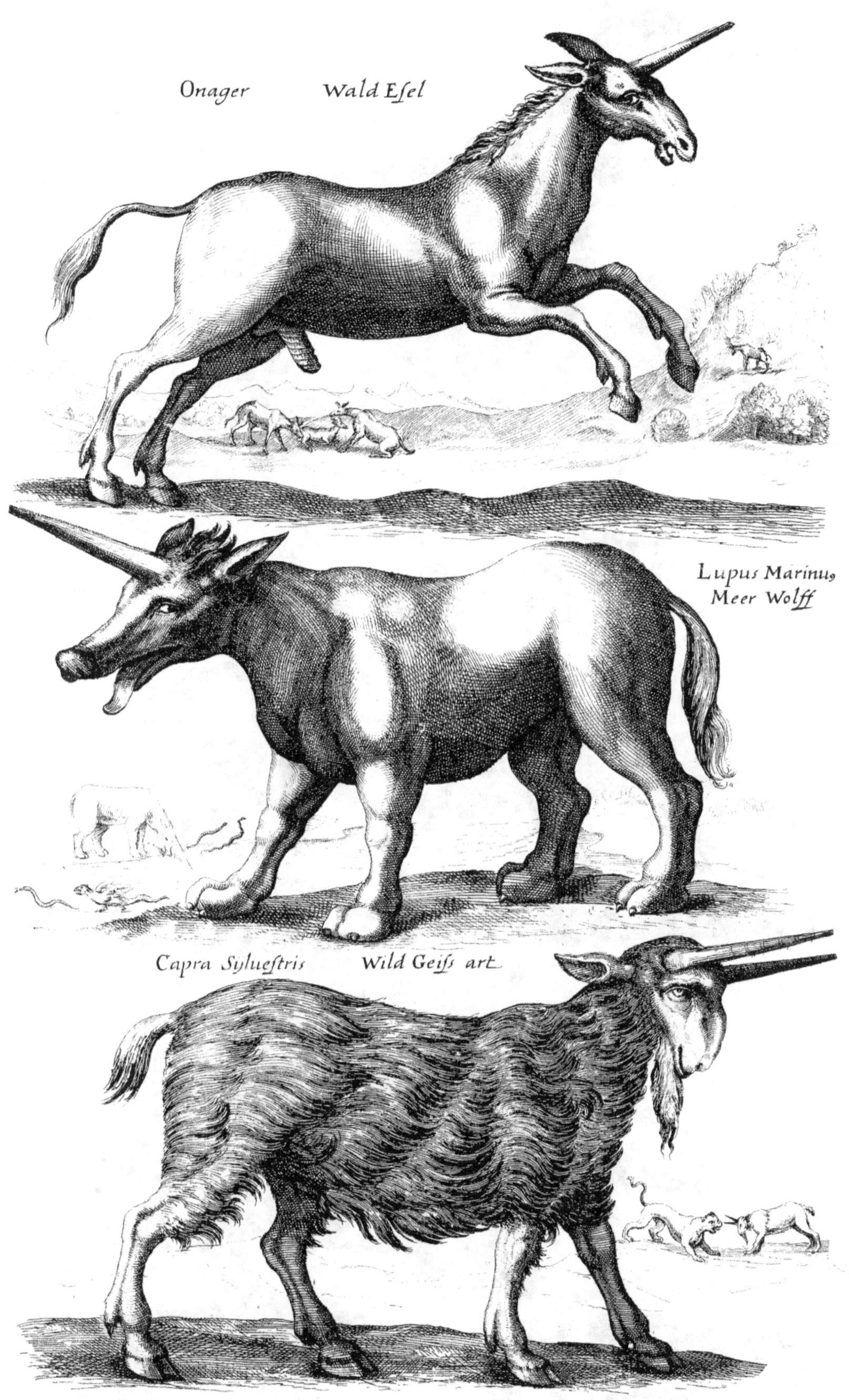
Onager   Wald Eſel
Lupus Marinu₉
Meer Wolff
Capra Sylueſtris   Wild Geiſs art

A56

Camelo - Pardalis

A57

Dama-Cervu
Damhirsch

Porcus pumilo Taxus porcing

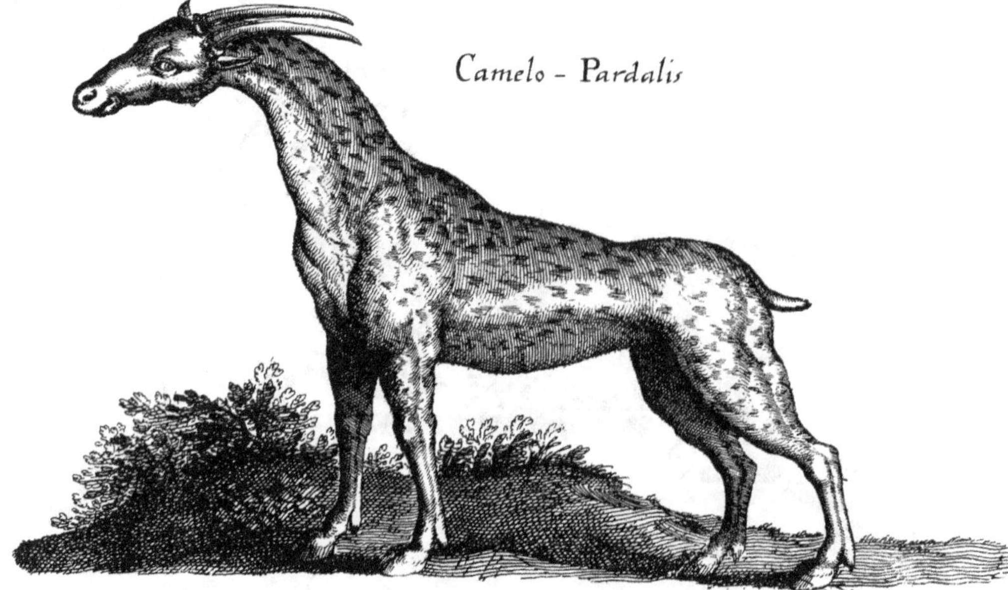

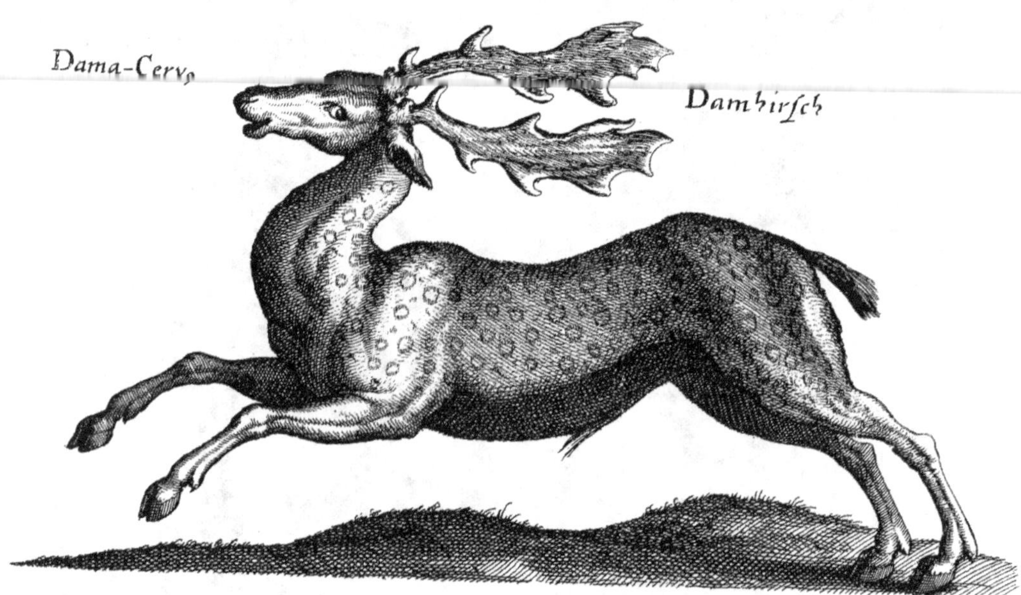

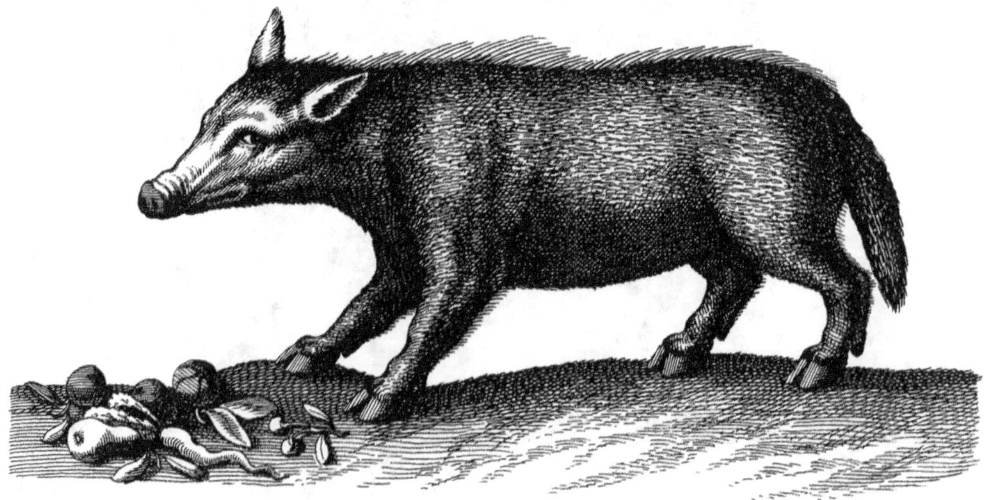

A58

A59

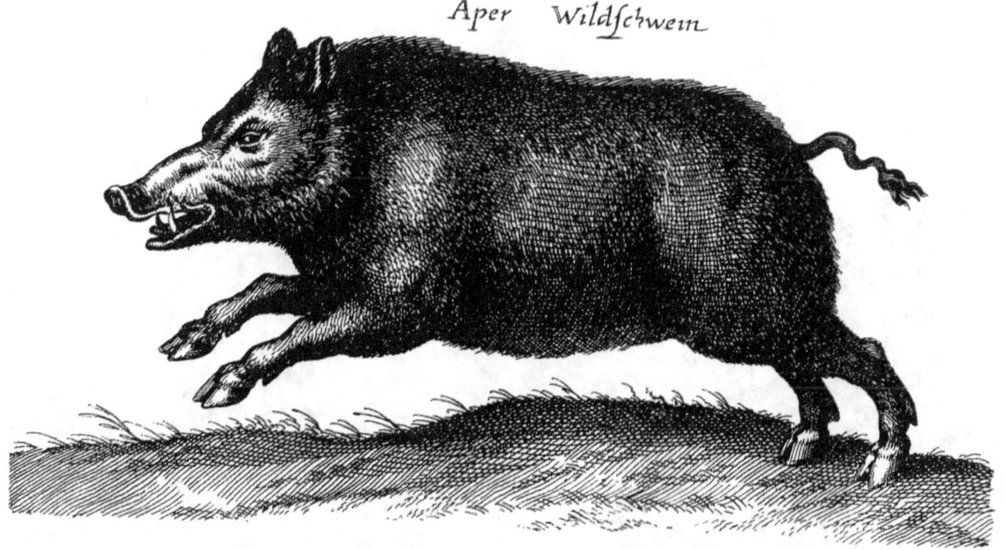

A60

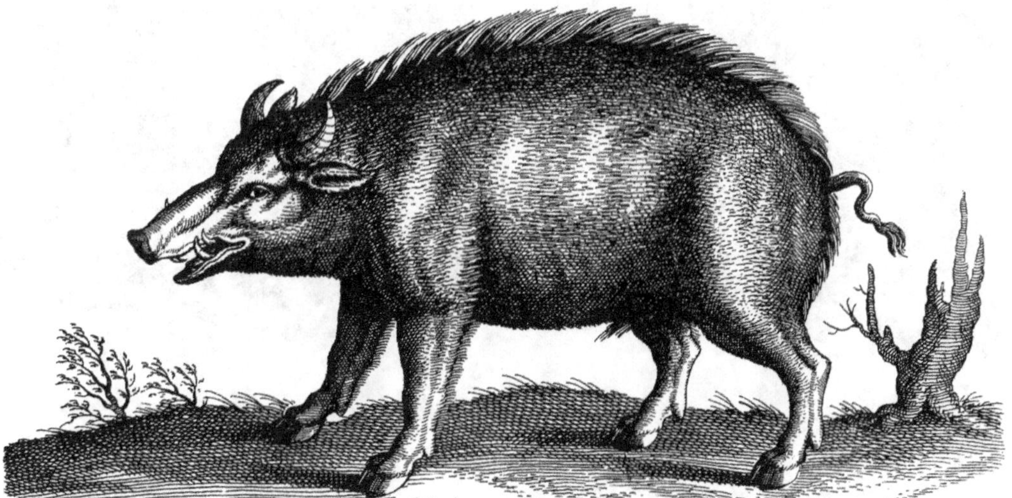

A61

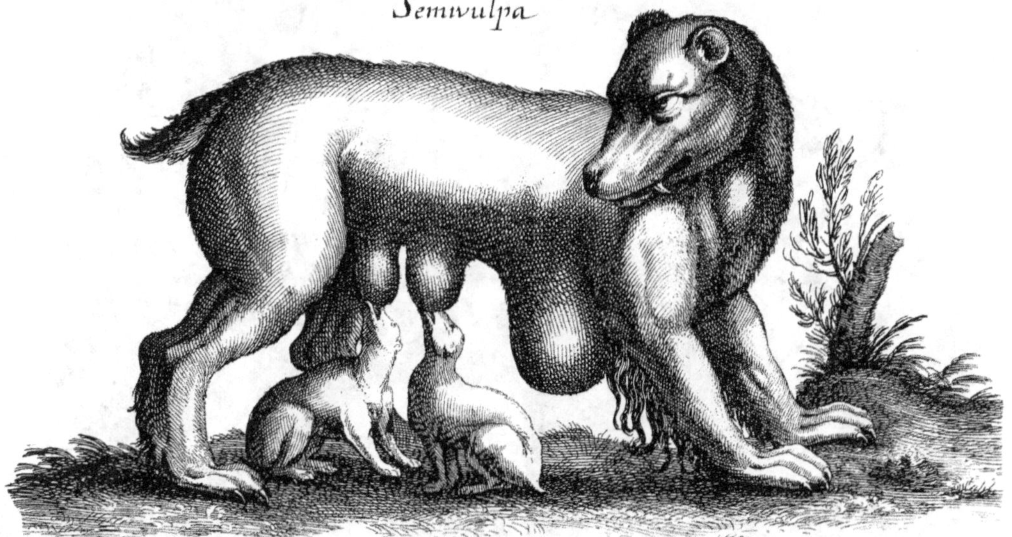

Elephas .   Elephan   Elephas.   Elephant.

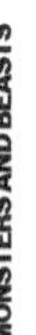

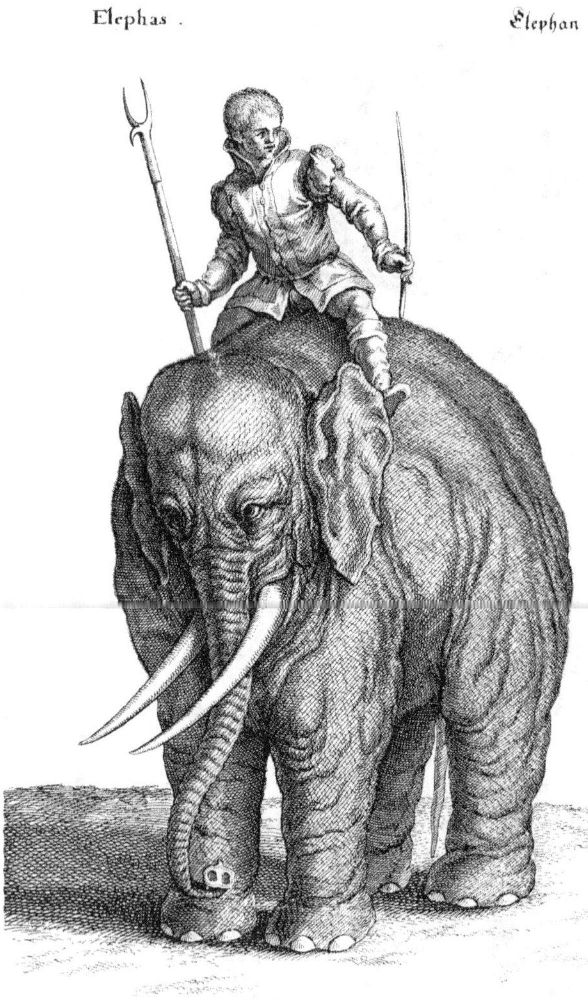

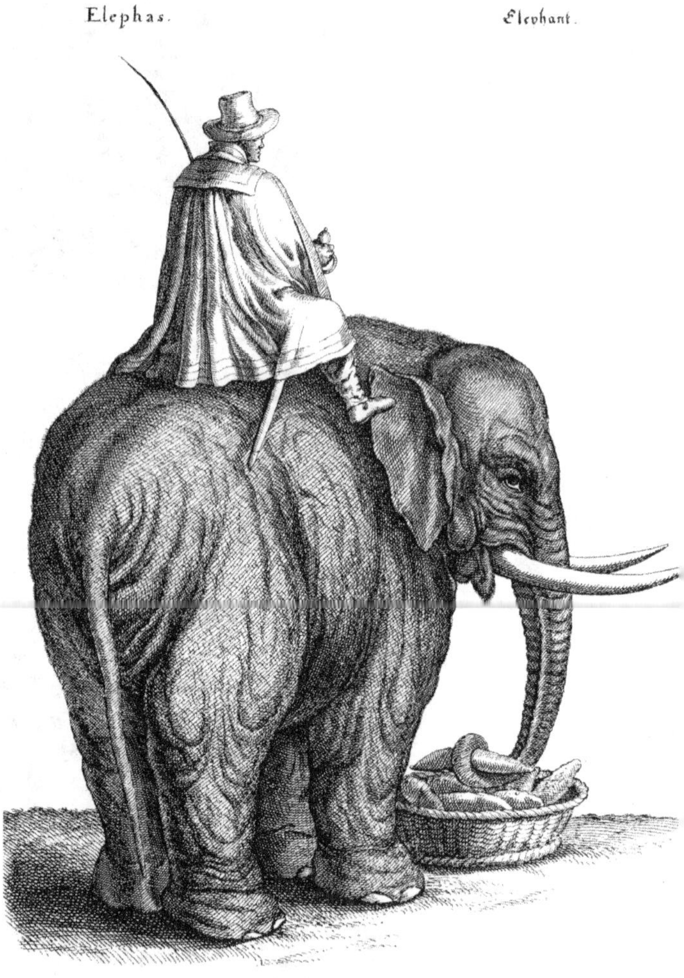

RHINOCEROS. Hornnafe Rhinocer

A63

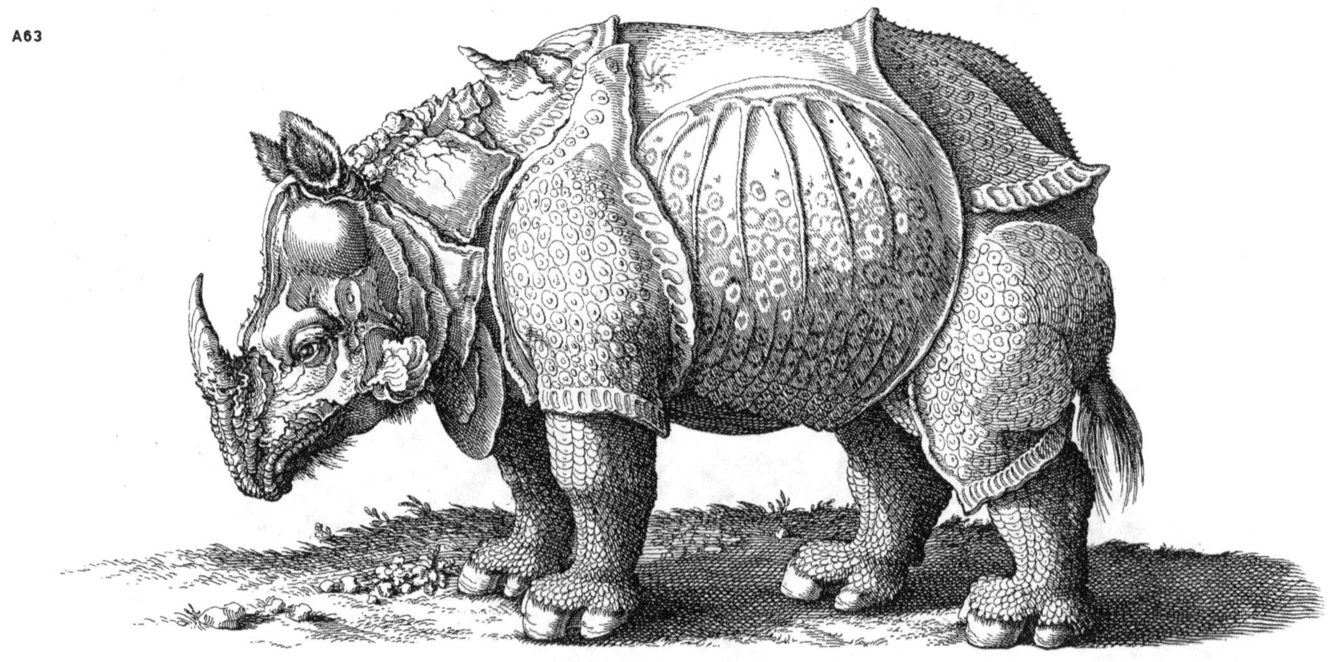

Pardus . Leopardus .
Parderthier   Leopard .

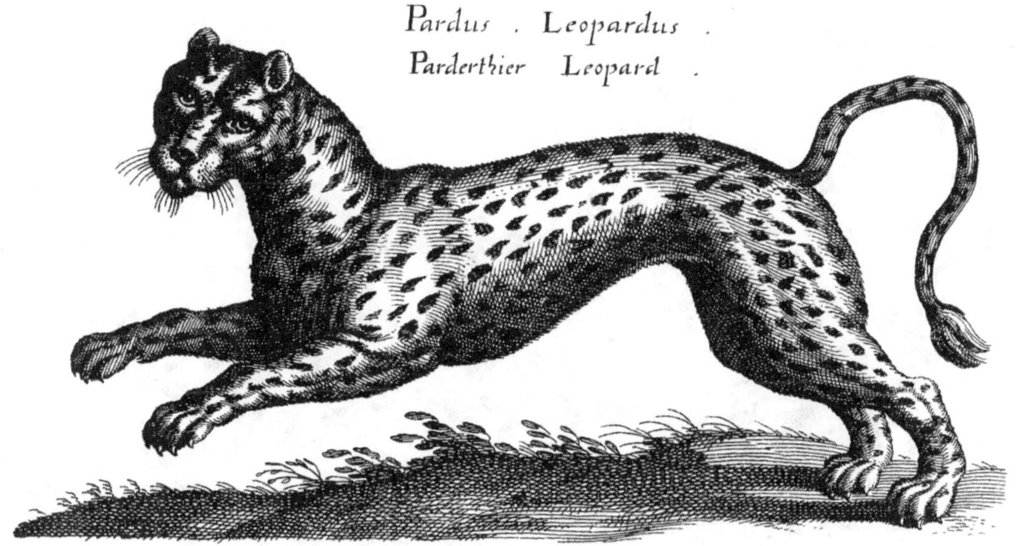

Pardus . Parderthier

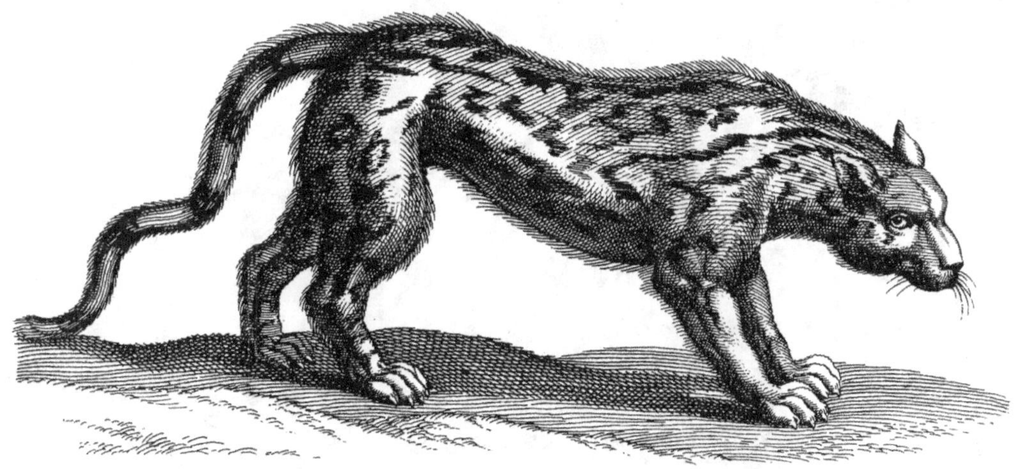

Tigris . Tigerthier

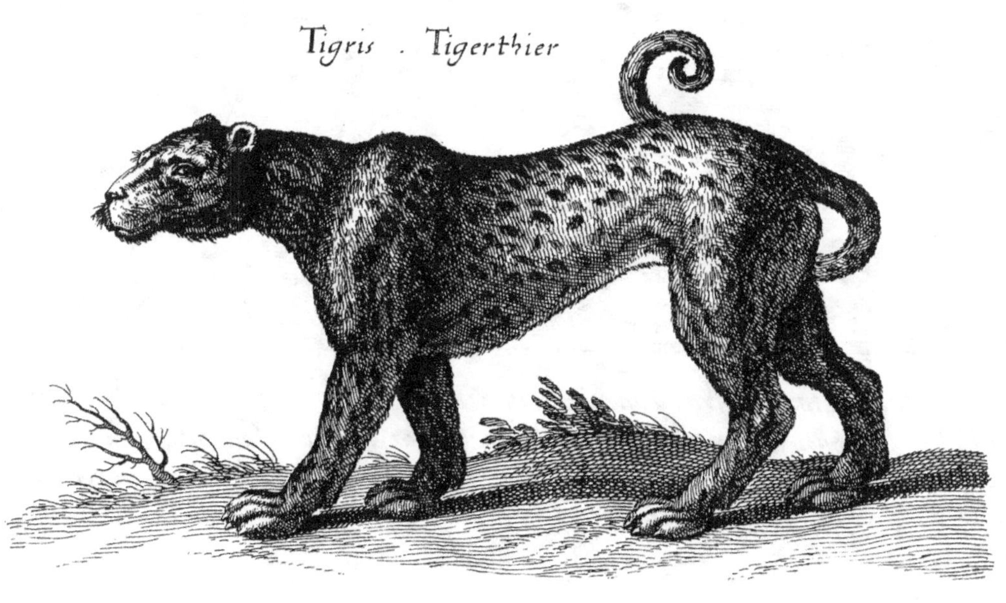

A68

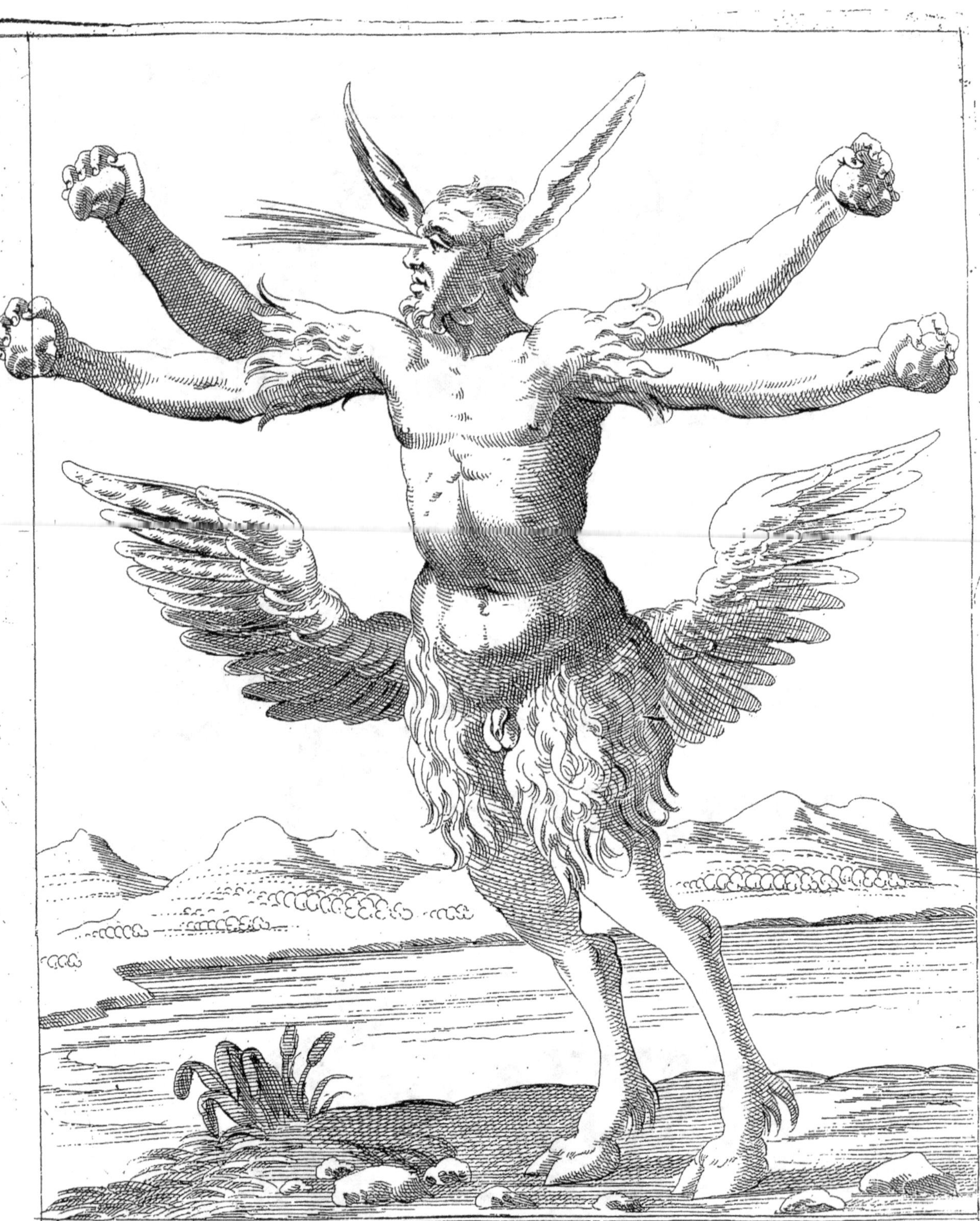

Vn marauiglioso mostro aparso nouamente nelle riue del danubio apreso à
buda. et si comincio à uedere alli.11.di febraro il quale faceua grádisimo strepito
ucideua animali è getaua fuoco/da gli ochi, è tiraua gui quátita di pietre có tutte qua
tro le mani có grádis.º terore. et spauento di queli del paese.

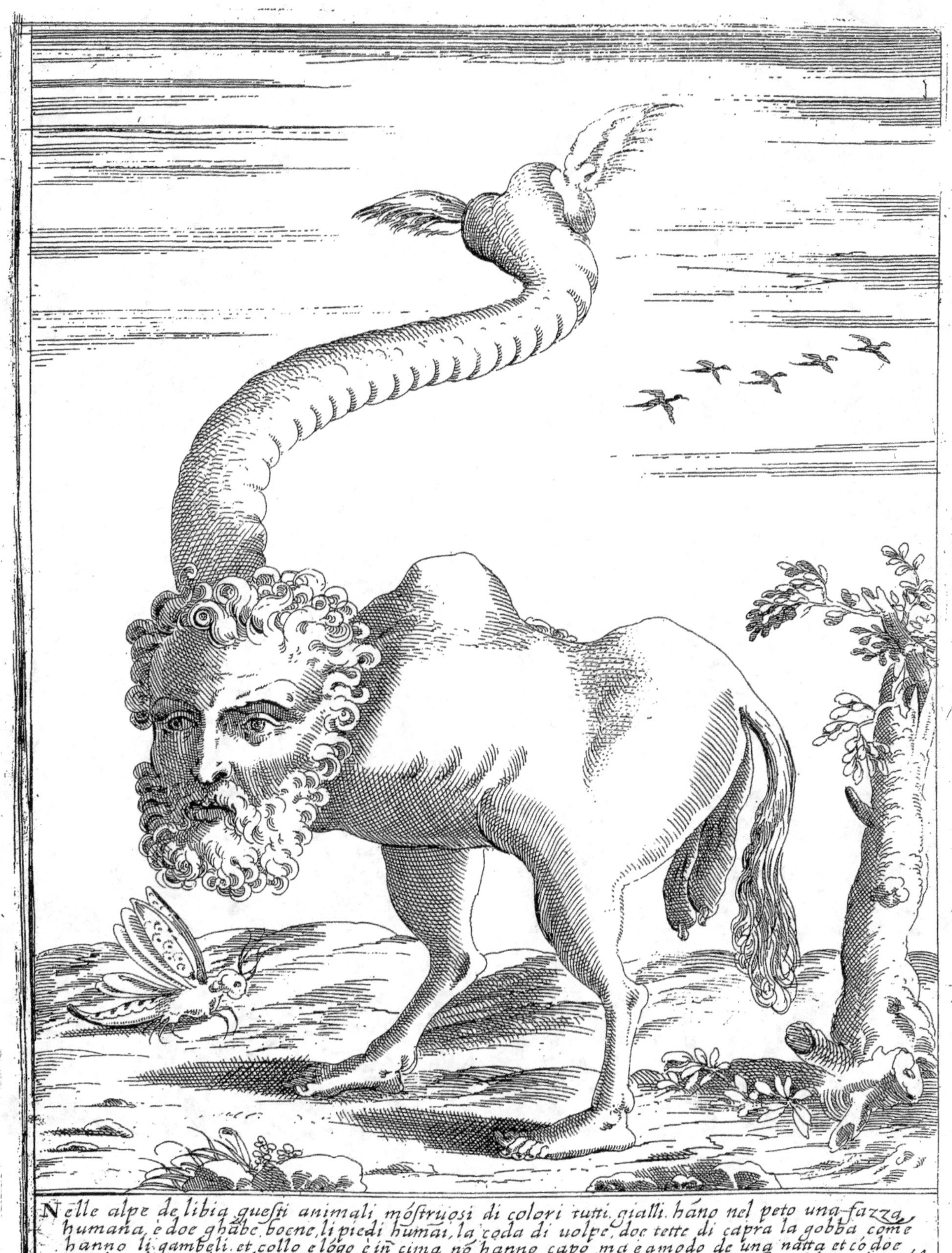

Nelle alpe de libia questi animali móstruosi di colori tutti gialli háno nel peto una fazza
humaña, e doe ghābe boene, li piedi humai, la coda di uolpe, doe tette di capra la gobba come
hanno li gambeli, et collo e lógo e iñ cima nó hanno capo ma e amodo de una nátta et có doe
orechie de porcho, e hano la barba di becco, e uiueno de erbe e radice et sono forte saluatichi, quádo
sono picoli sono buoni da mazare, e il usa el grá cane, et quando sono grádi sono durissimi da
padire et pero se manzano picholi, sono meglori questi là, che qui li capretj.

A70

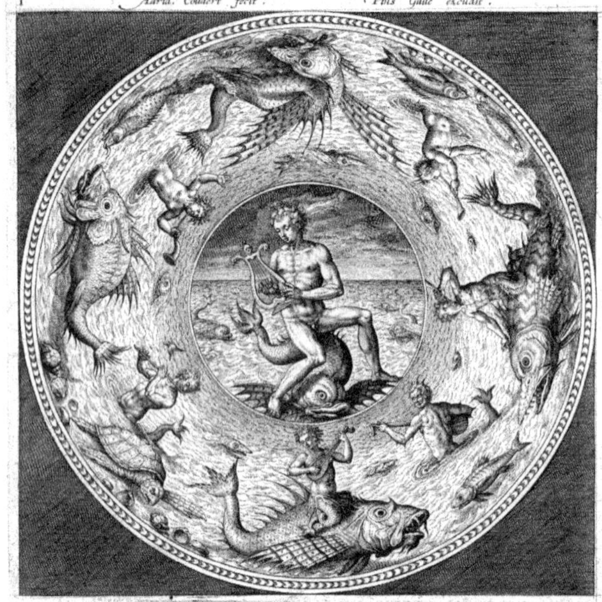

A74

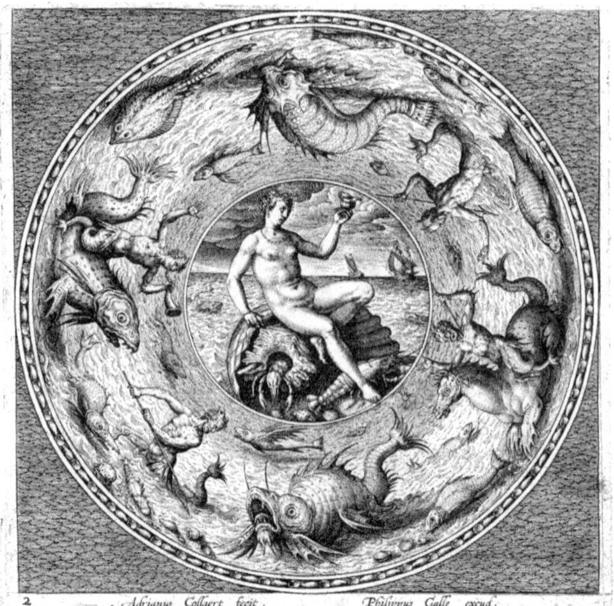

A71

A75

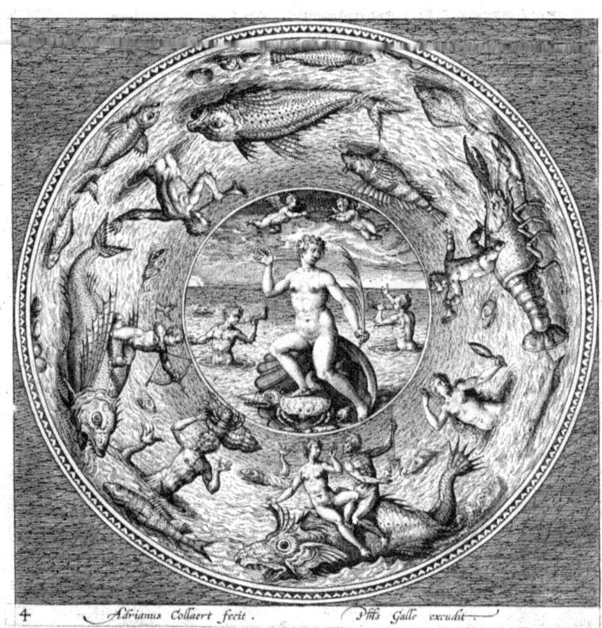

A72

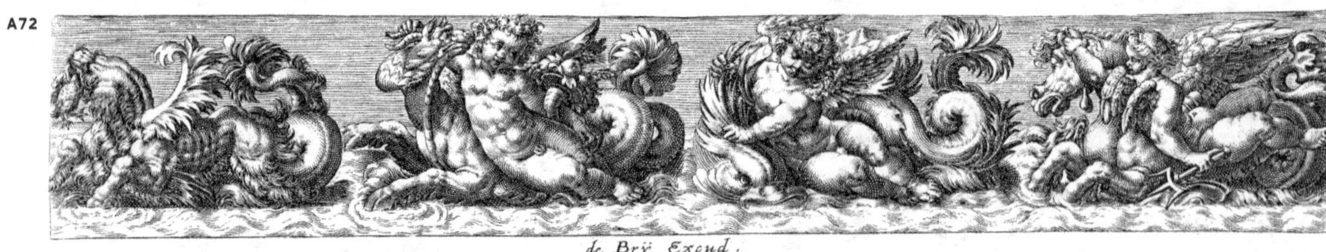

A73

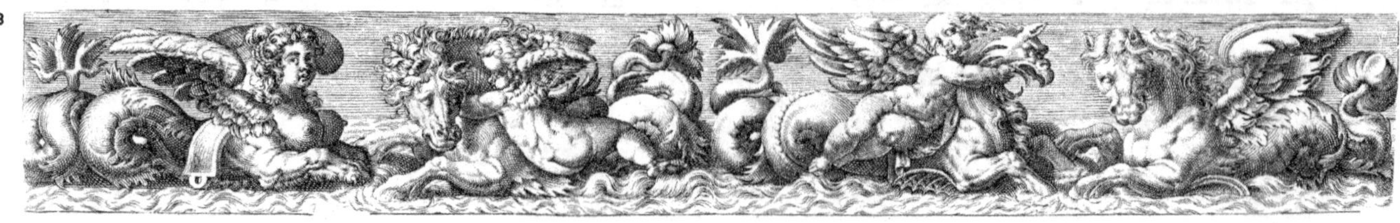

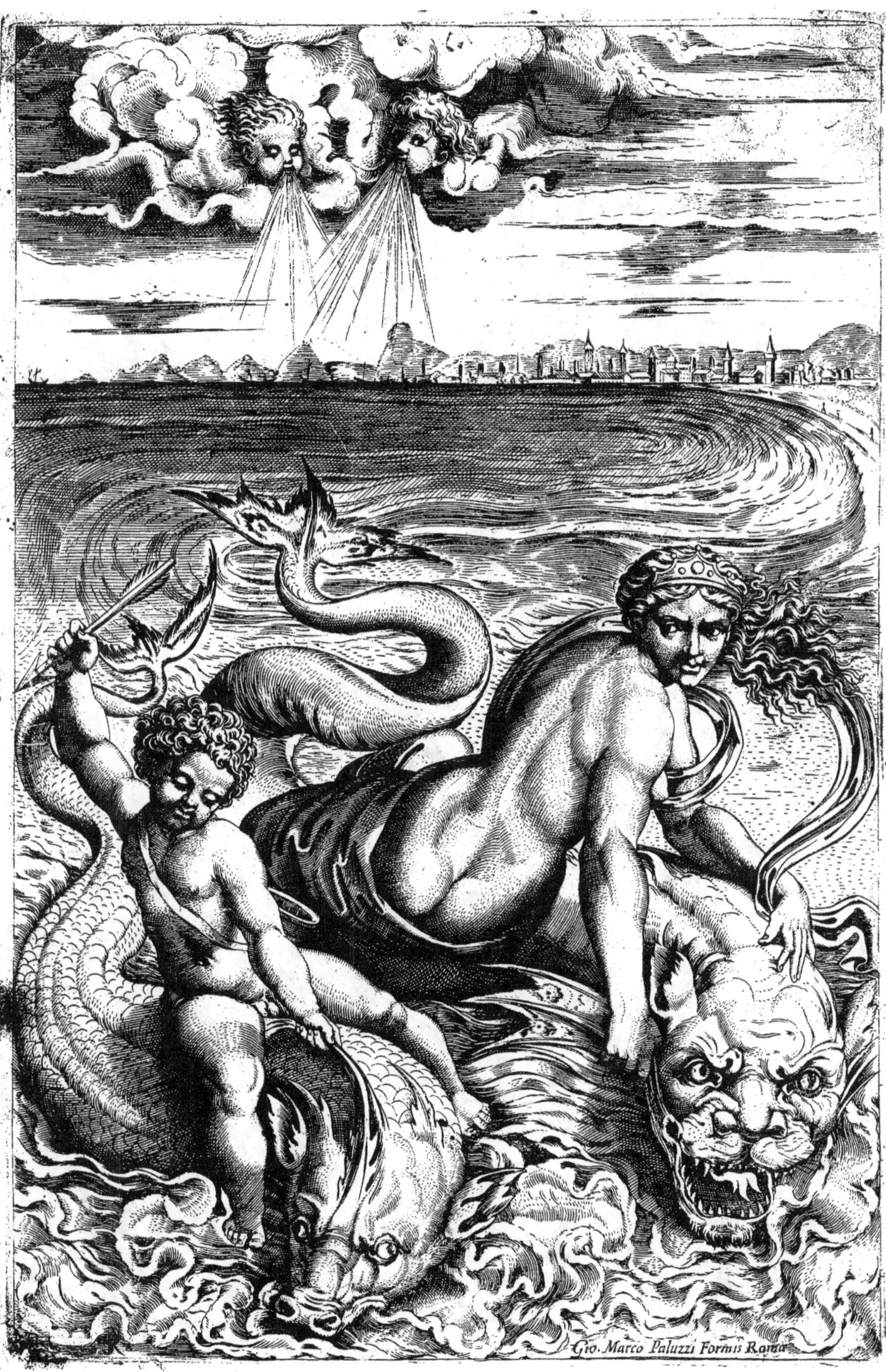
Gio. Marco Paluzzi Formis Roma

A77

A79

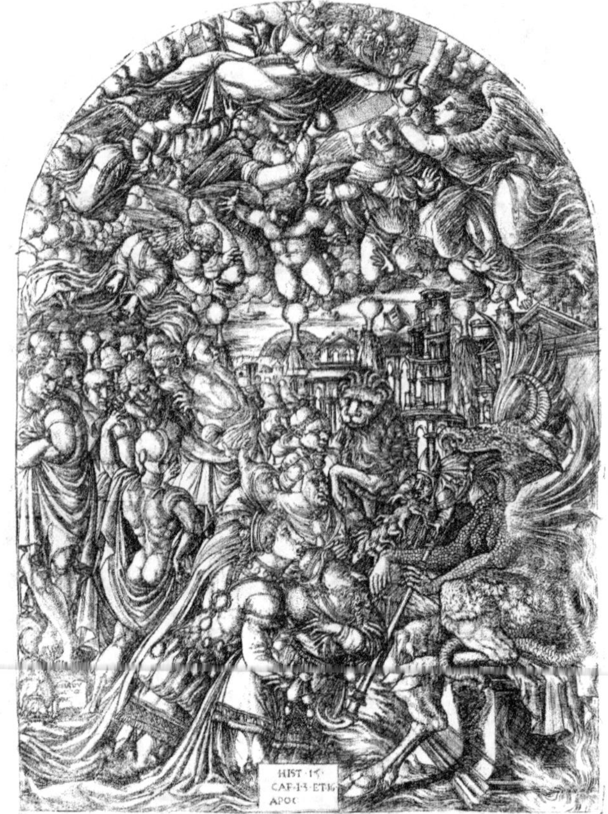

A78

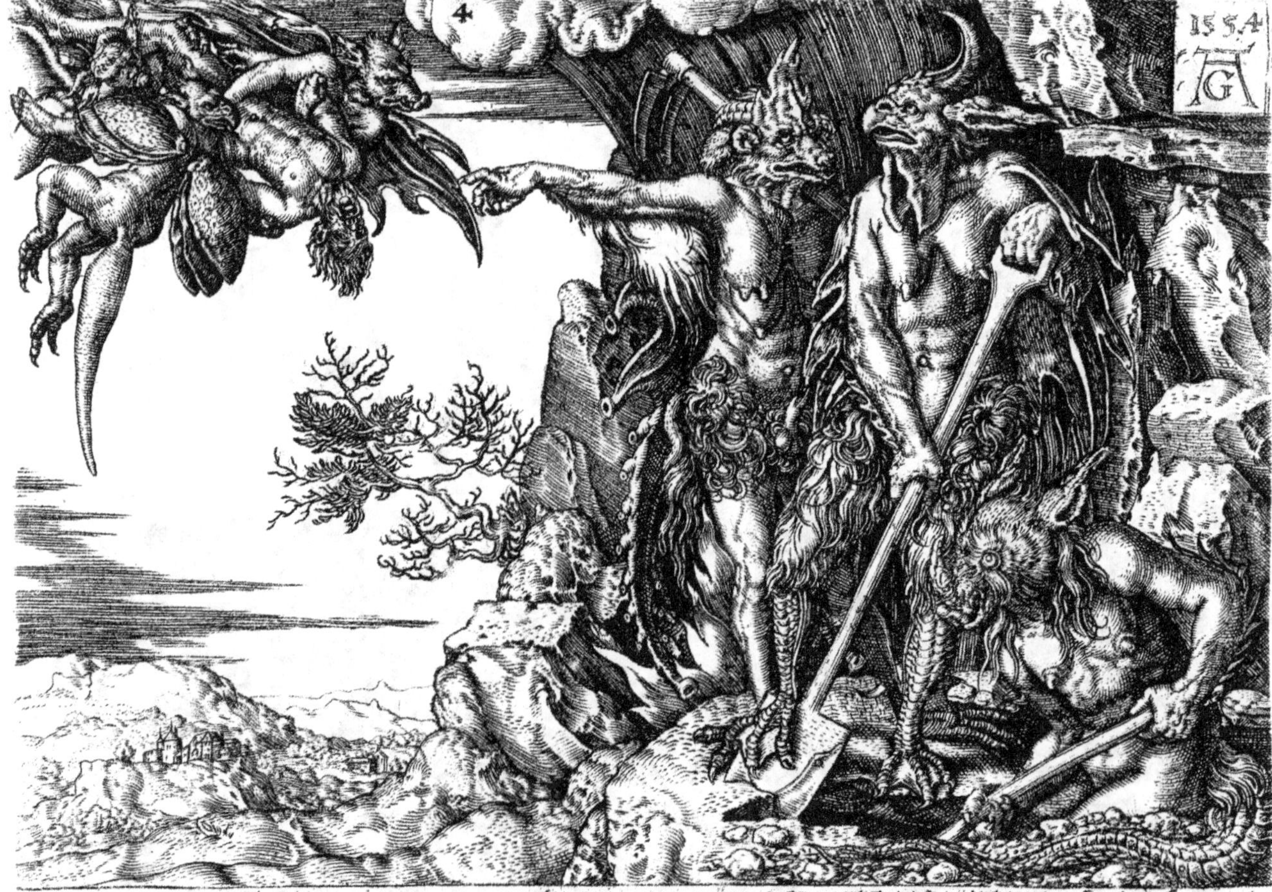

· DIVITEM · EPVLONEM · APVD · INFEROS · SEPVLTVM · HEC · TABELLA · REFERT · LVC · 16 ·

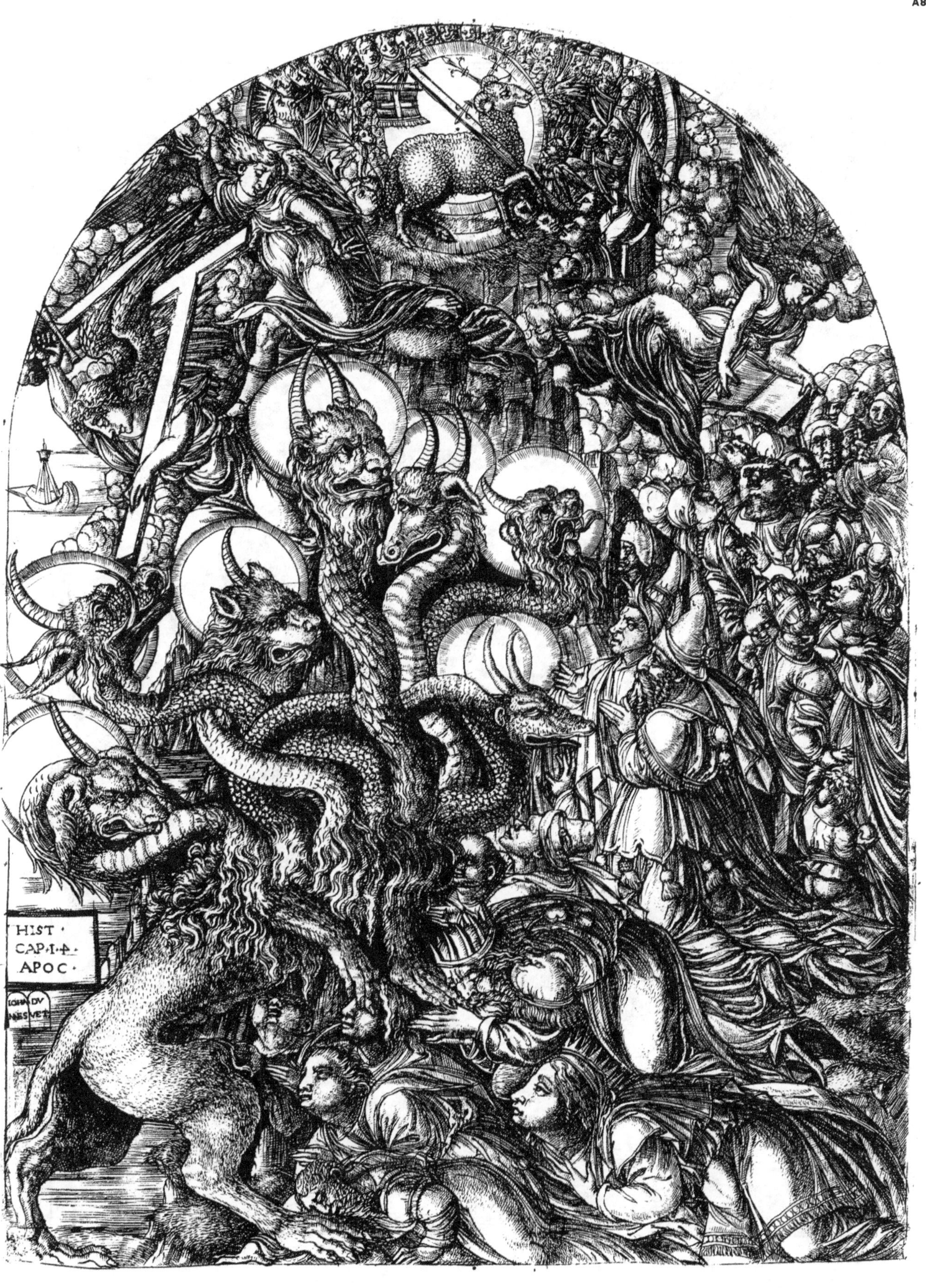

HIST ·
CAP·I·4·
APOC·
IOHA DV
NESVE

A81

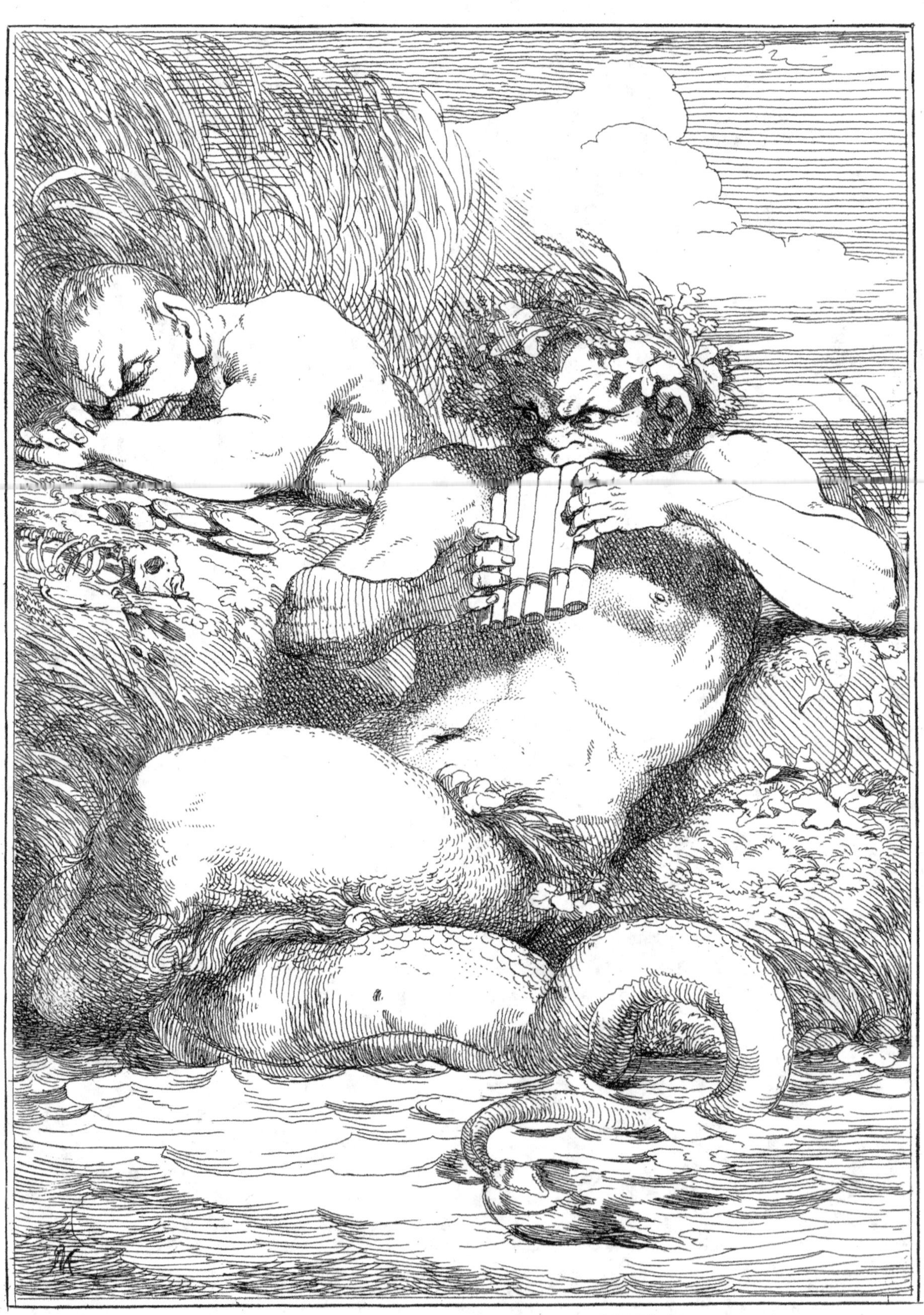

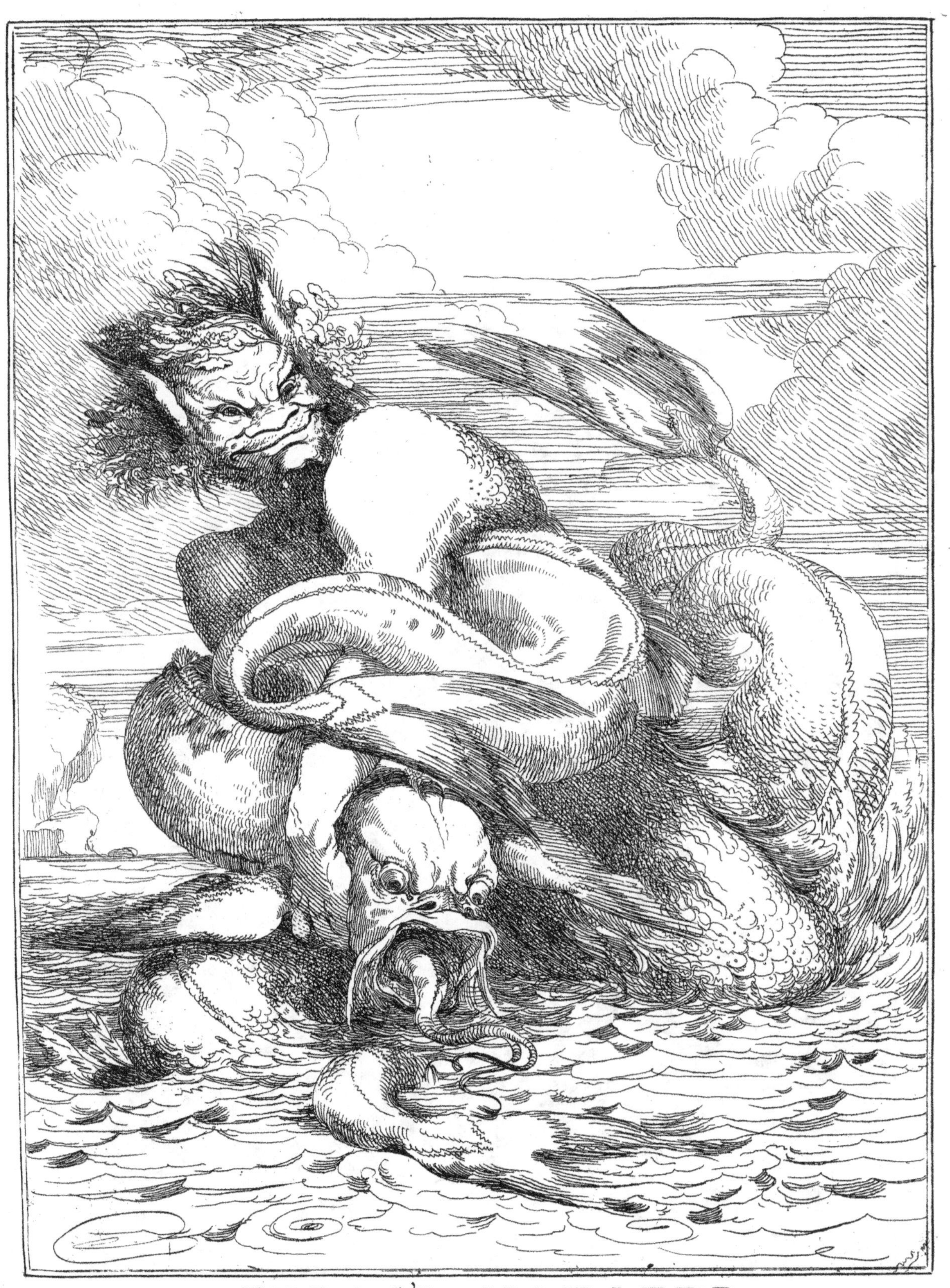

ENRAG'D MONSTER.

Publish'd Dec.r 8, 1778

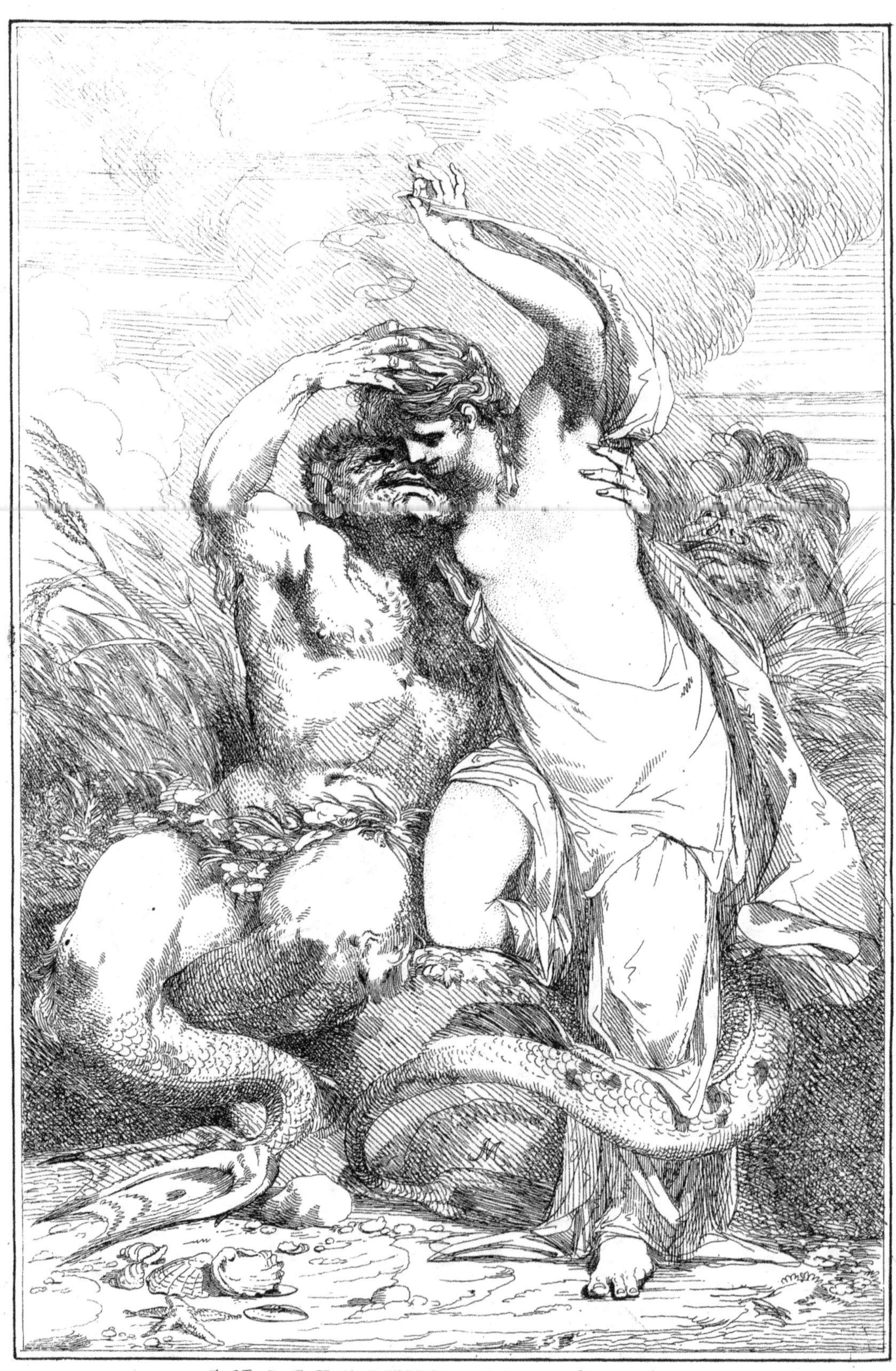

SUCCESSFUL MONSTER.
Published Dec.r 8. 1778

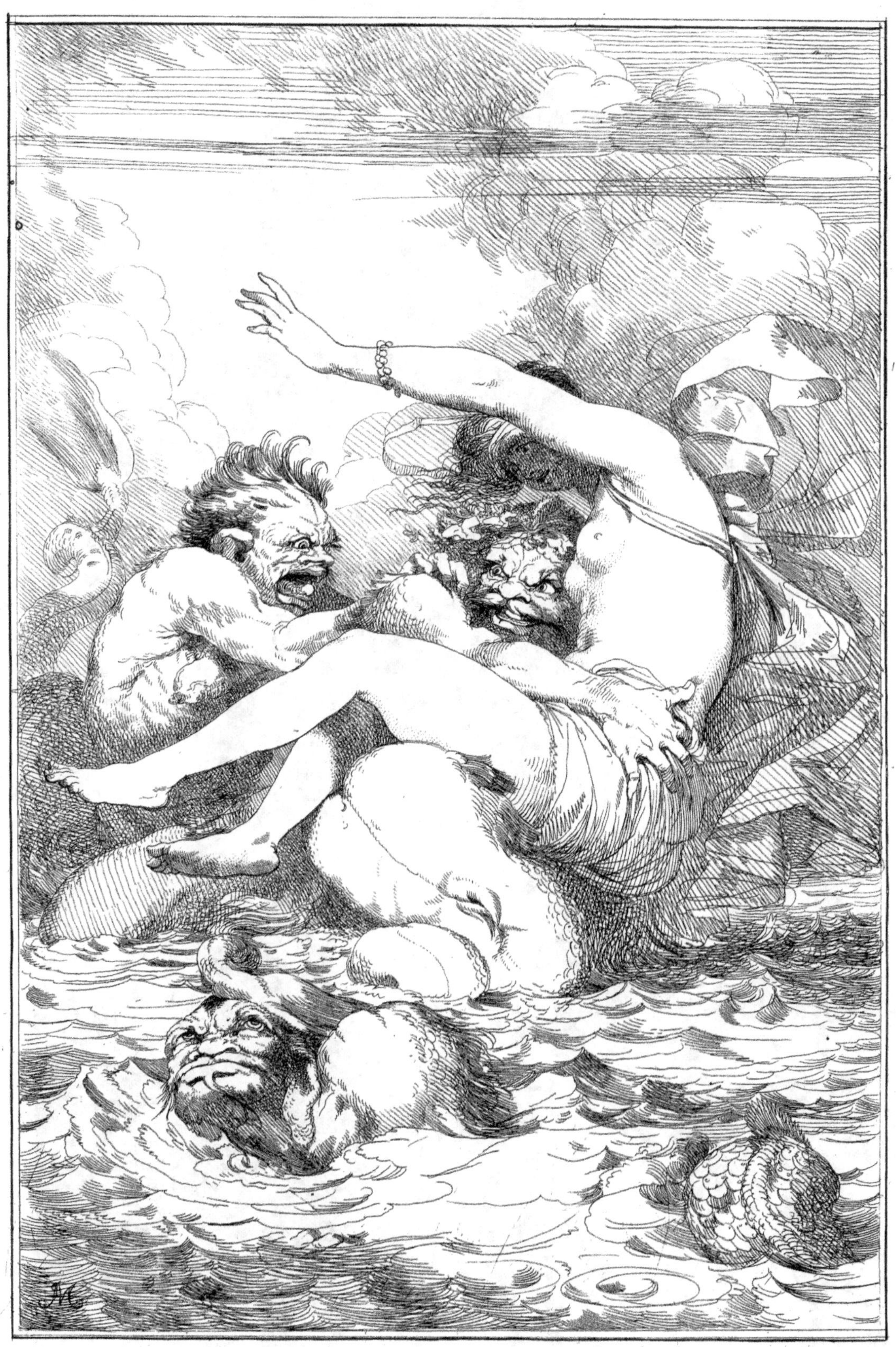

JEALOUS MONSTER.

Publish'd Dec.ʳ 8.1778

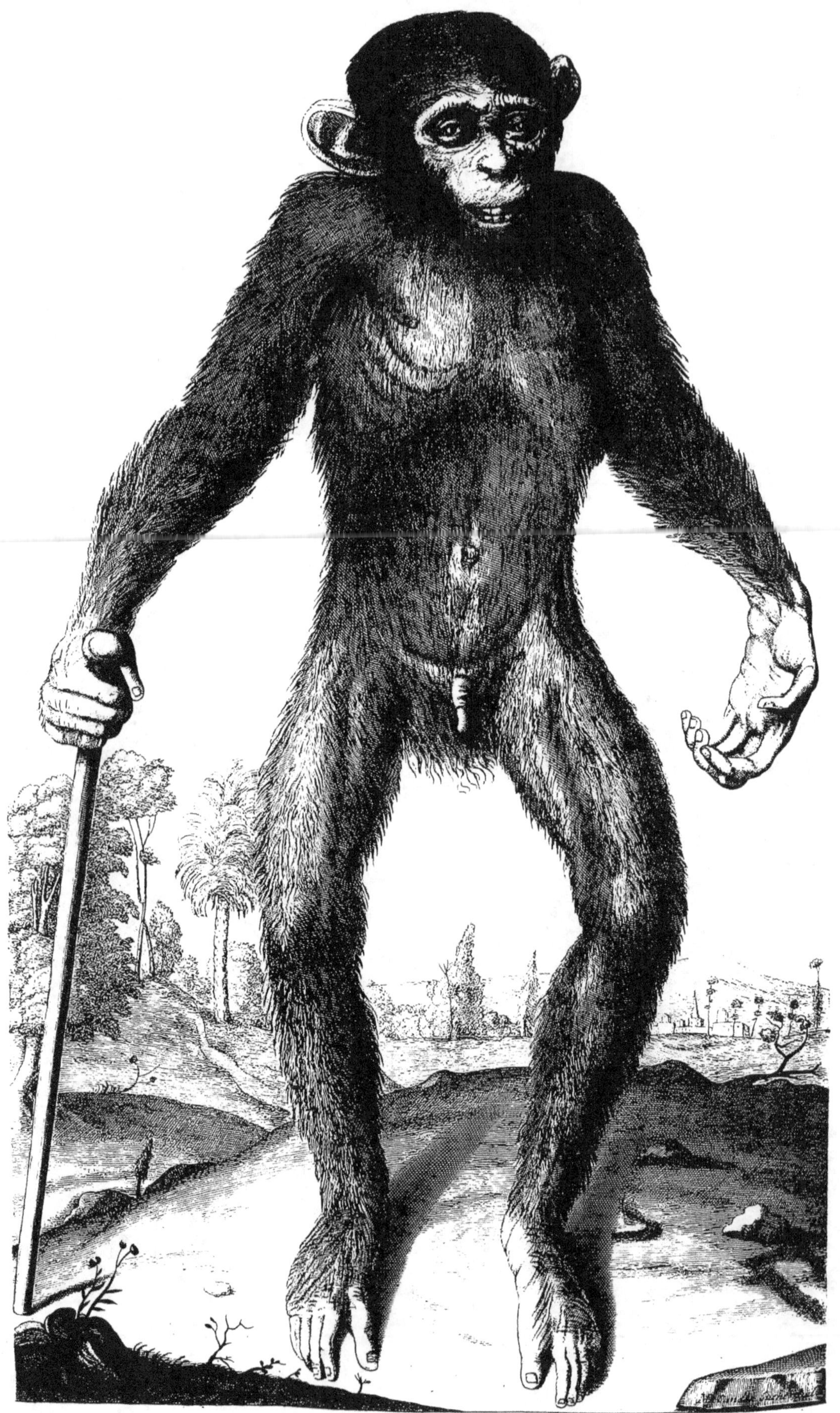

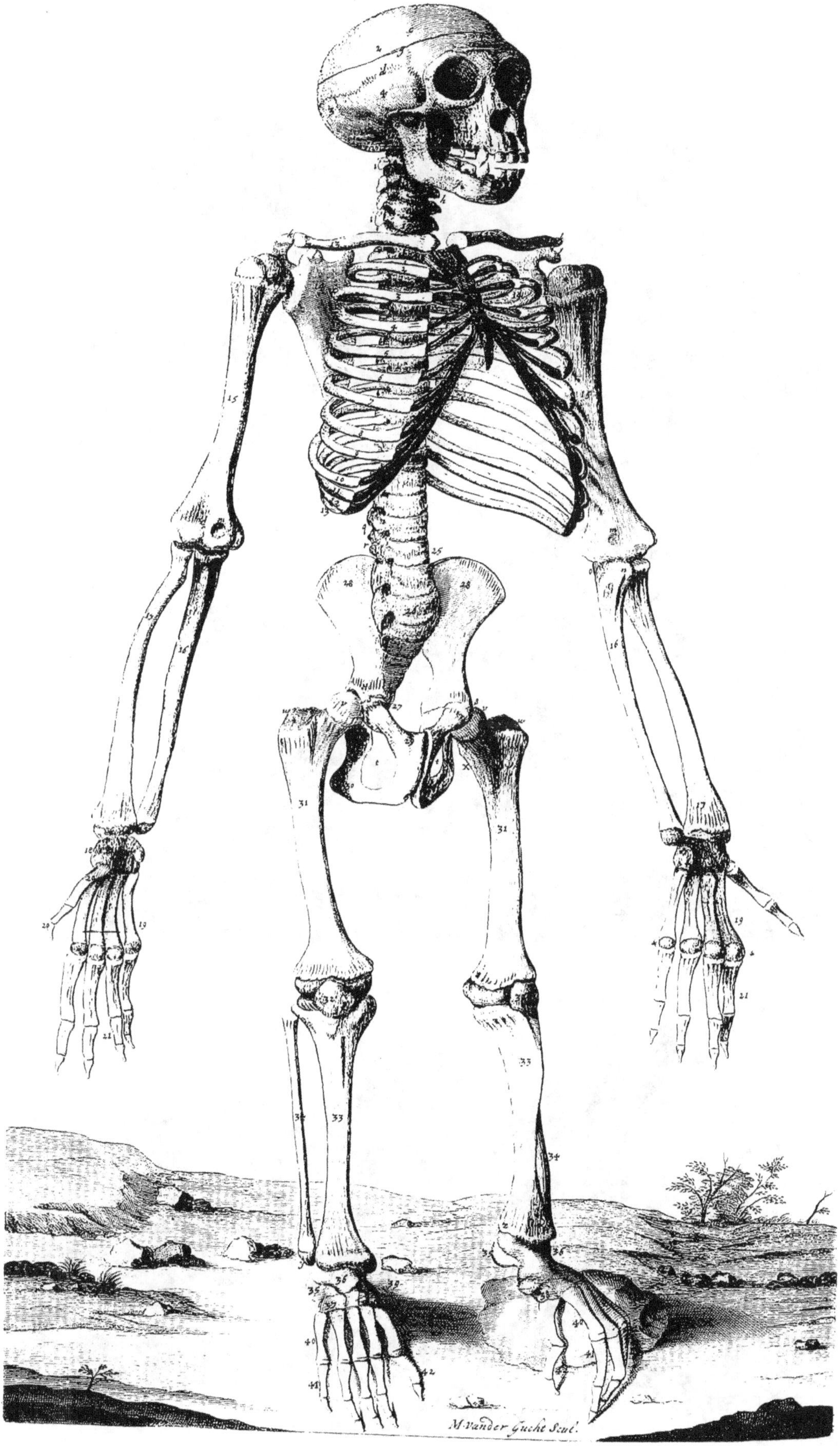

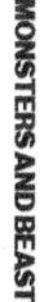

M. Vander Gucht Scul.

A87

Cercopithecus Major seu Manticora

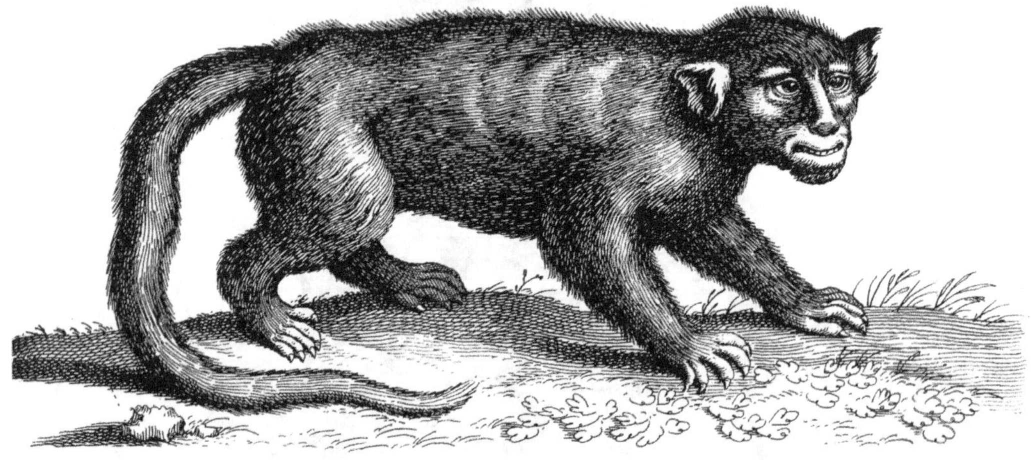

A88

Papio . Pavion . 1

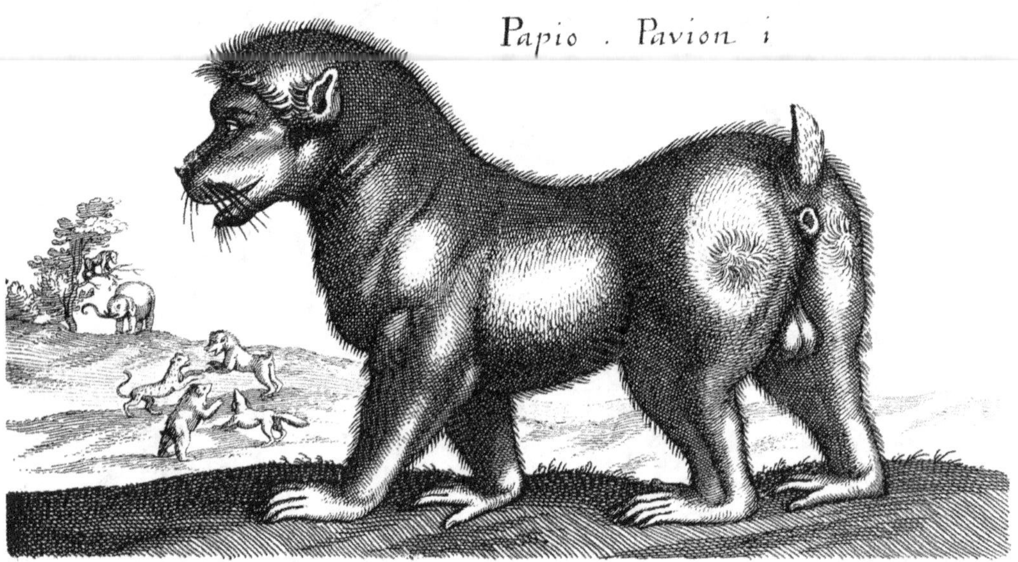

A89

Papio . 2

Cercopithecus Meer Katz

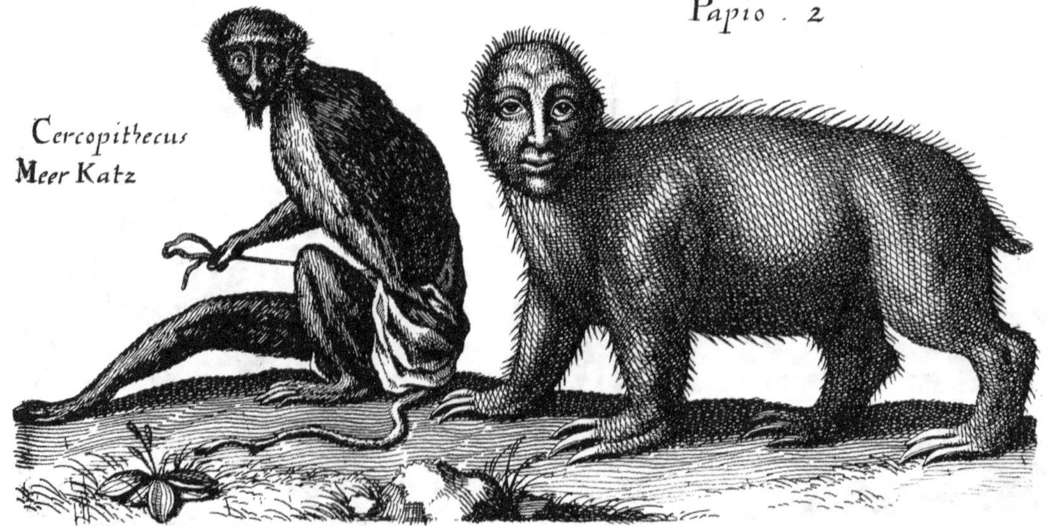

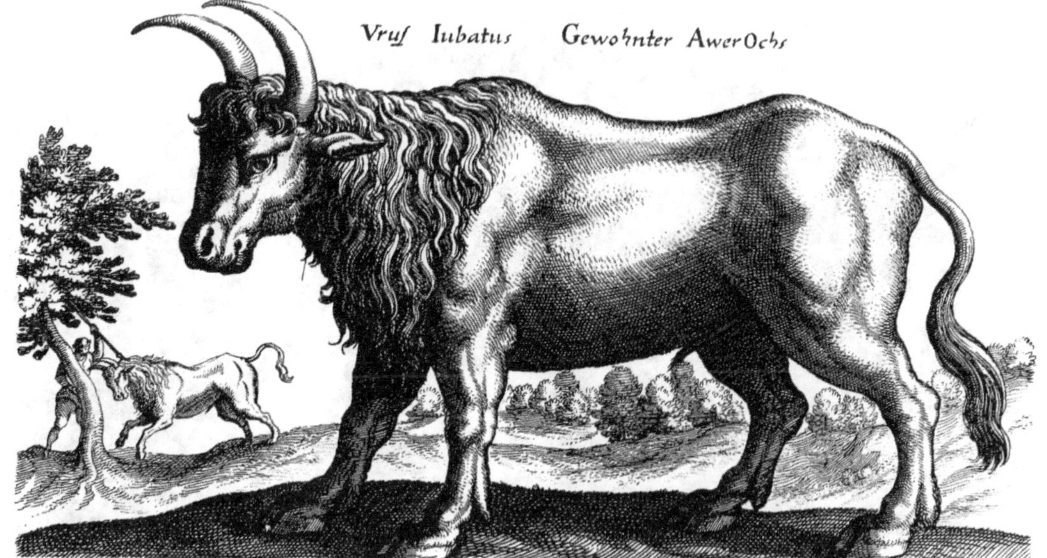
Vruʃ Iubatus   Gewohnter AwerOchs

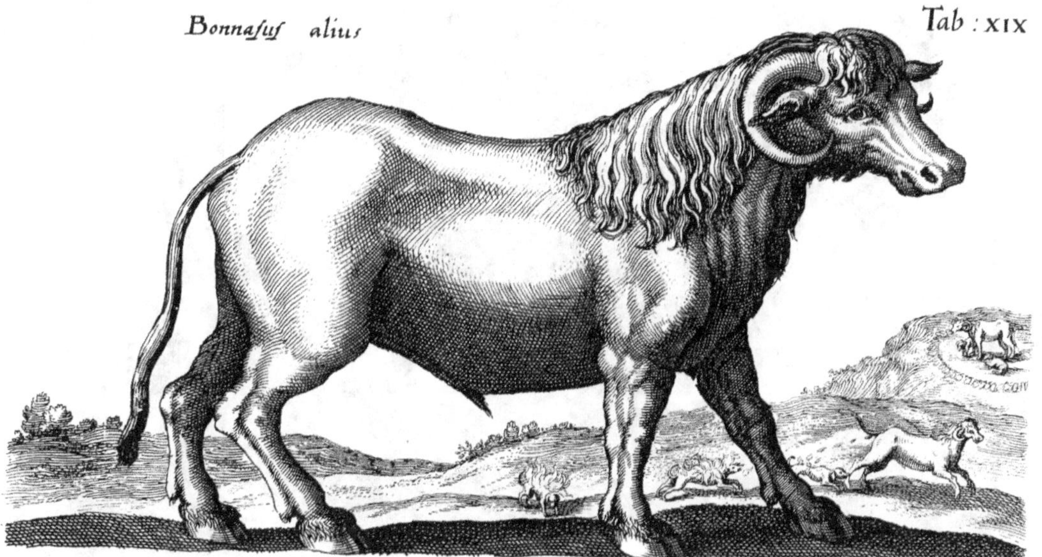
Bonnaʃuʃ alius
Tab : XIX

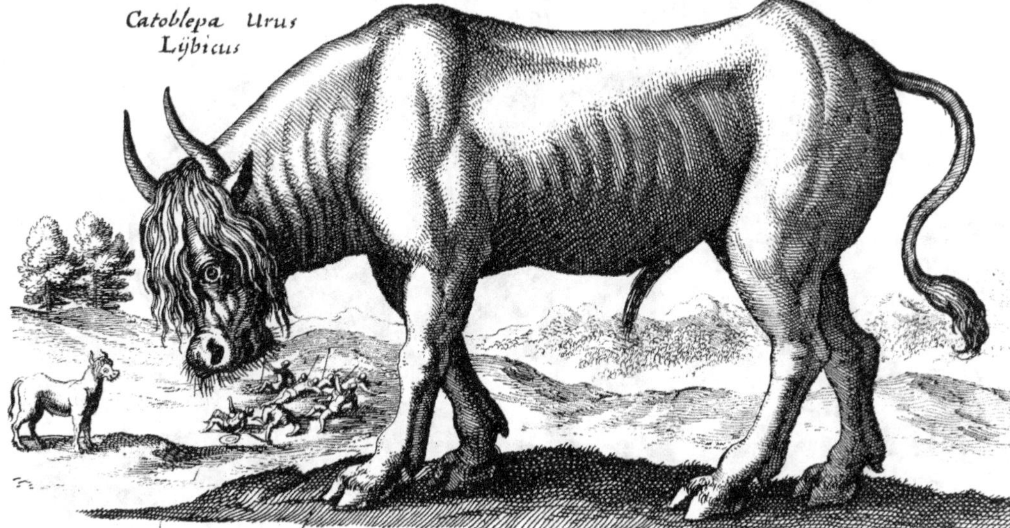
Catoblepa Urus
Lÿbicus

A93

Bison Iubatus .

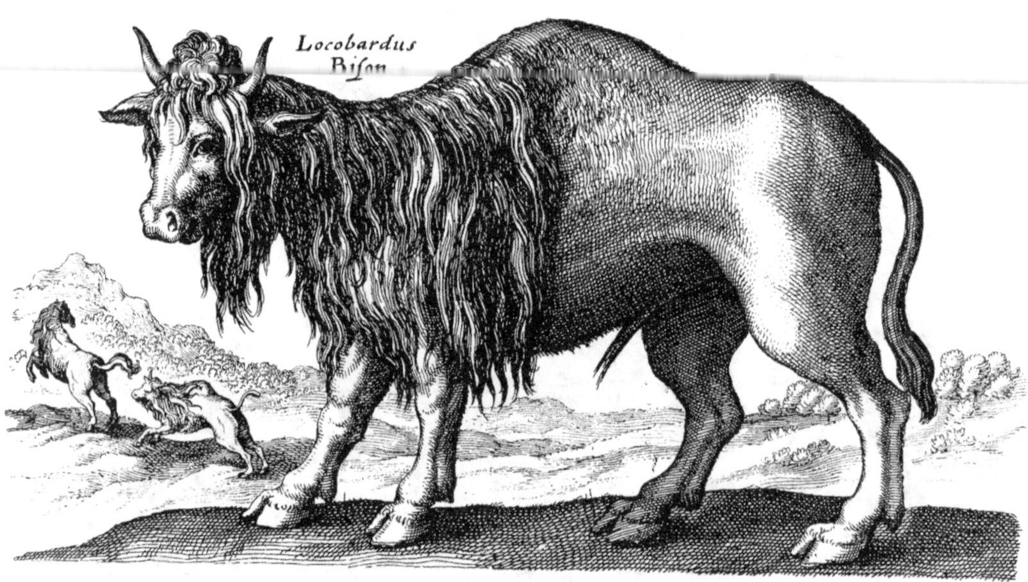

A94

A95

Bisons Magnus

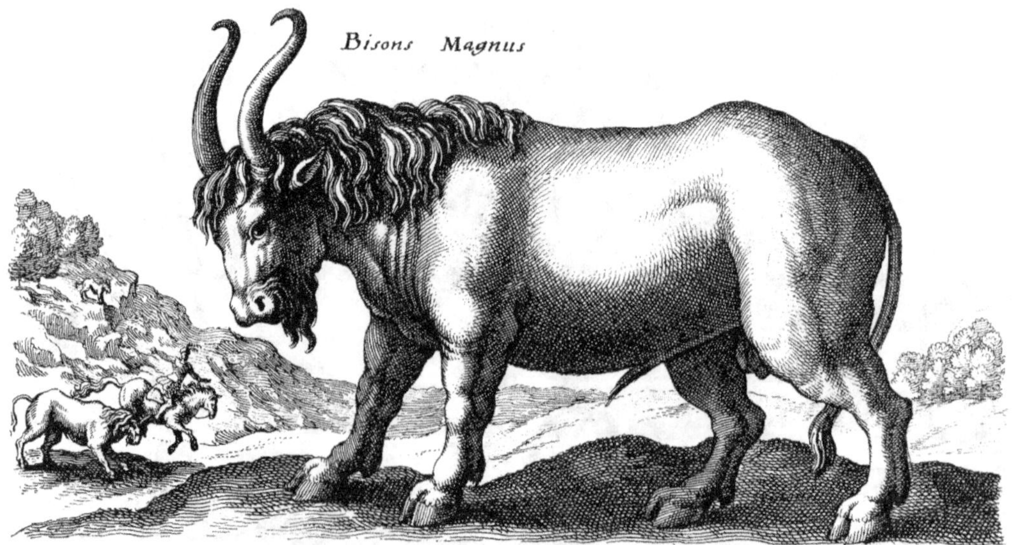

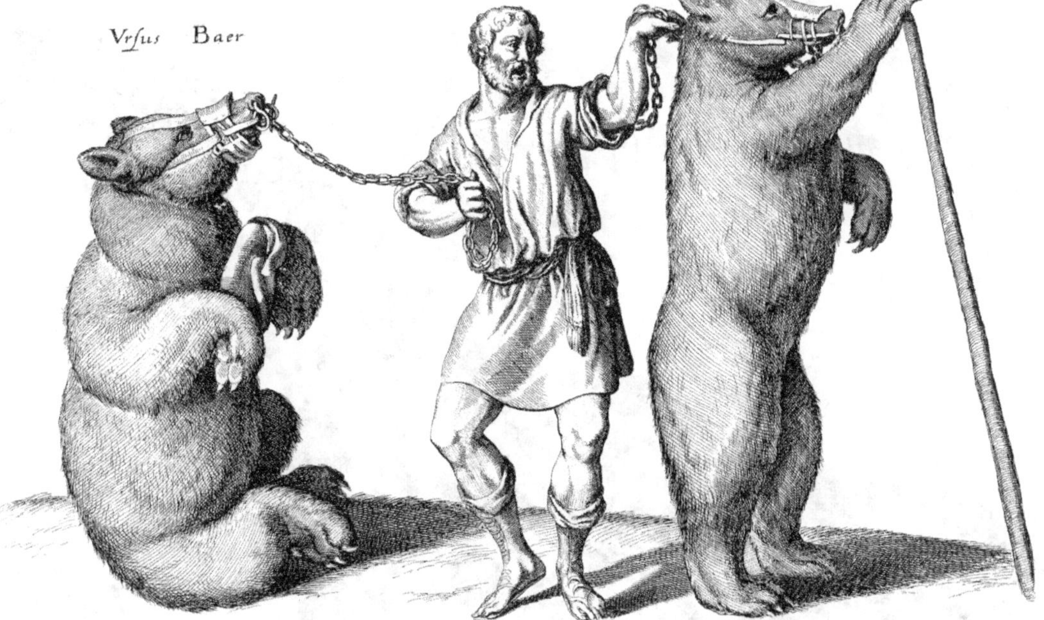
Vrfus Baer

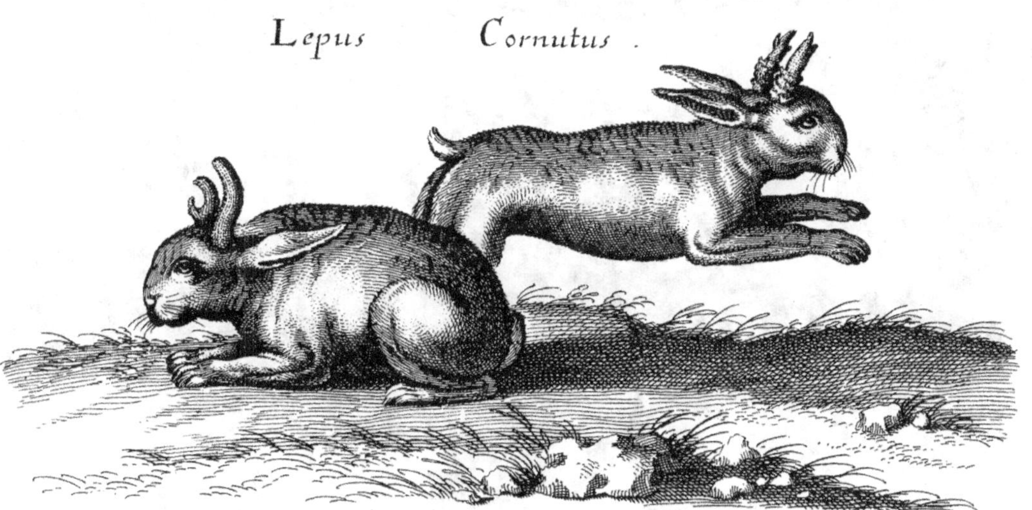
Lepus   Cornutus .

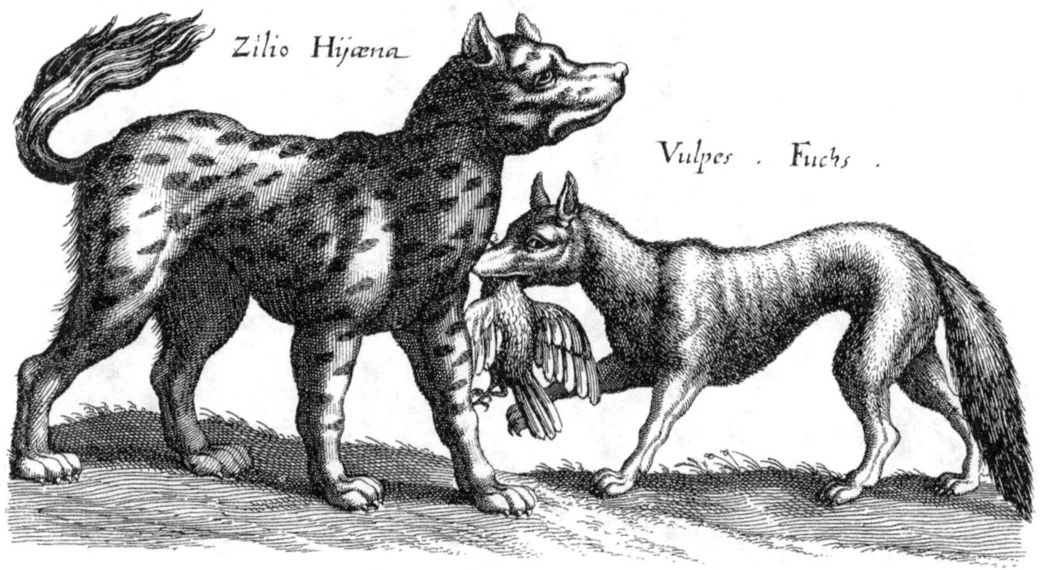
Zilio Hijæna
Vulpes . Fuchs .

A99

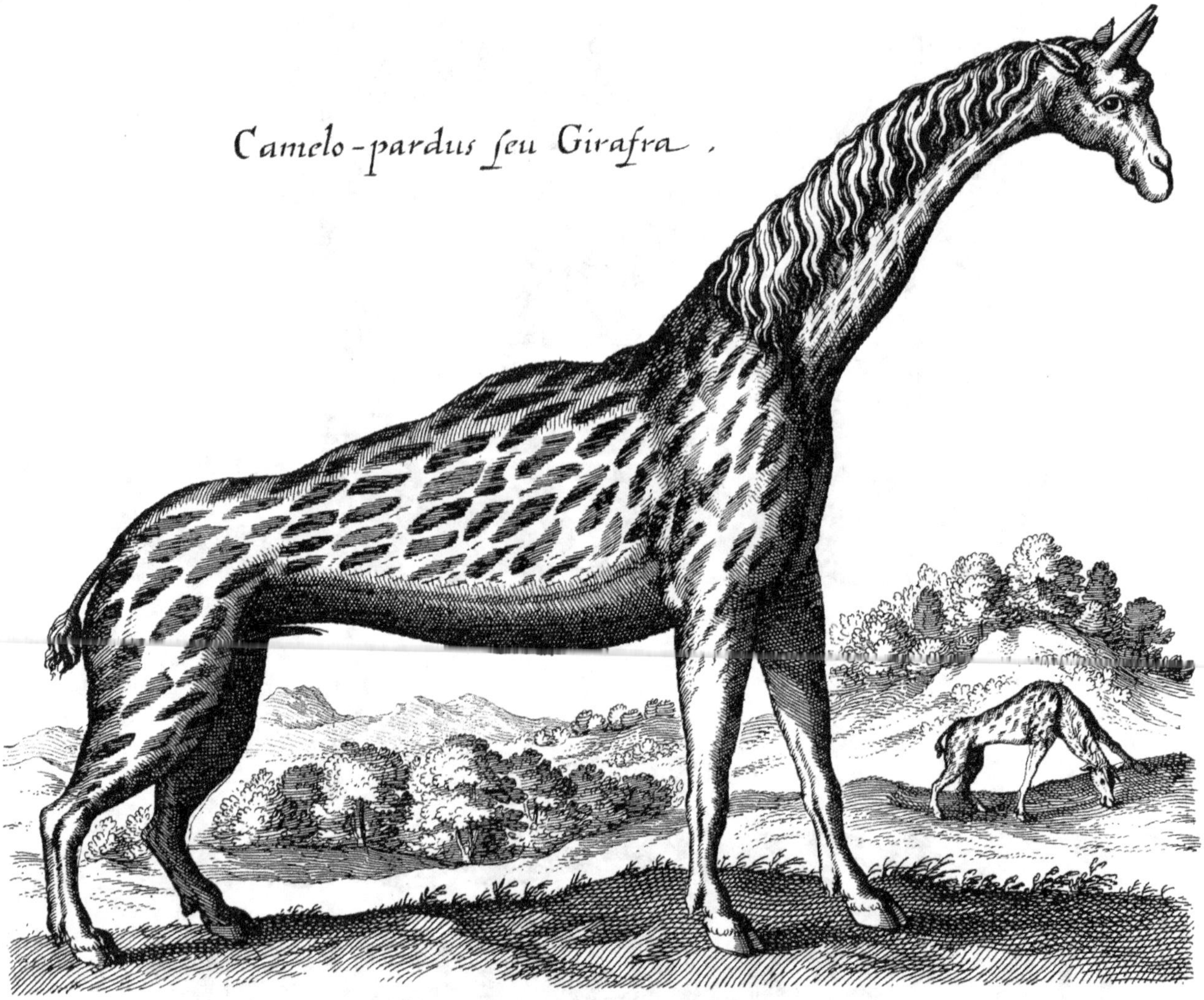

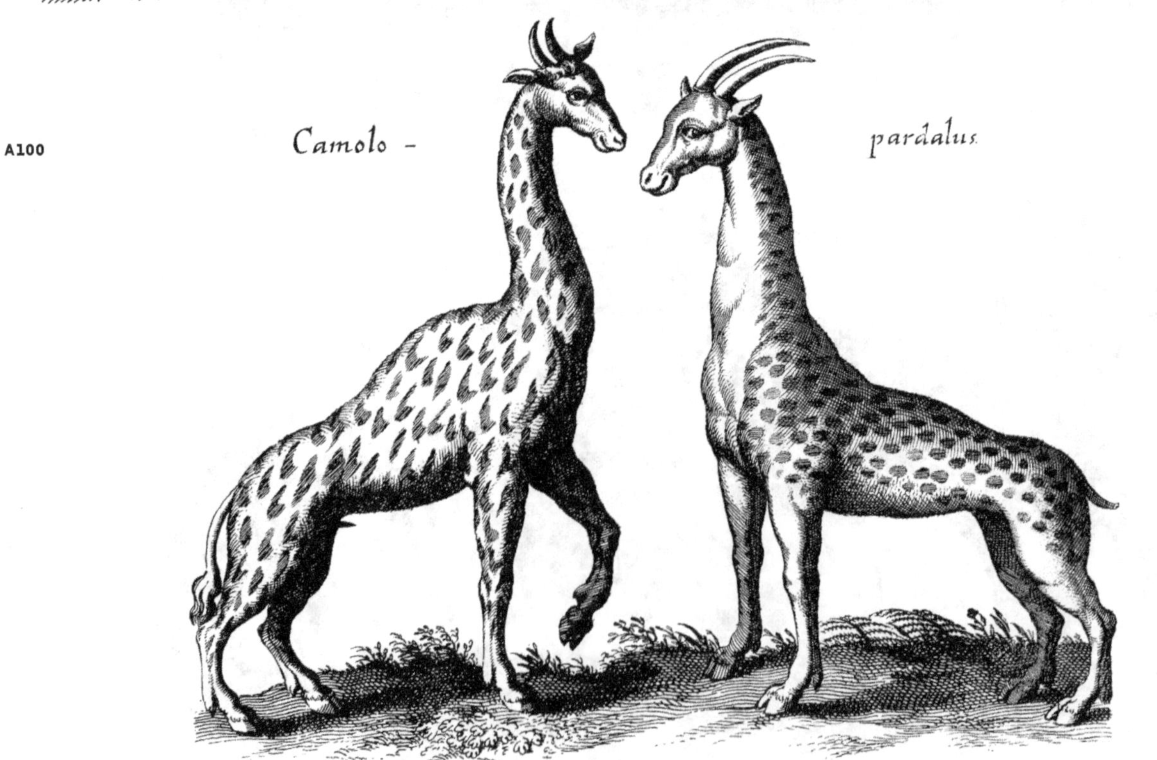

A100

Verres   Eber   **A101**

Aper   *Wildſchwein*   **A102**

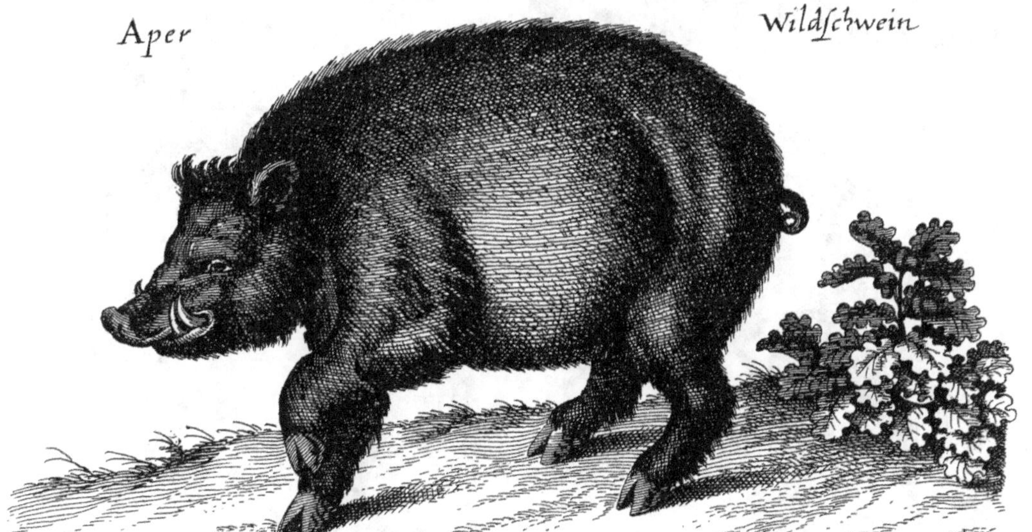

Scrofa   *Mock*   **A103**

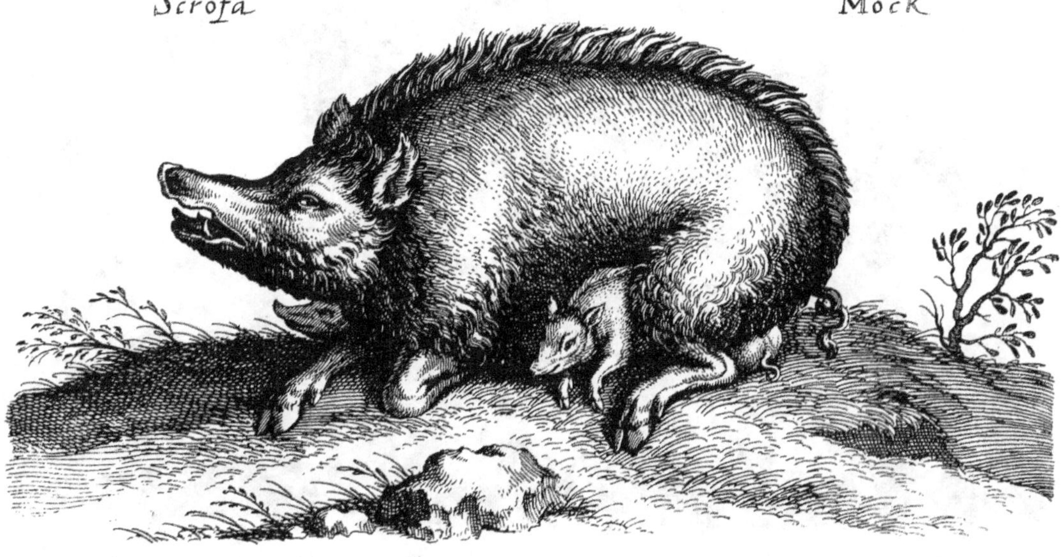

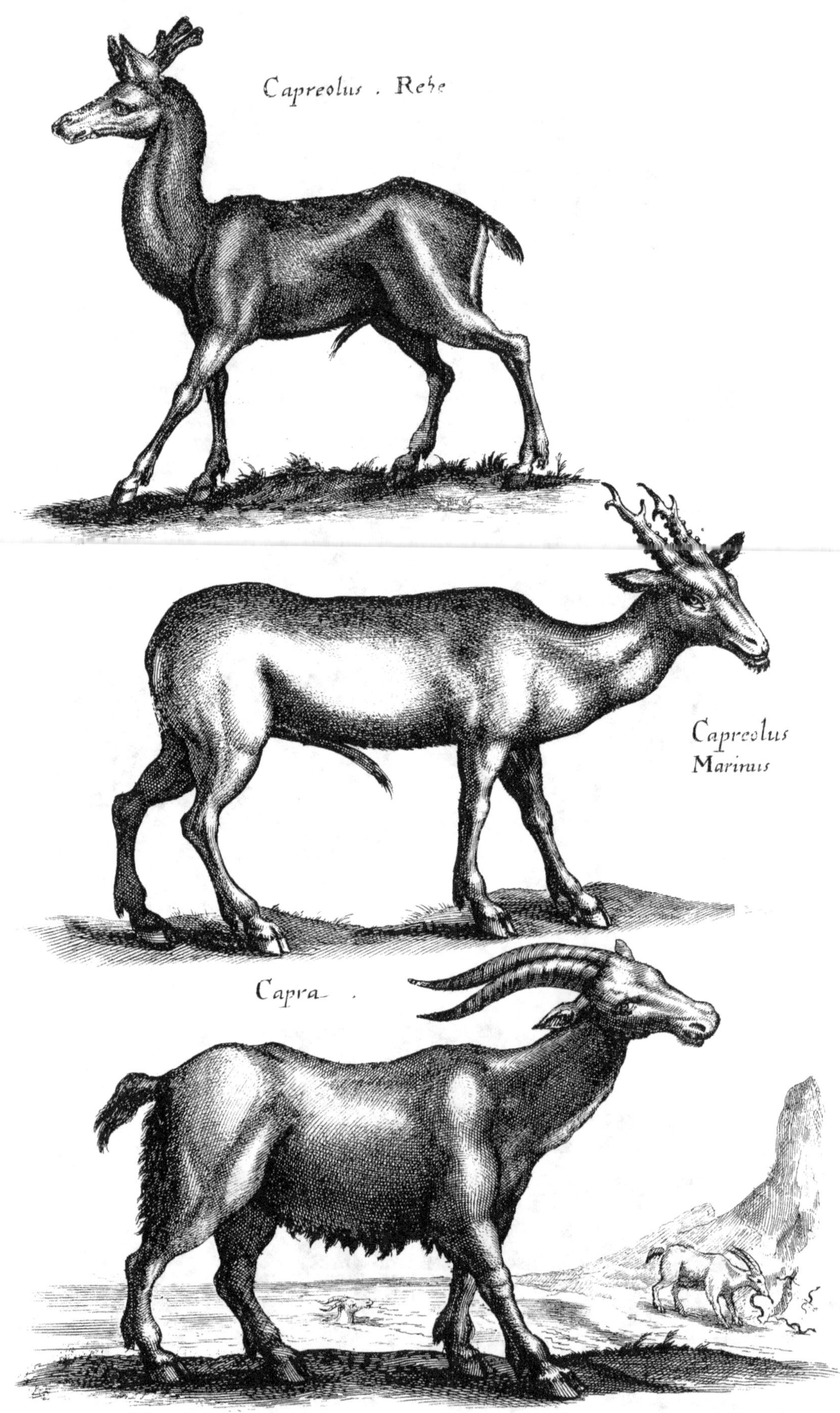
Capreolus . Rehe
Capreolus Marinus
Capra .

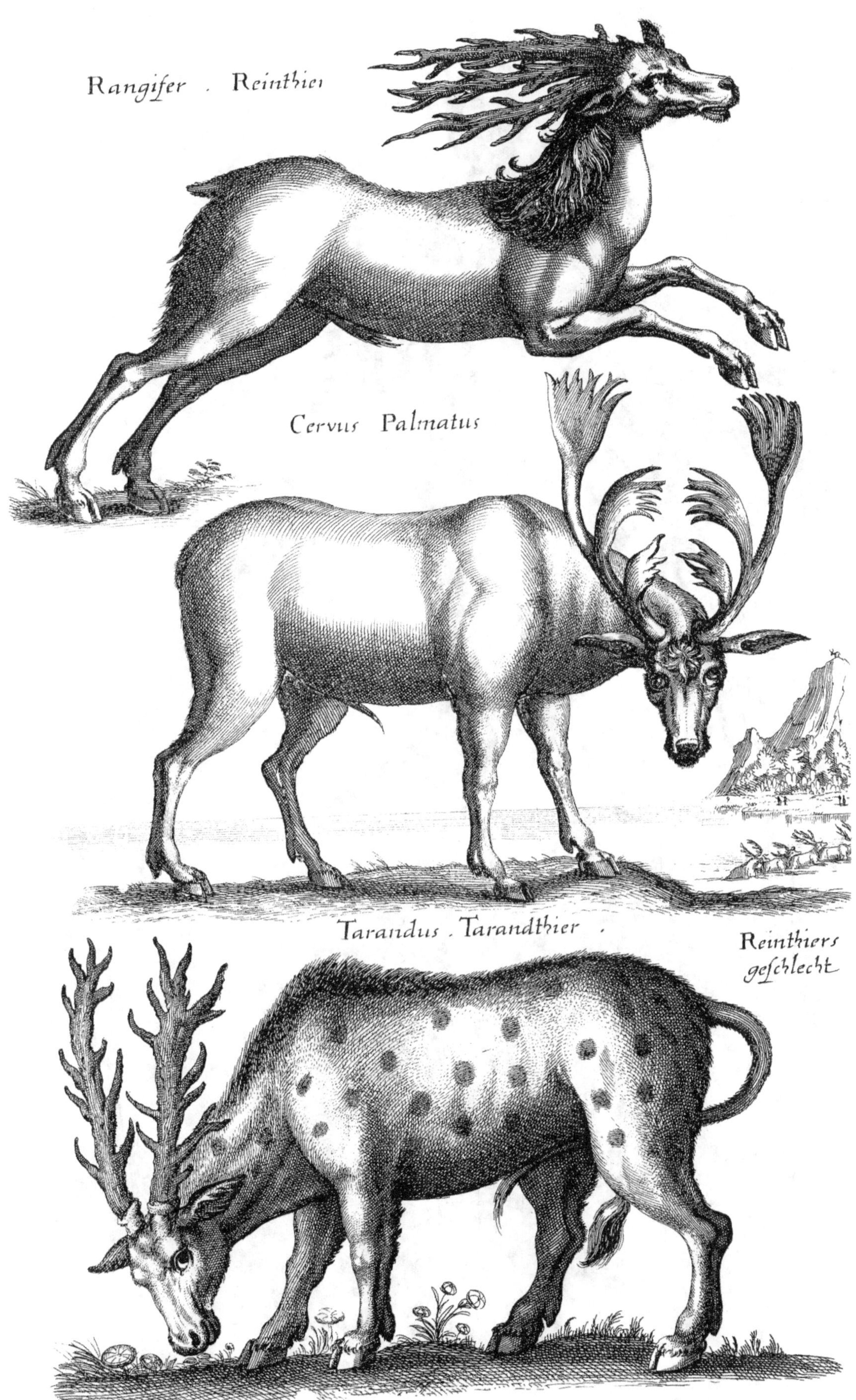
Rangifer . Reinthier

Cervus Palmatus

Tarandus . Tarandthier .

Reinthiers
gefchlecht

A106

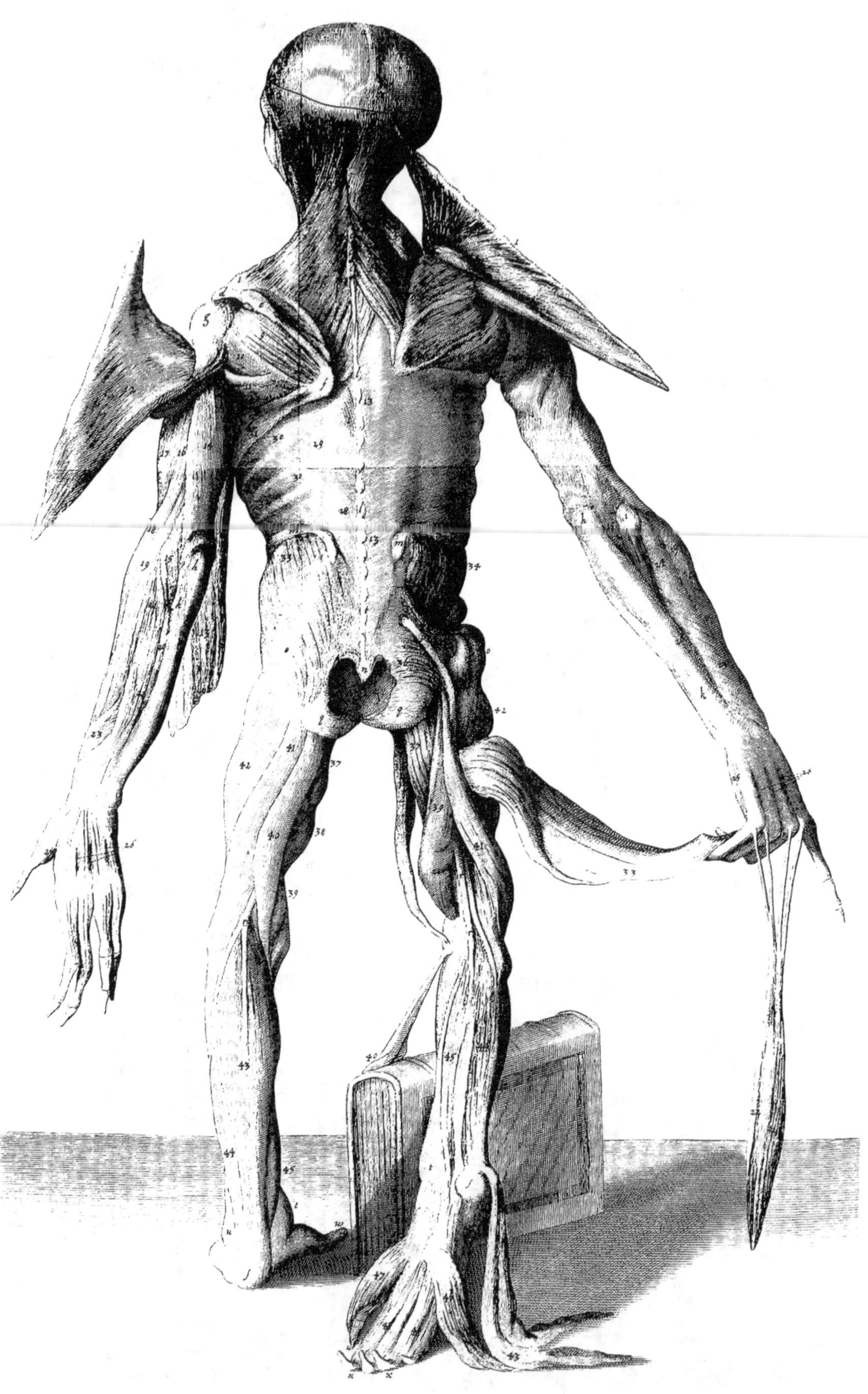

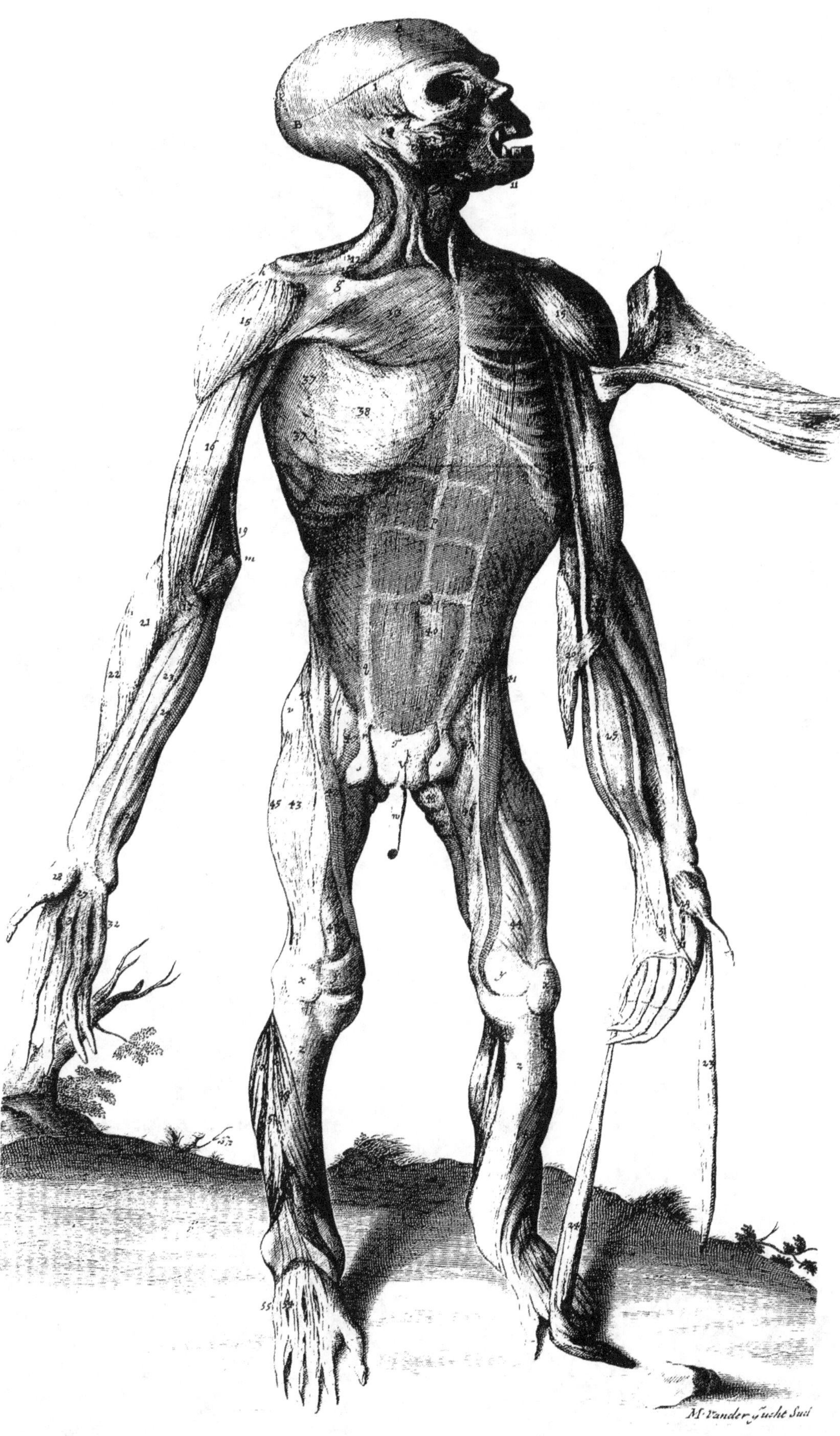

A108

A111

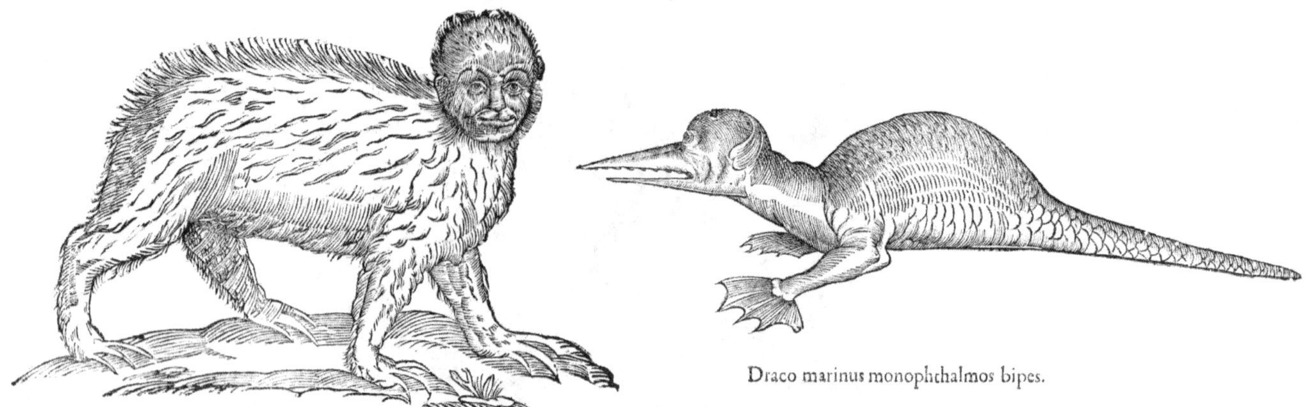

Draco marinus monophchalmos bipes.

A109

A112

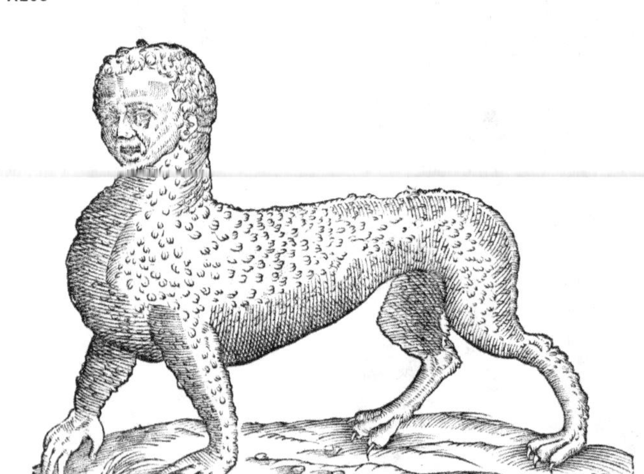

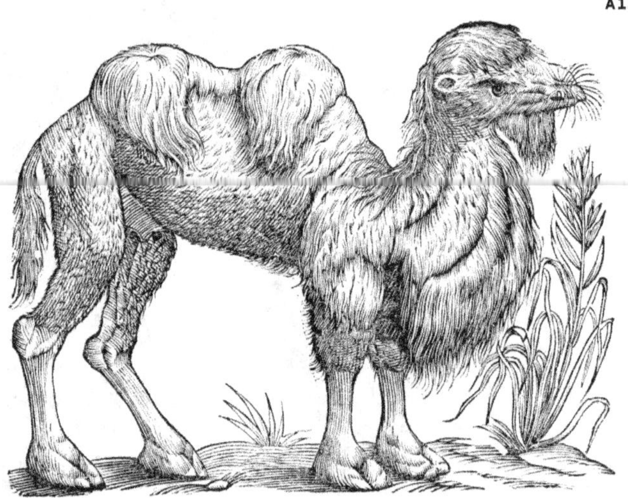

A110

A113

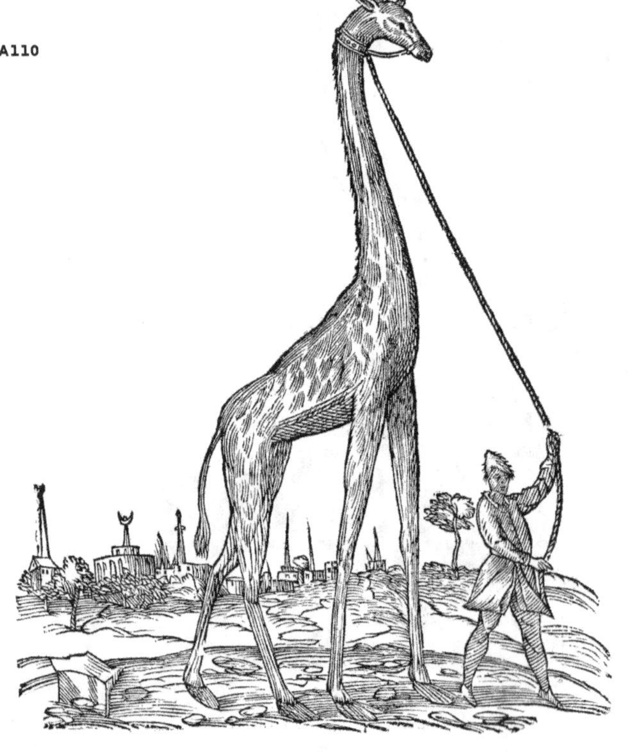

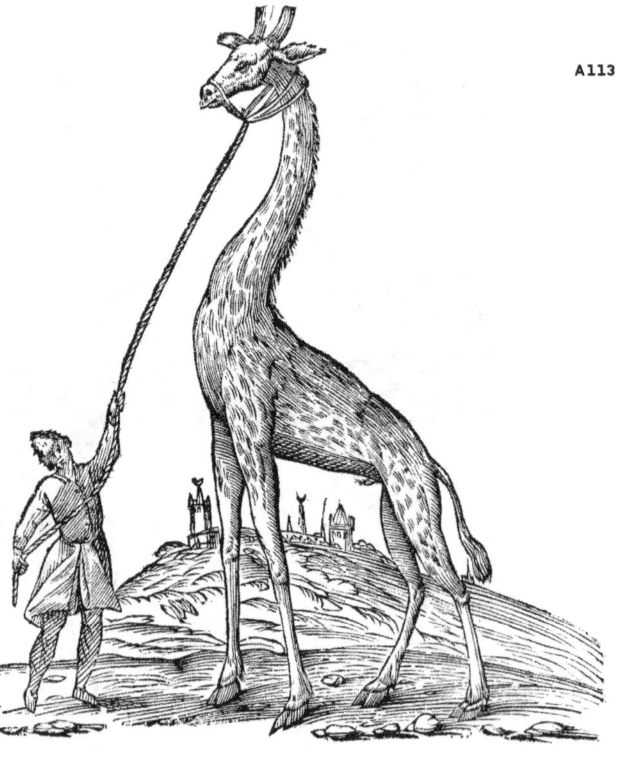

A114

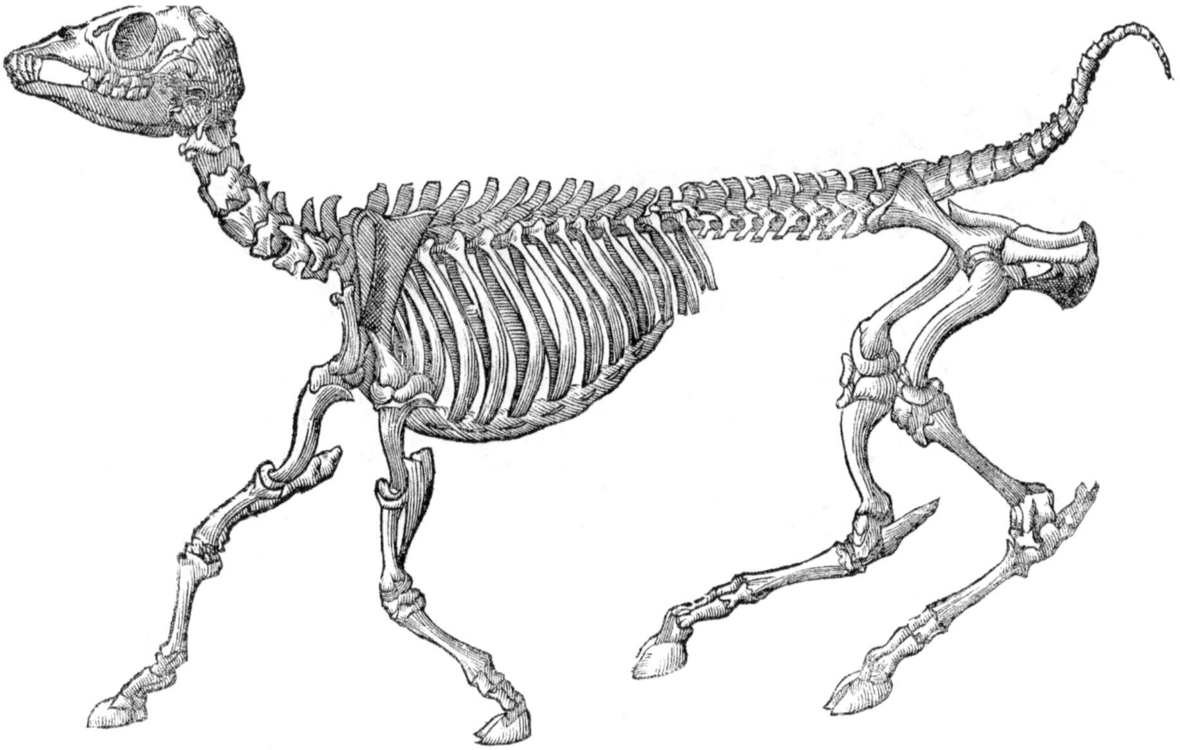

A115

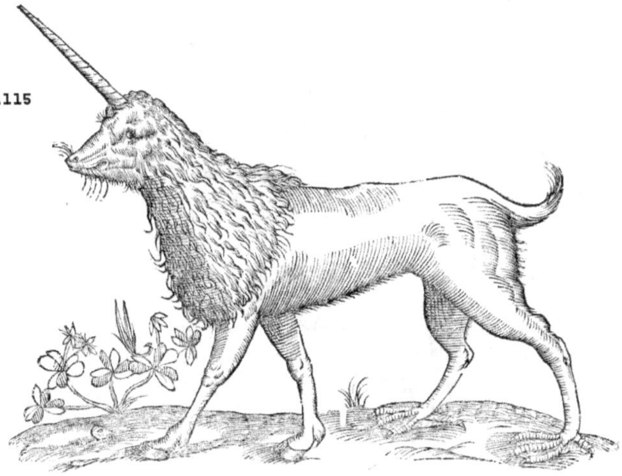

A117

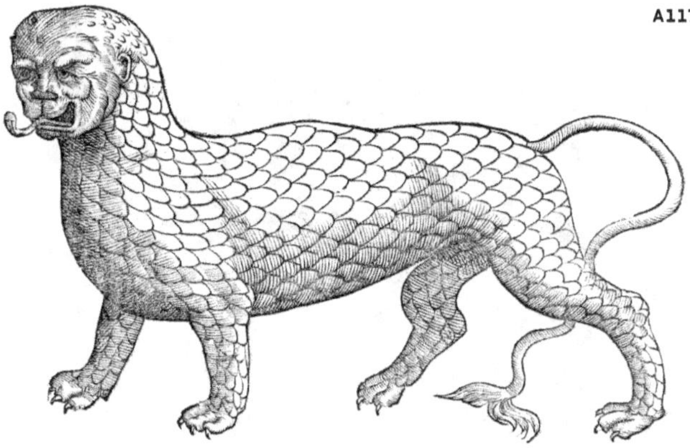

A116

A118

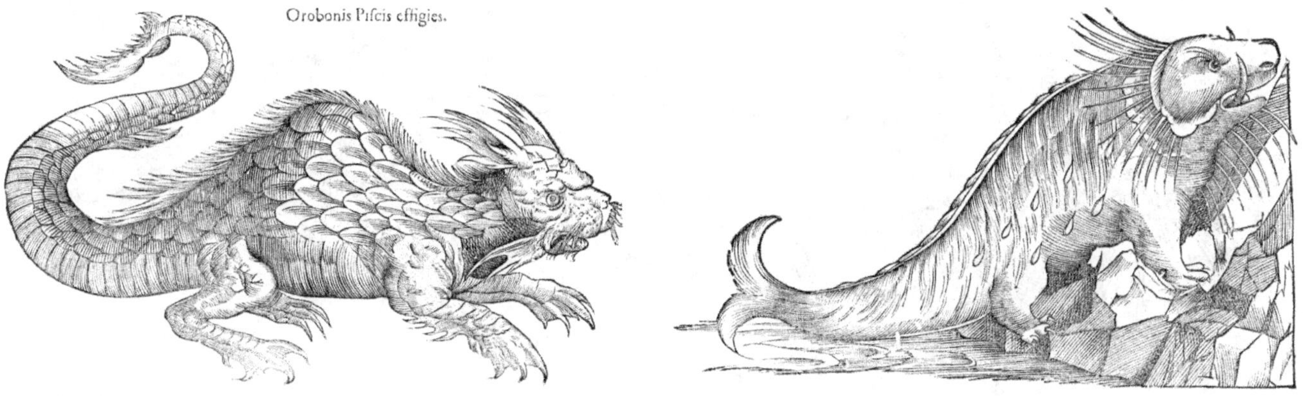

Orobonis Piscis effigies.

A119

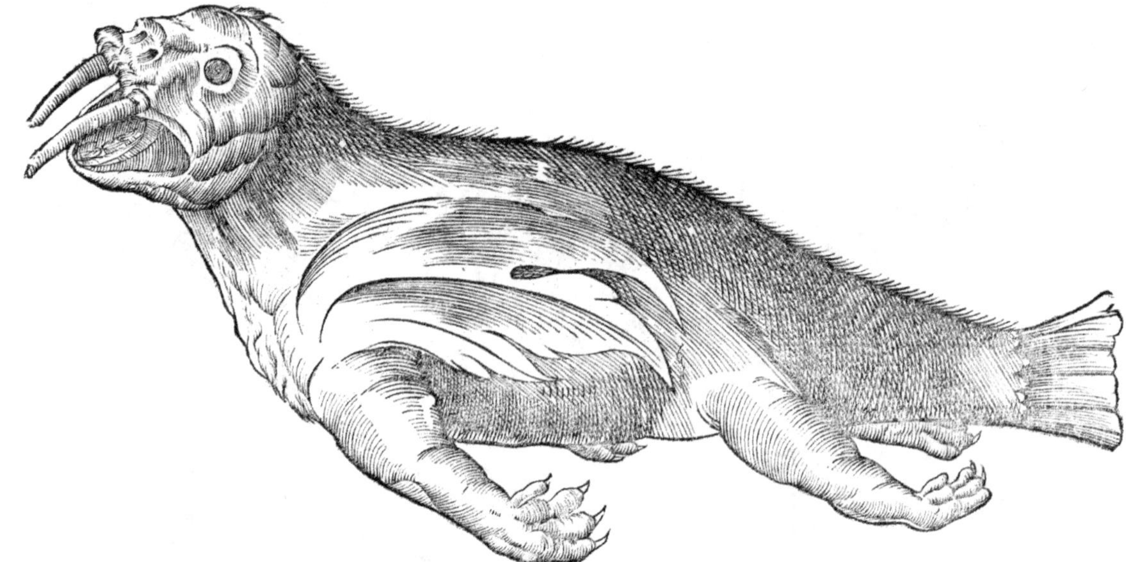

A120

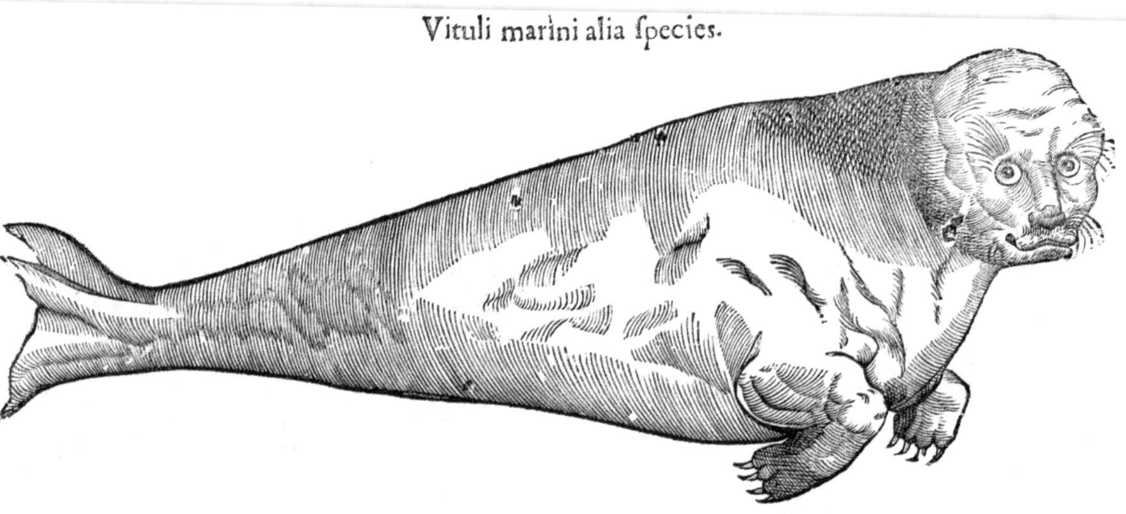

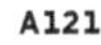

A121

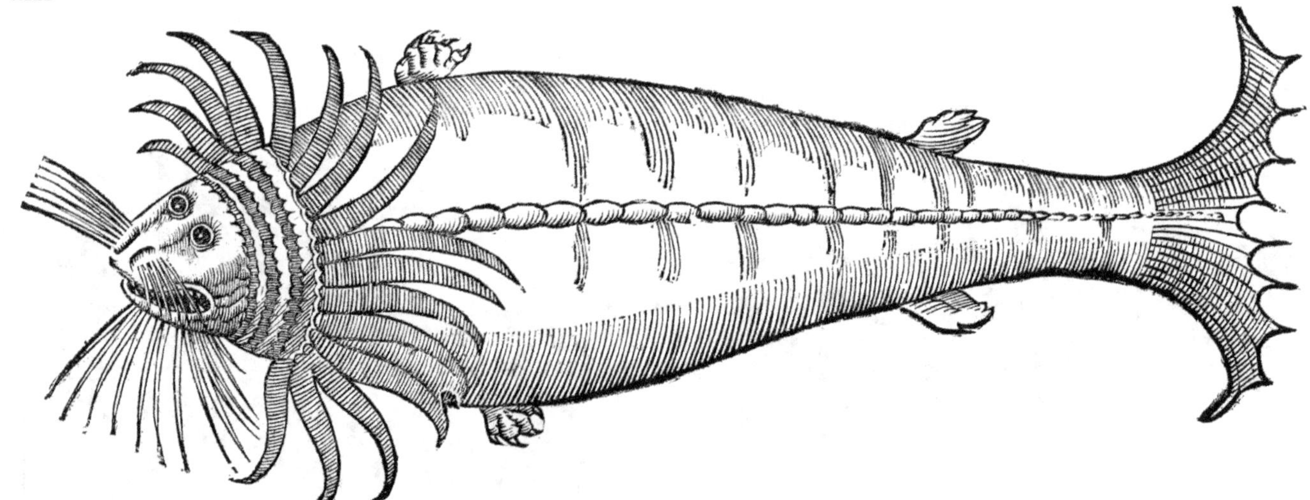

A122

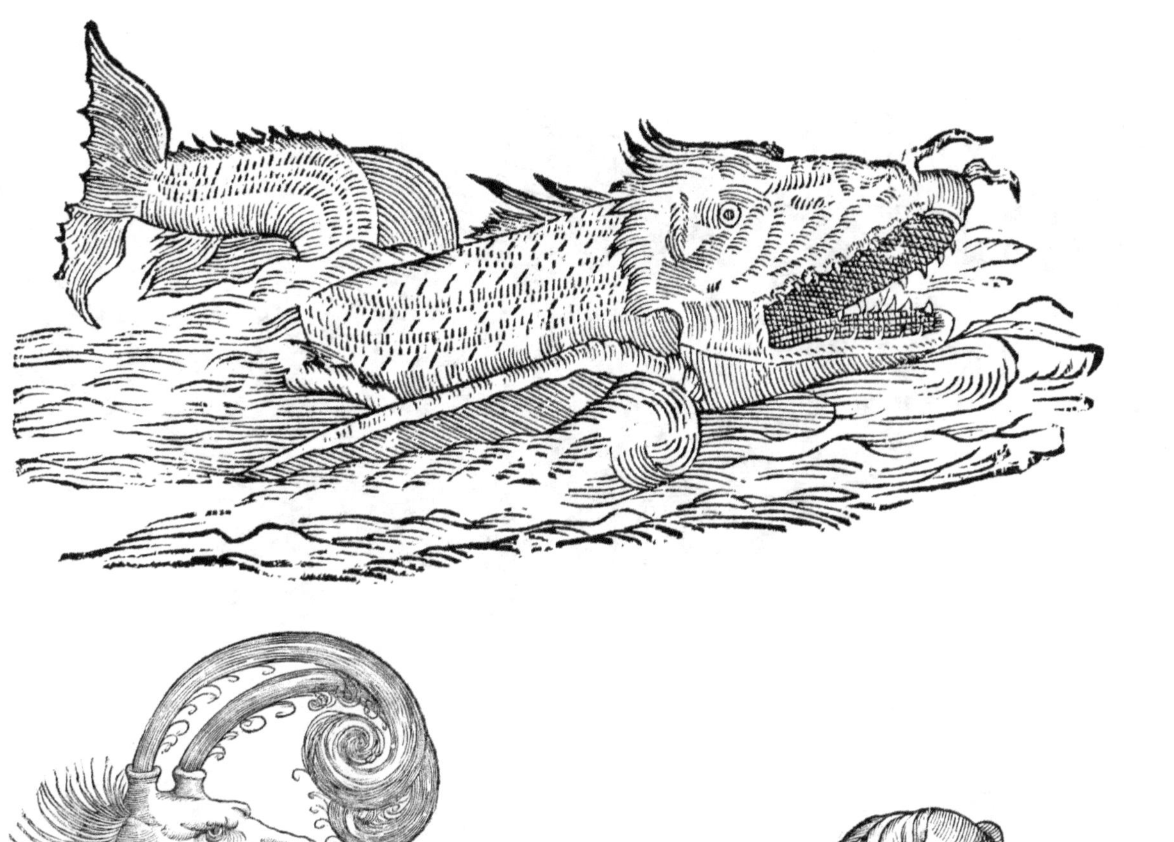

A123

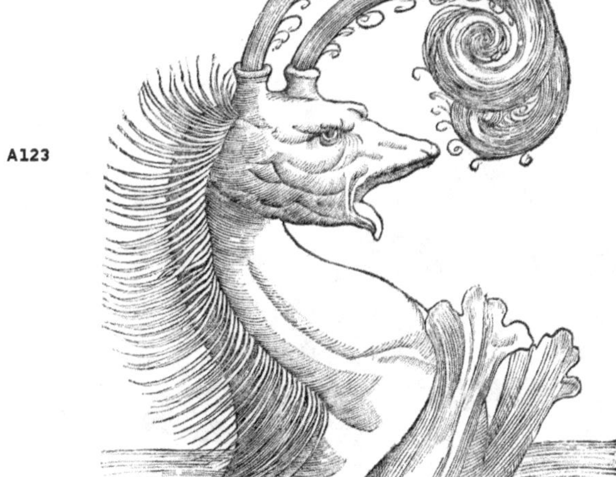

A124

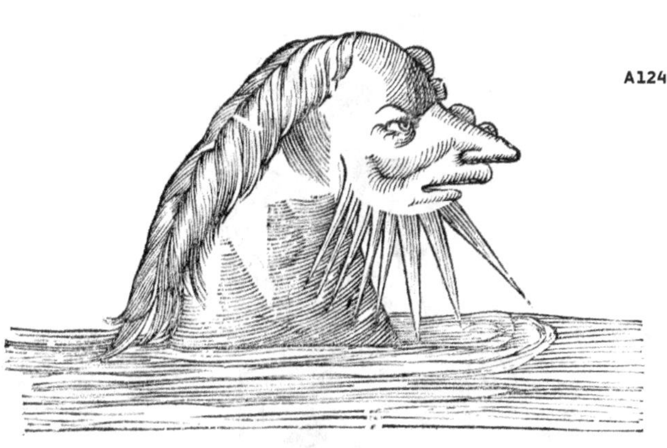

A125

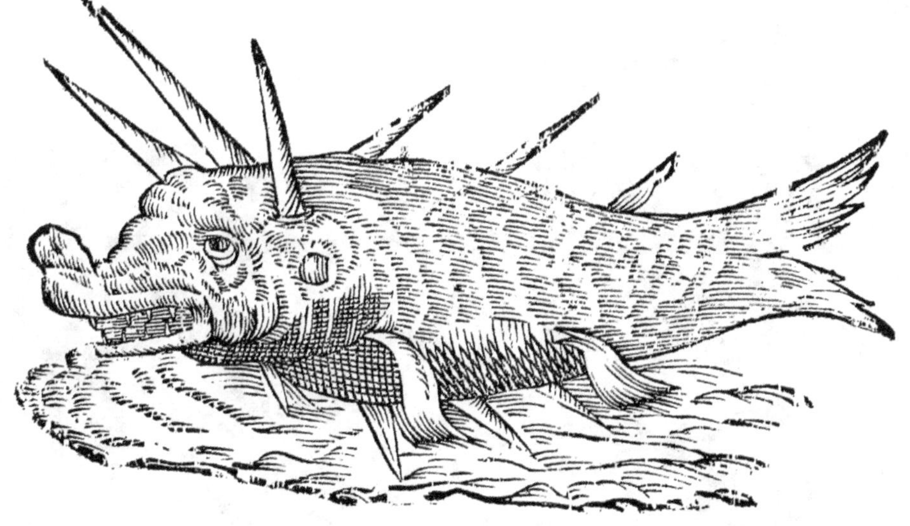

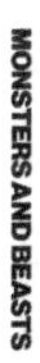

A126

A127

A128

A129

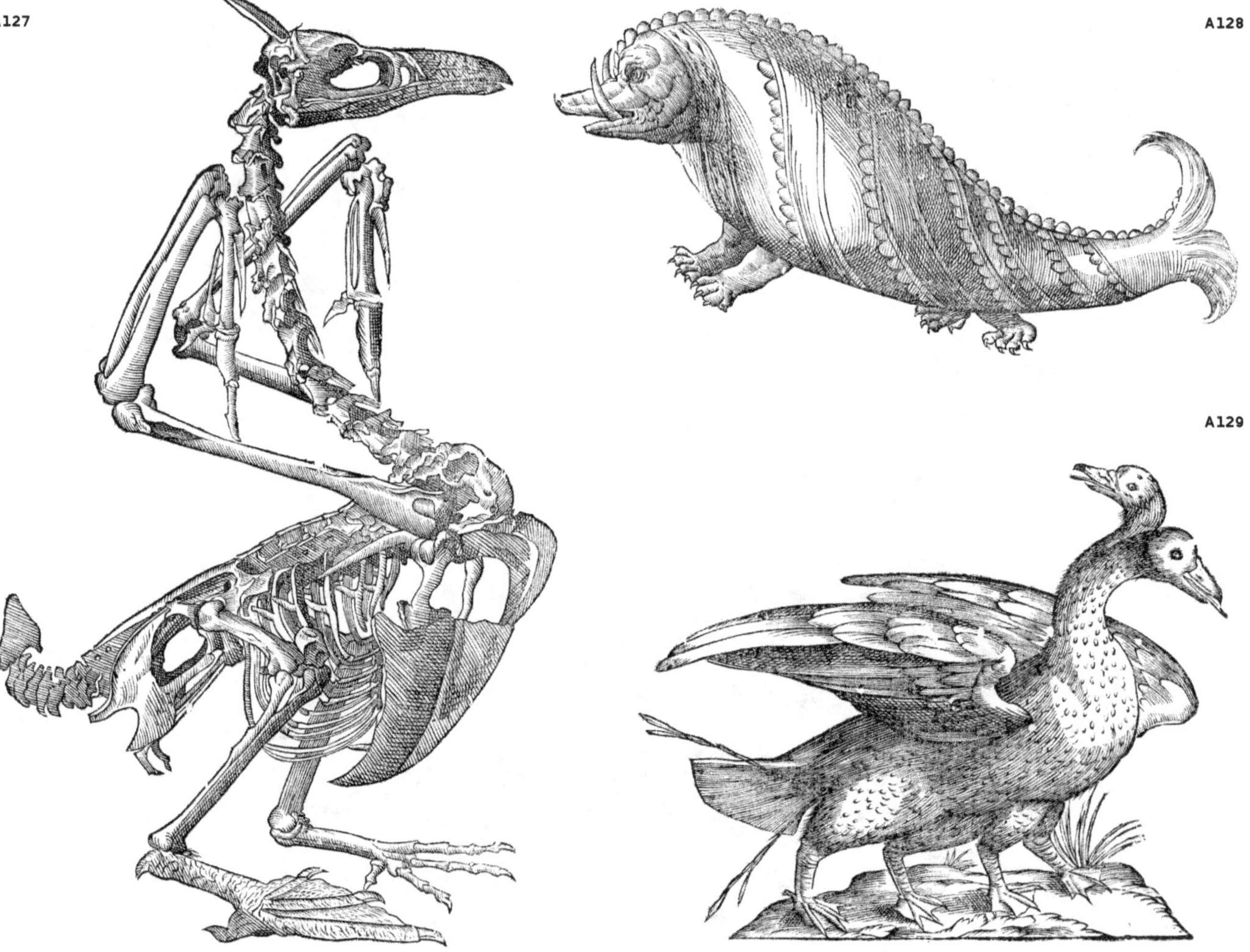

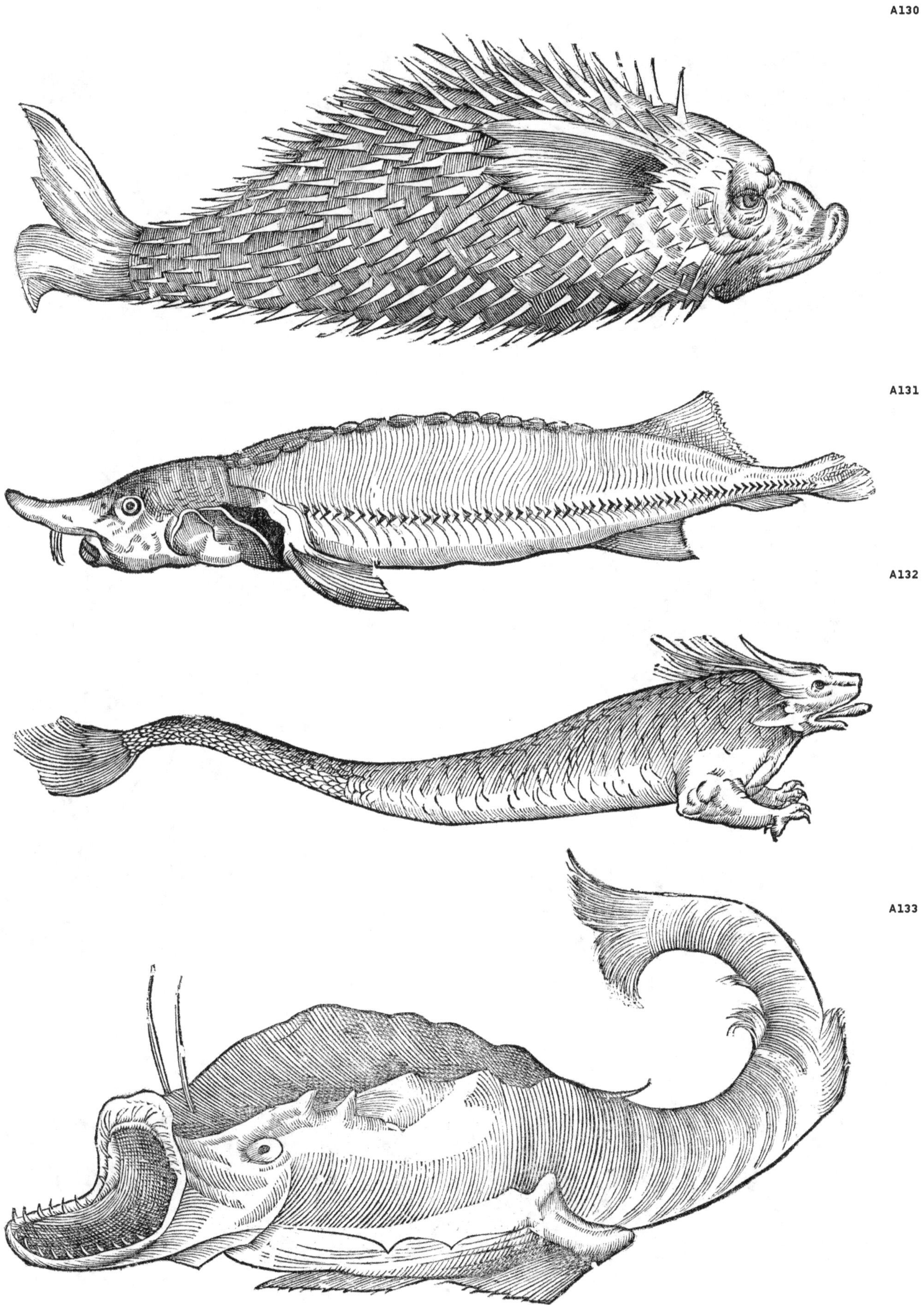

A130

A131

A132

A133

A134

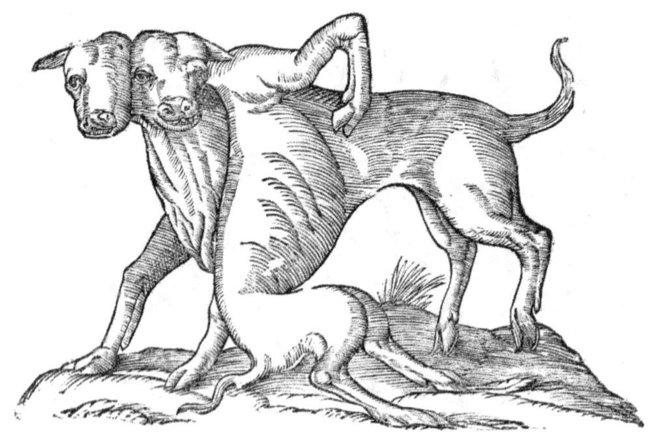

A136

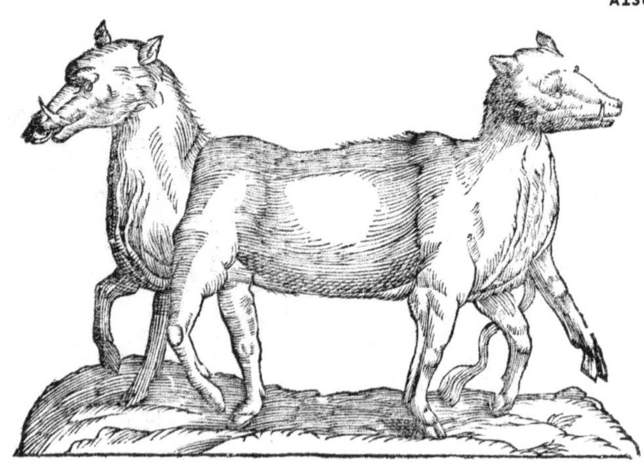

A135

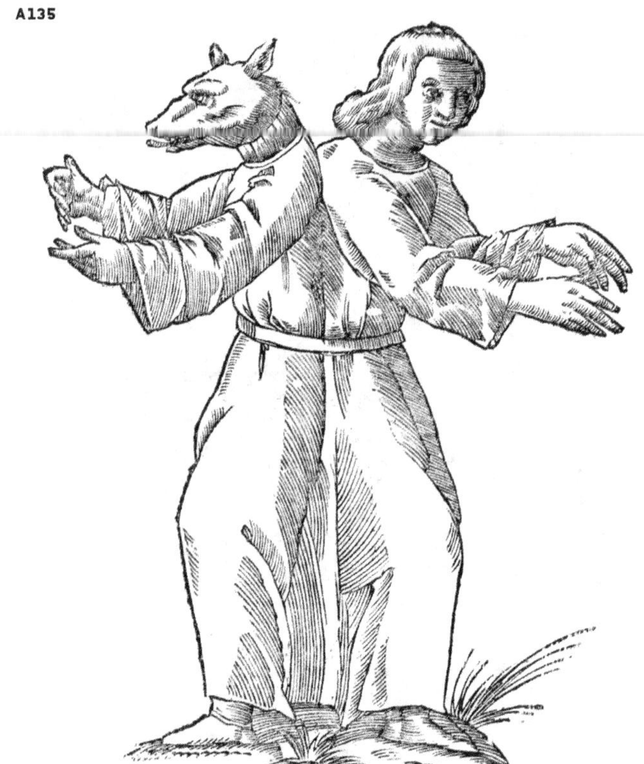

A137

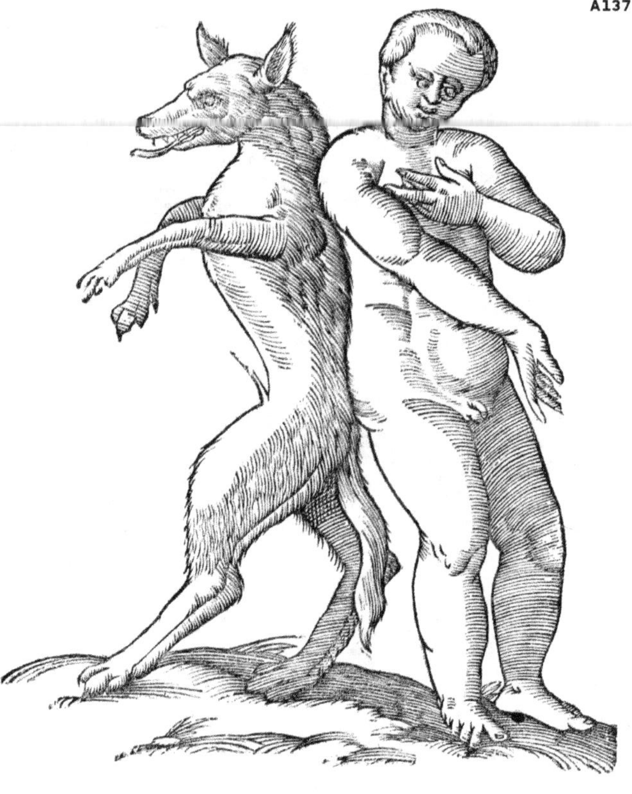

A138

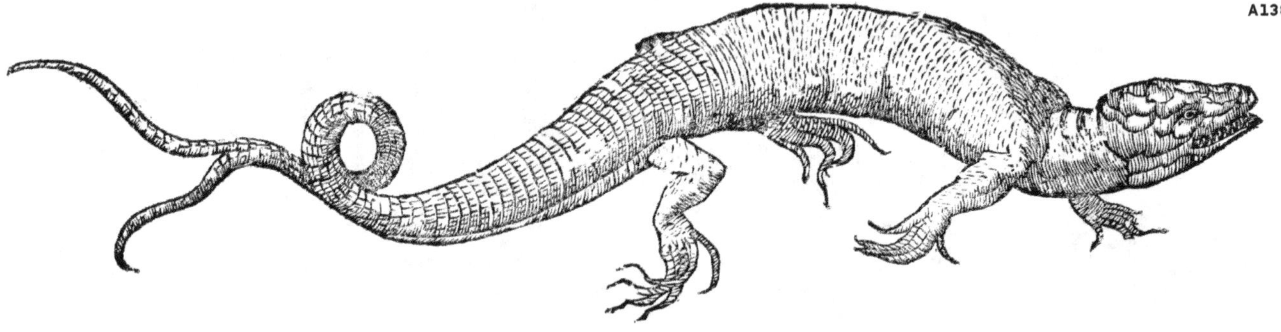

A139

A141

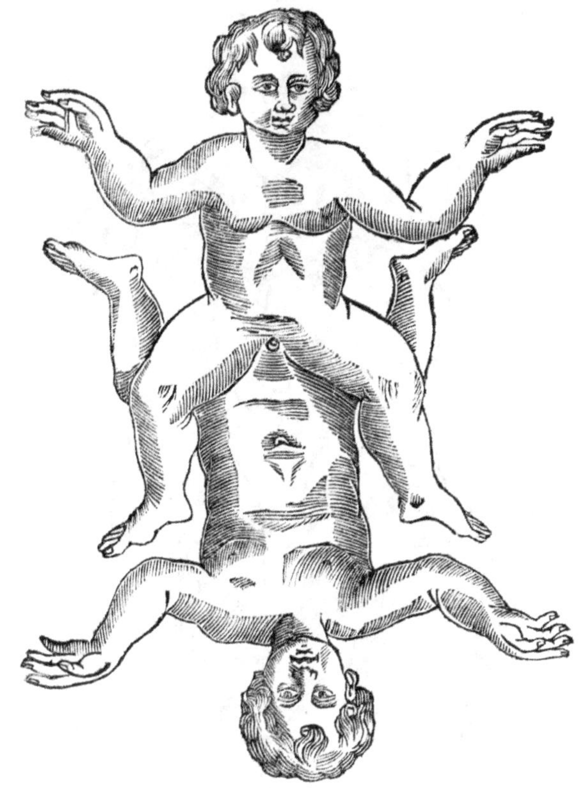

A140

A142

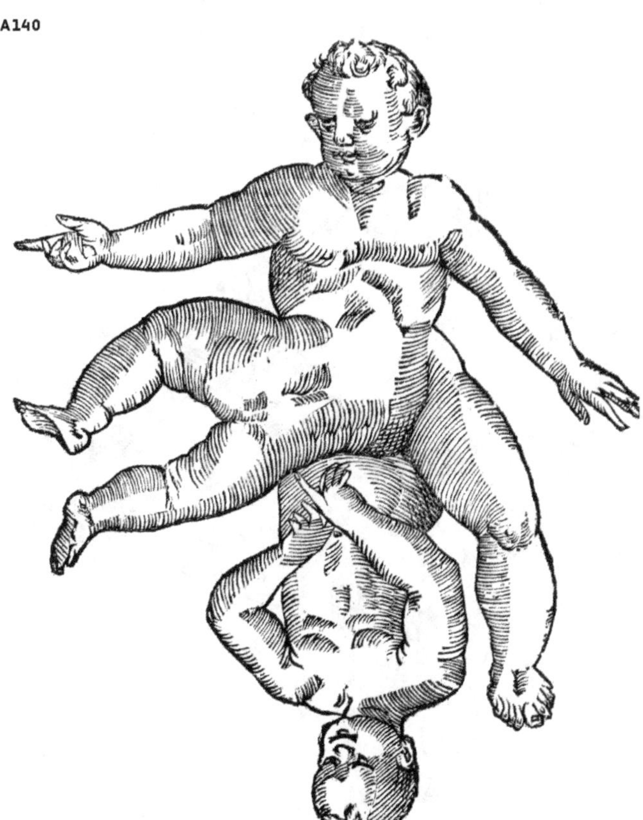

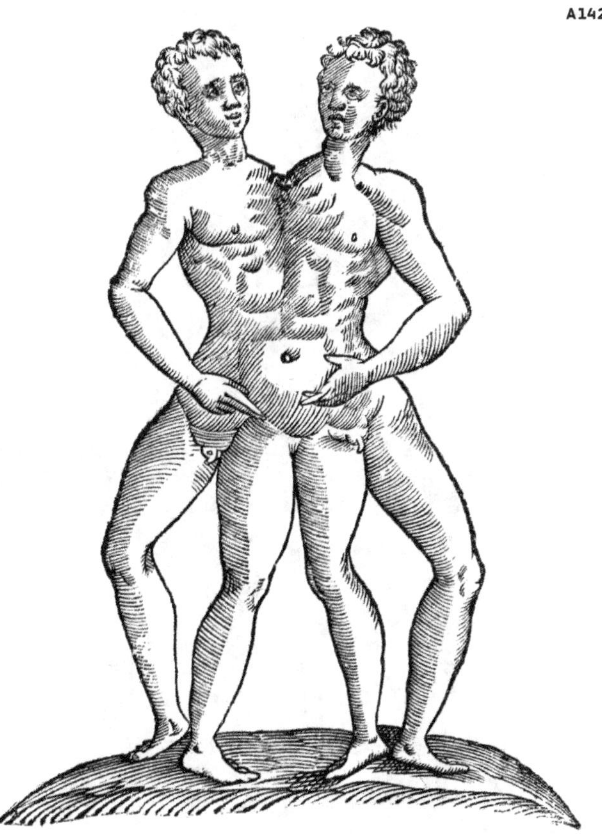

A143

A145

A144

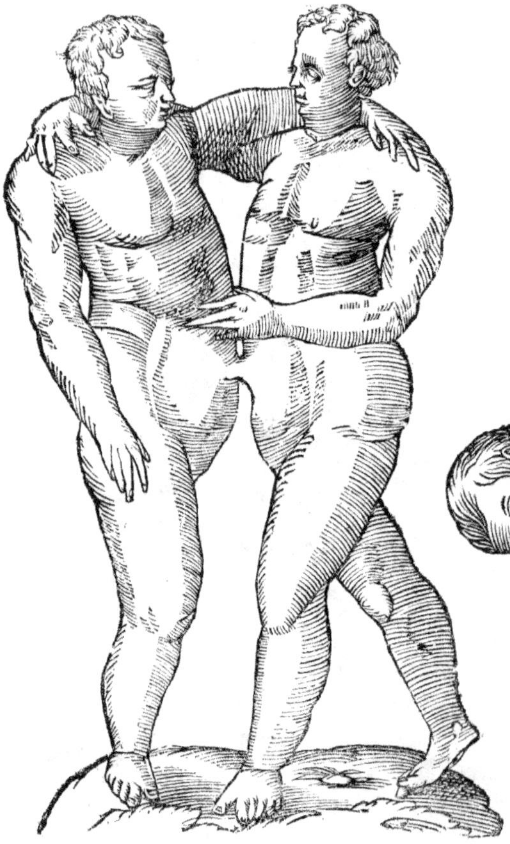

A146

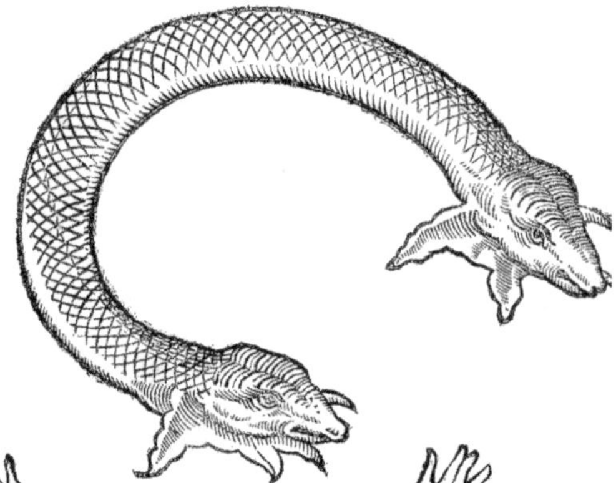

A147

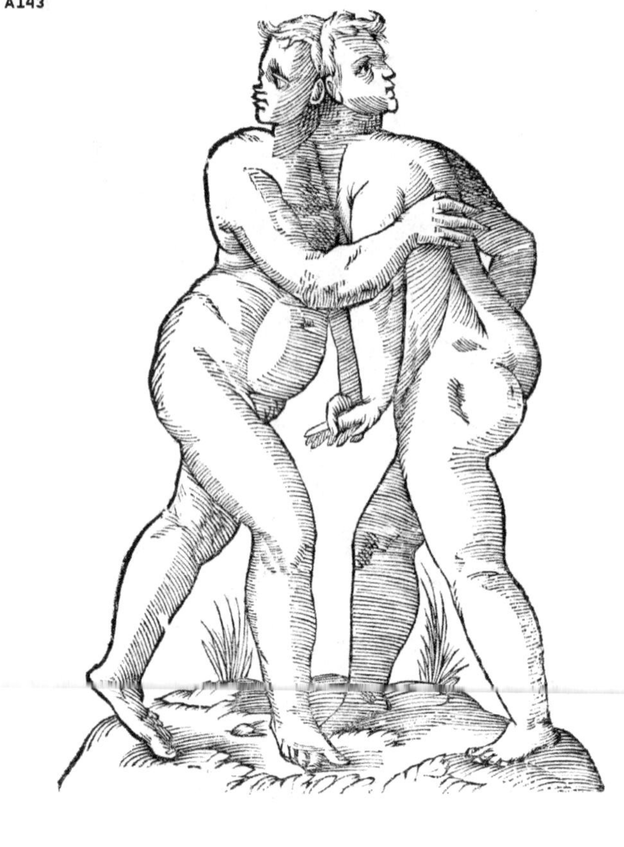

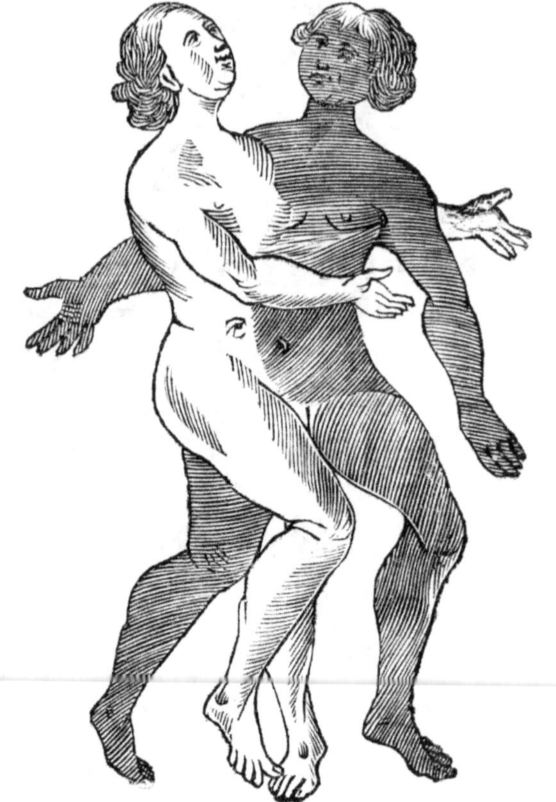

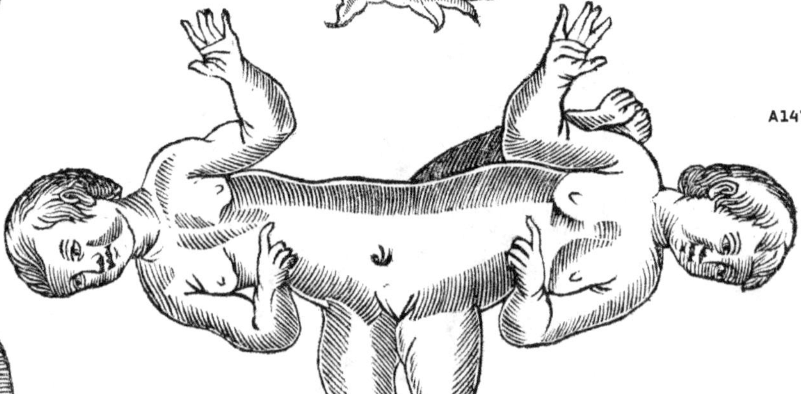

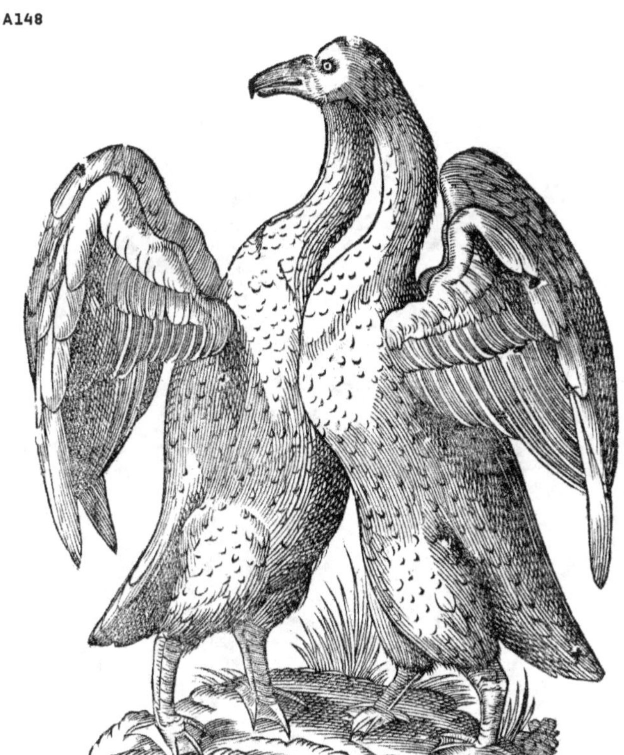

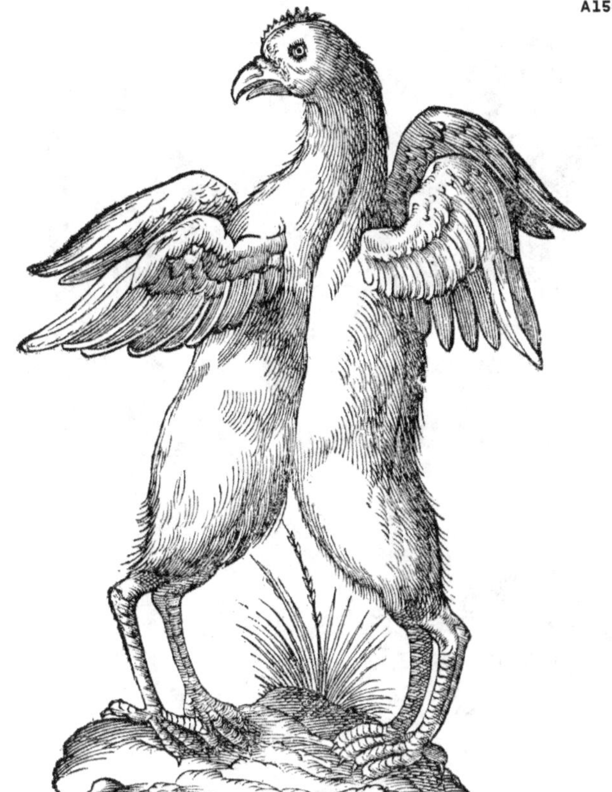

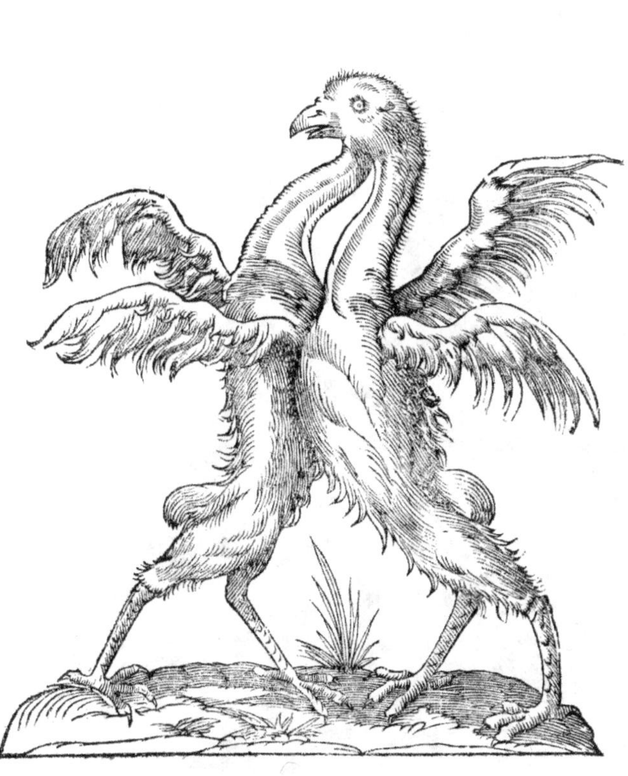

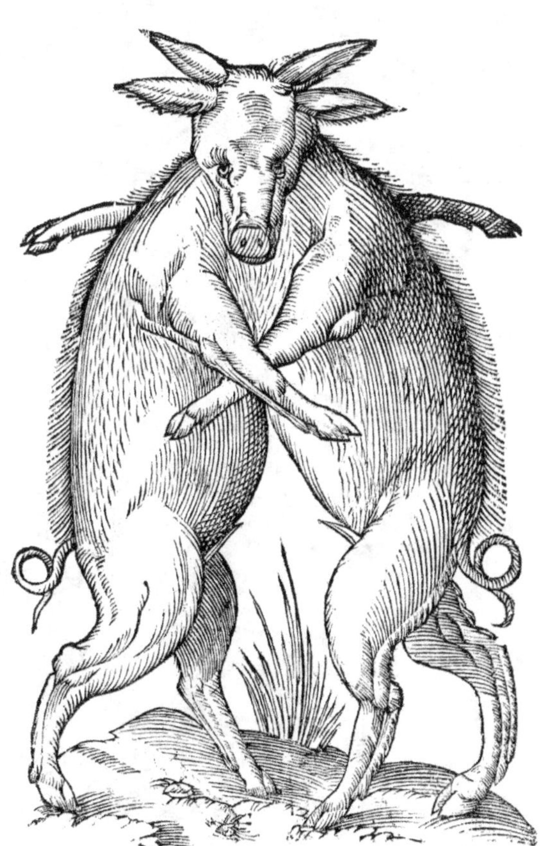

MONSTERS AND BEASTS

A152

A155

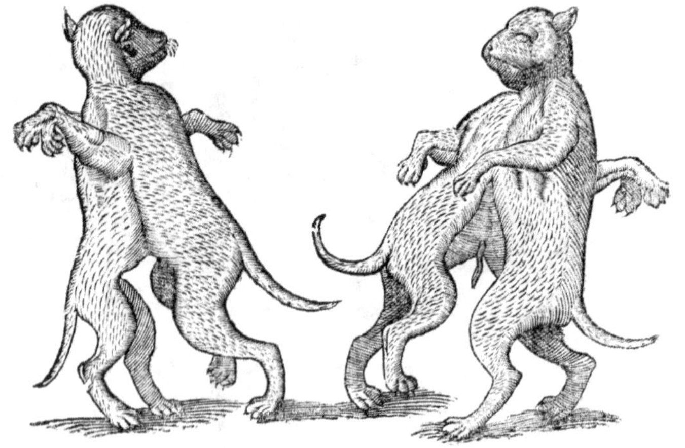

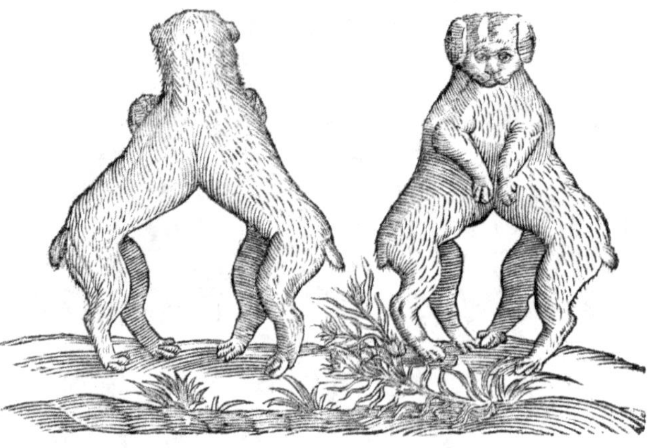

A153

A156

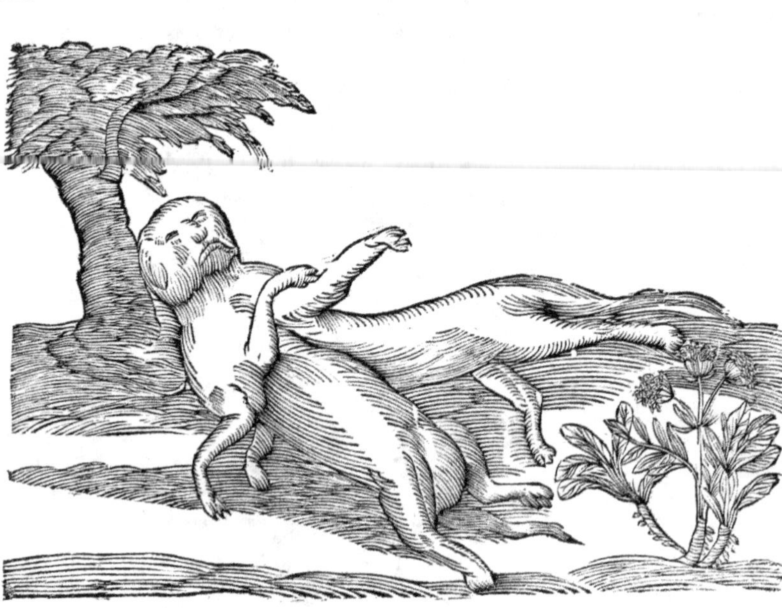

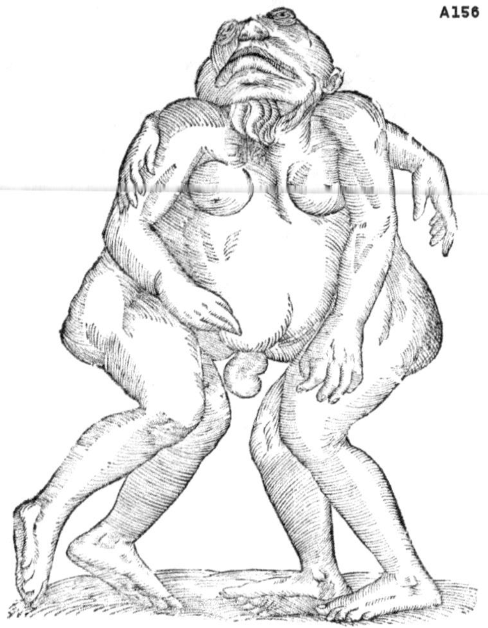

A154

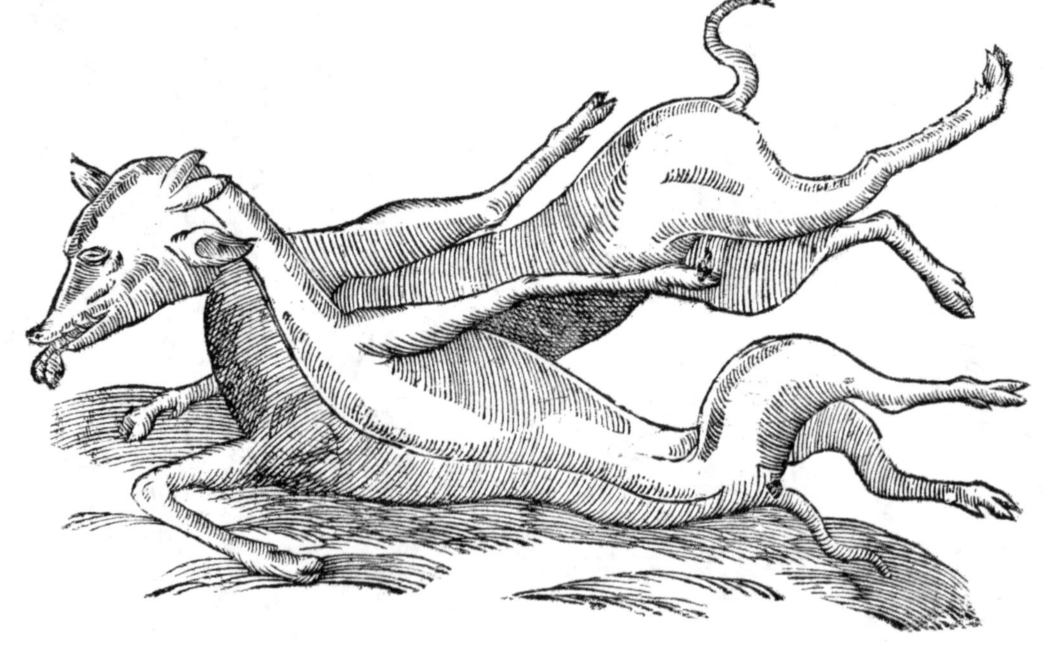

A157

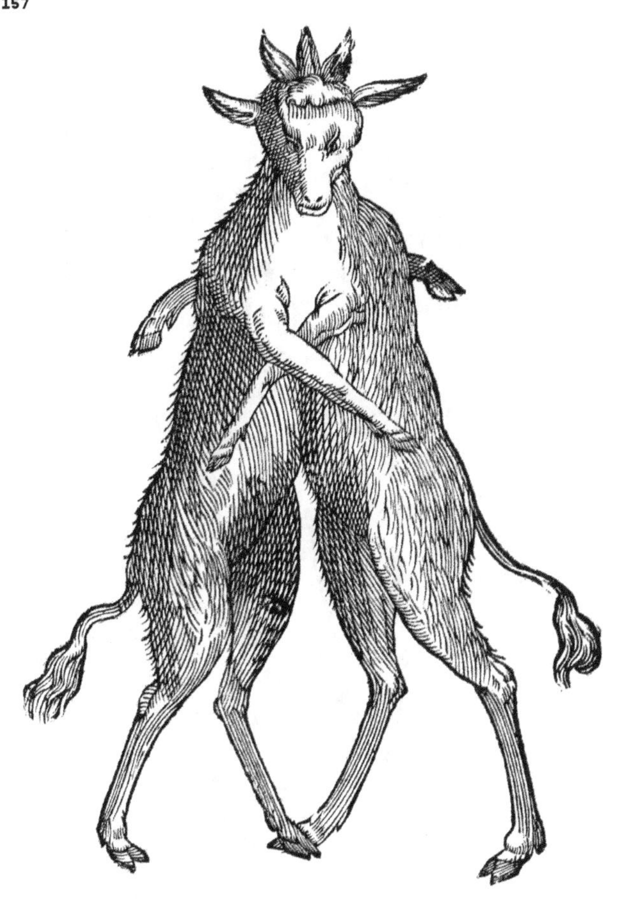

A159

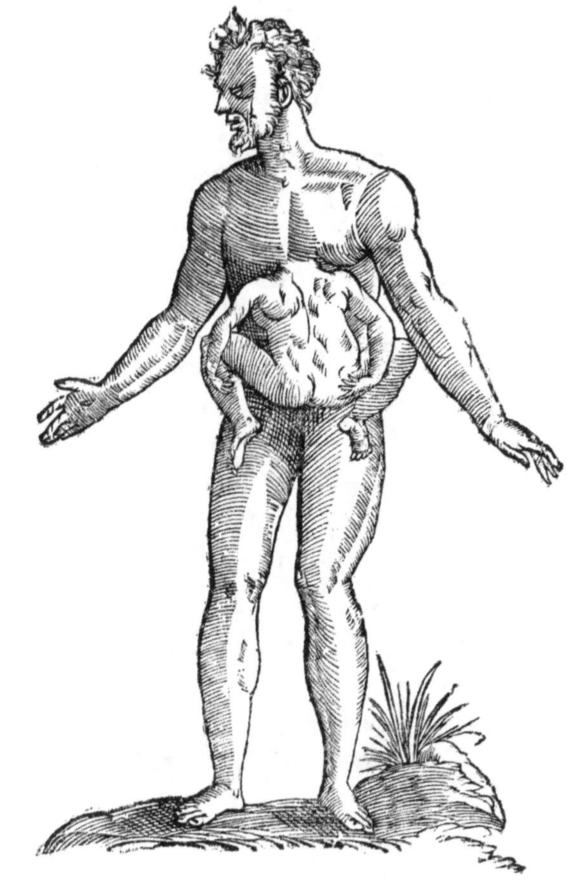

A158

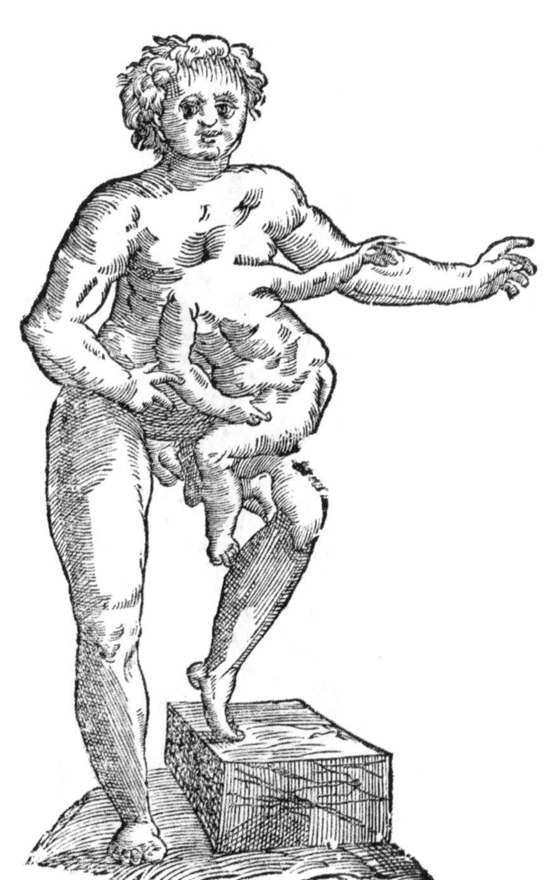

A160

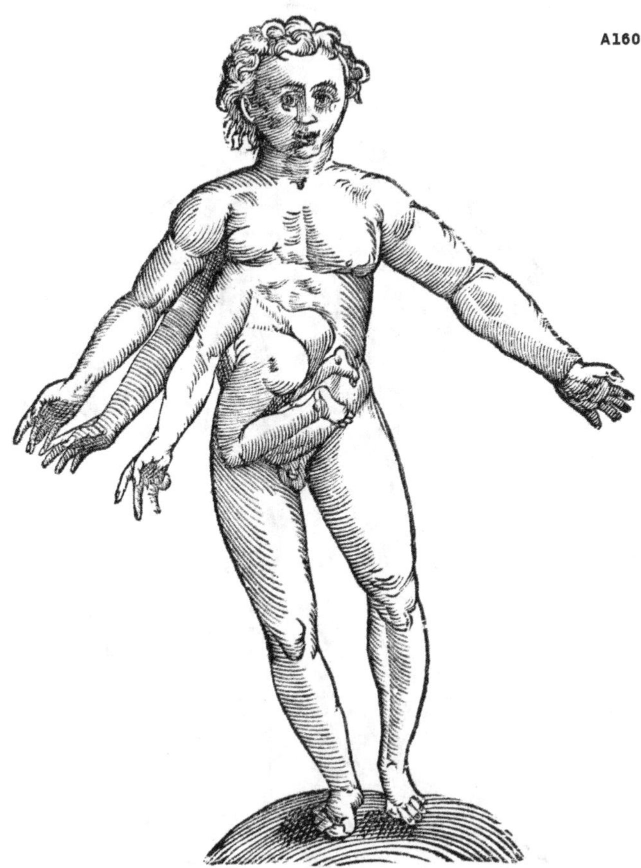

A161

A163

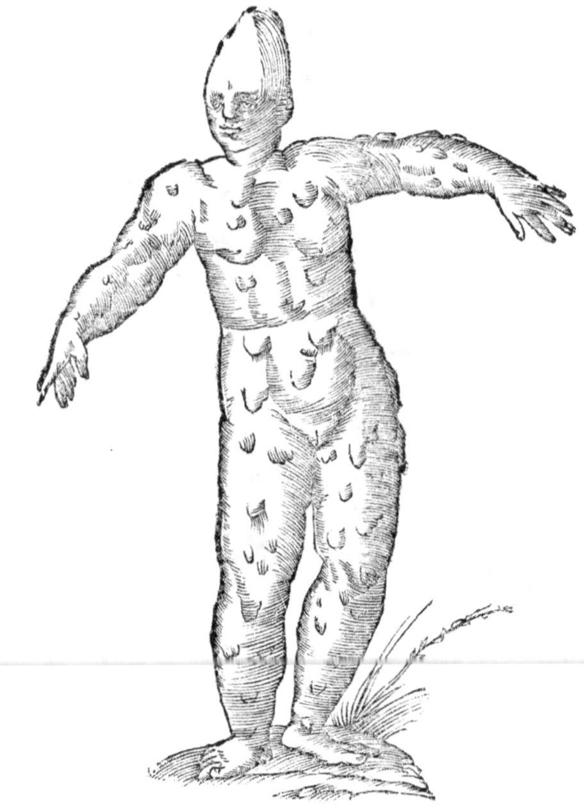

A162

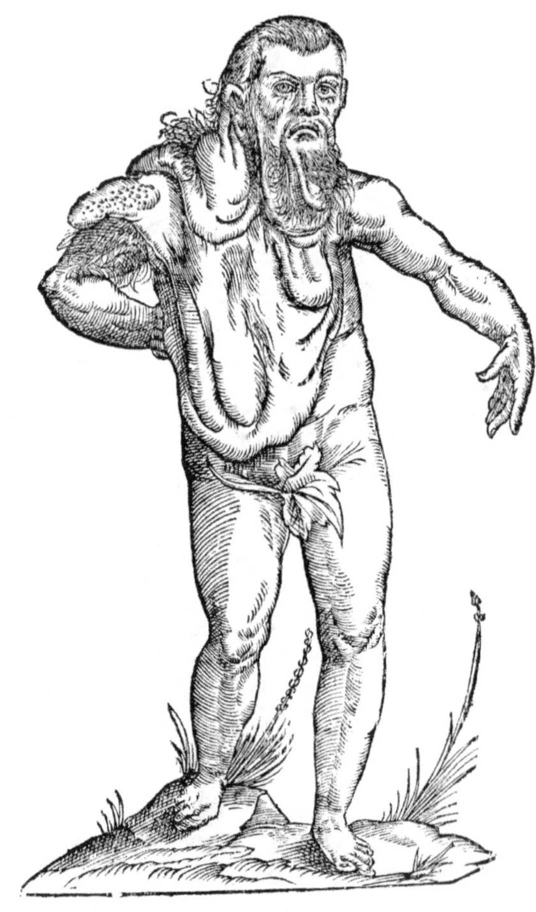

A164

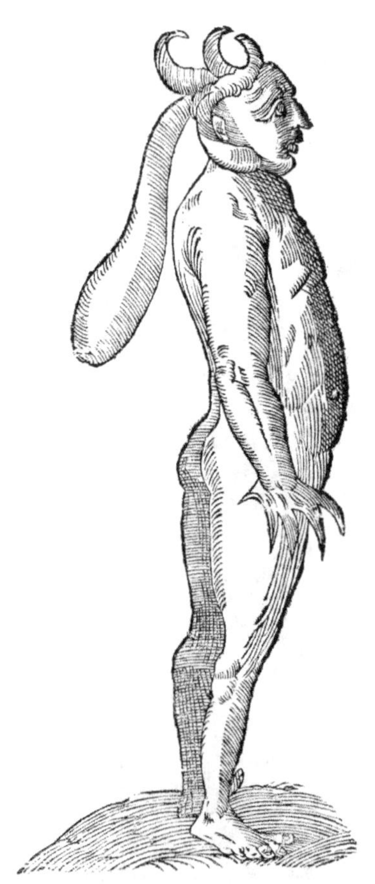

A165

A167

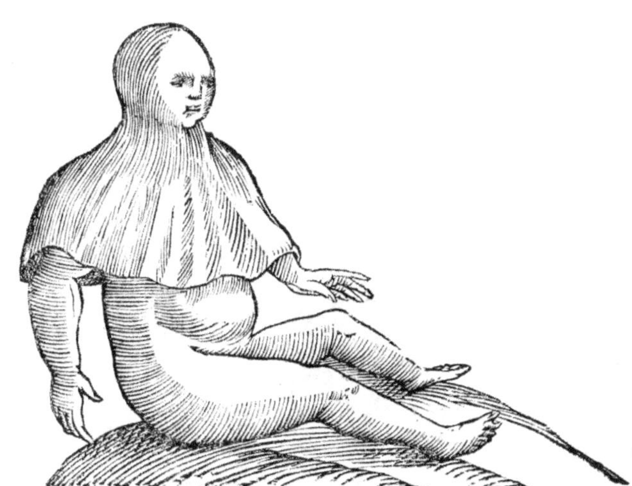

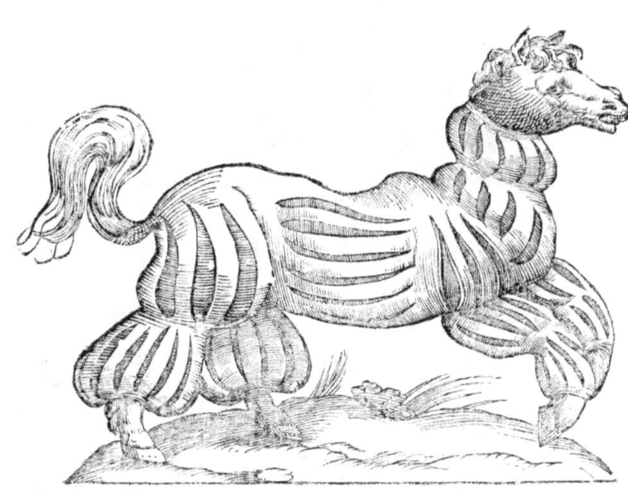

A166

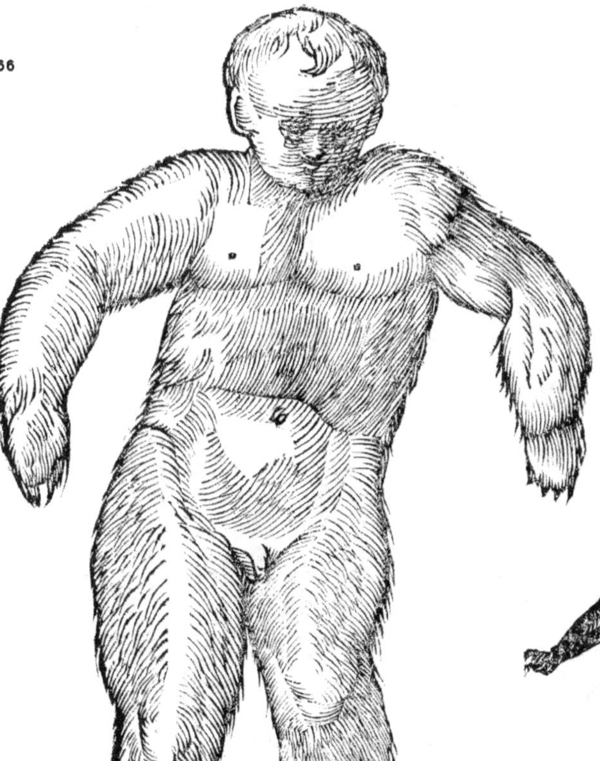

A168

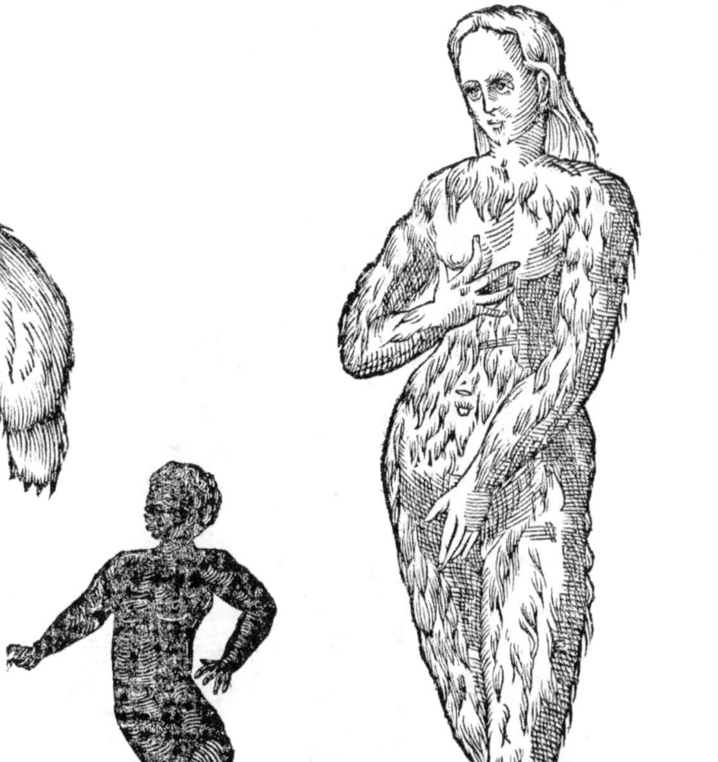

A169

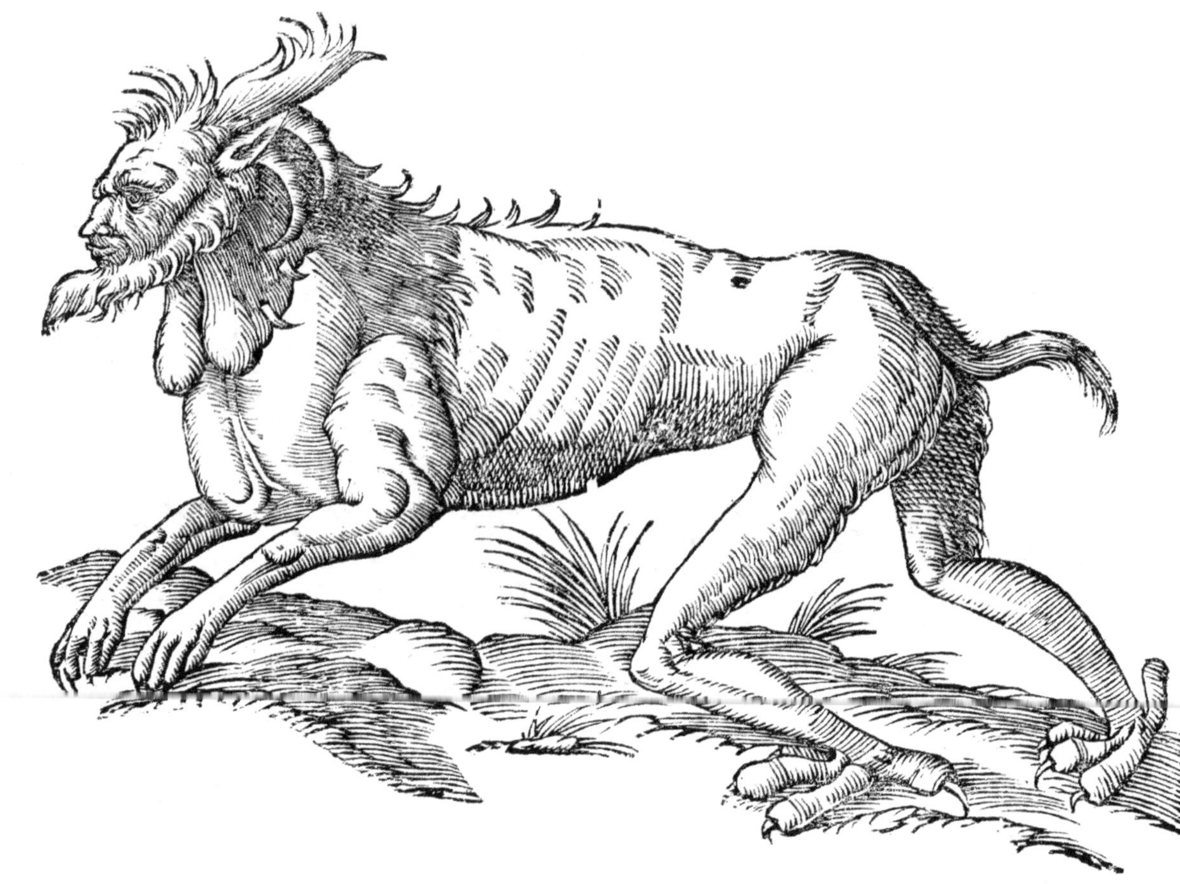

A170

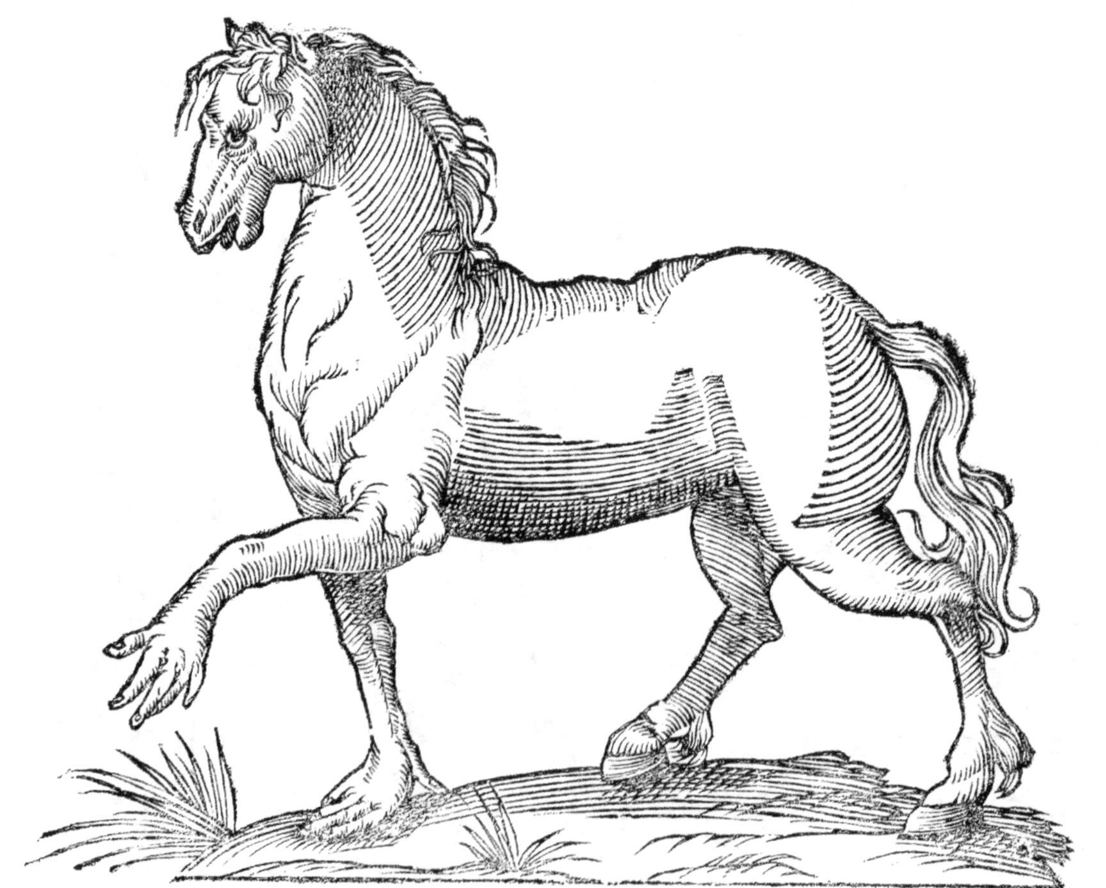

A171

A174

A172

A175

A173

A176

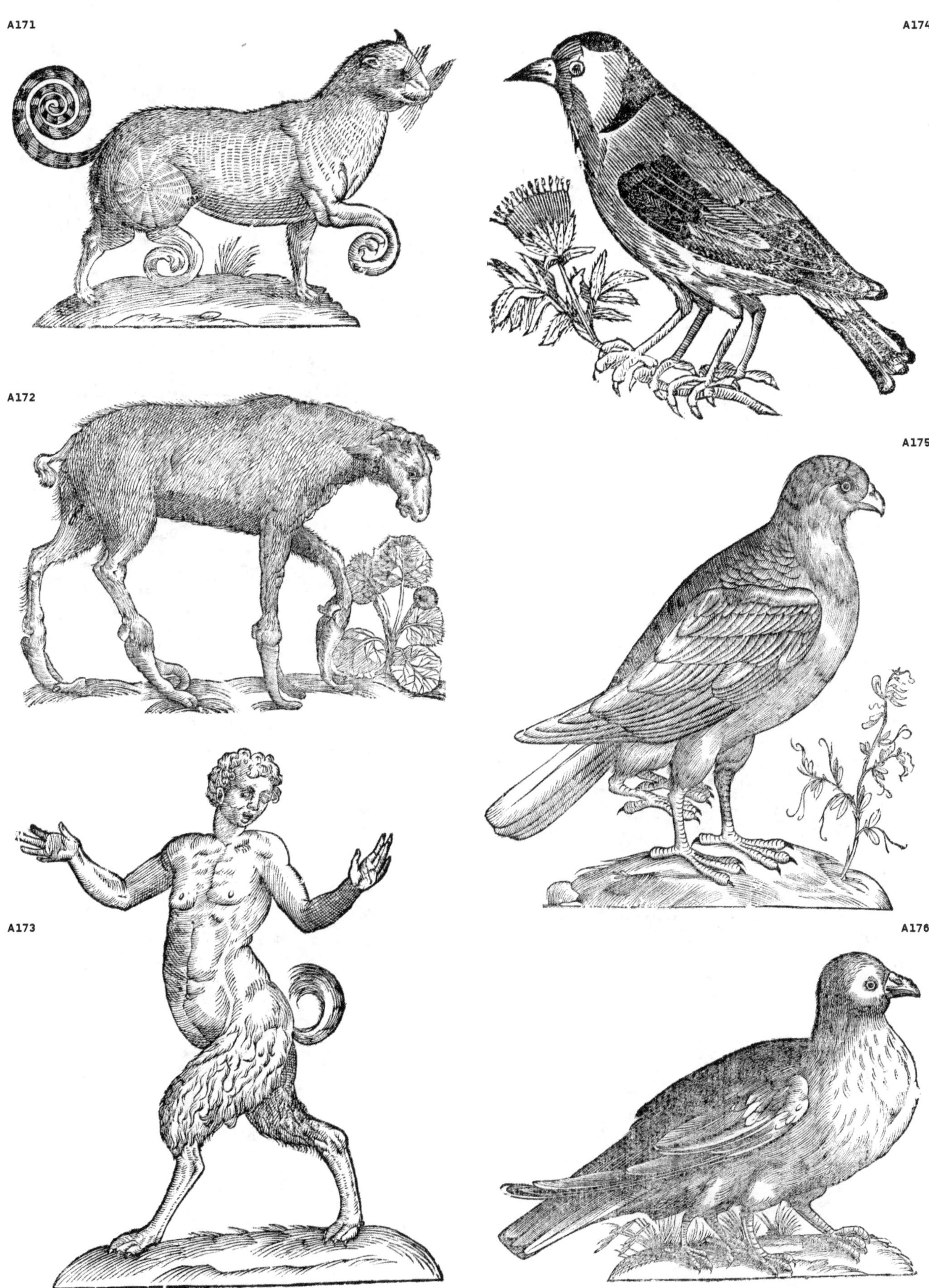

A177

A180

A178

A181

A182

A179

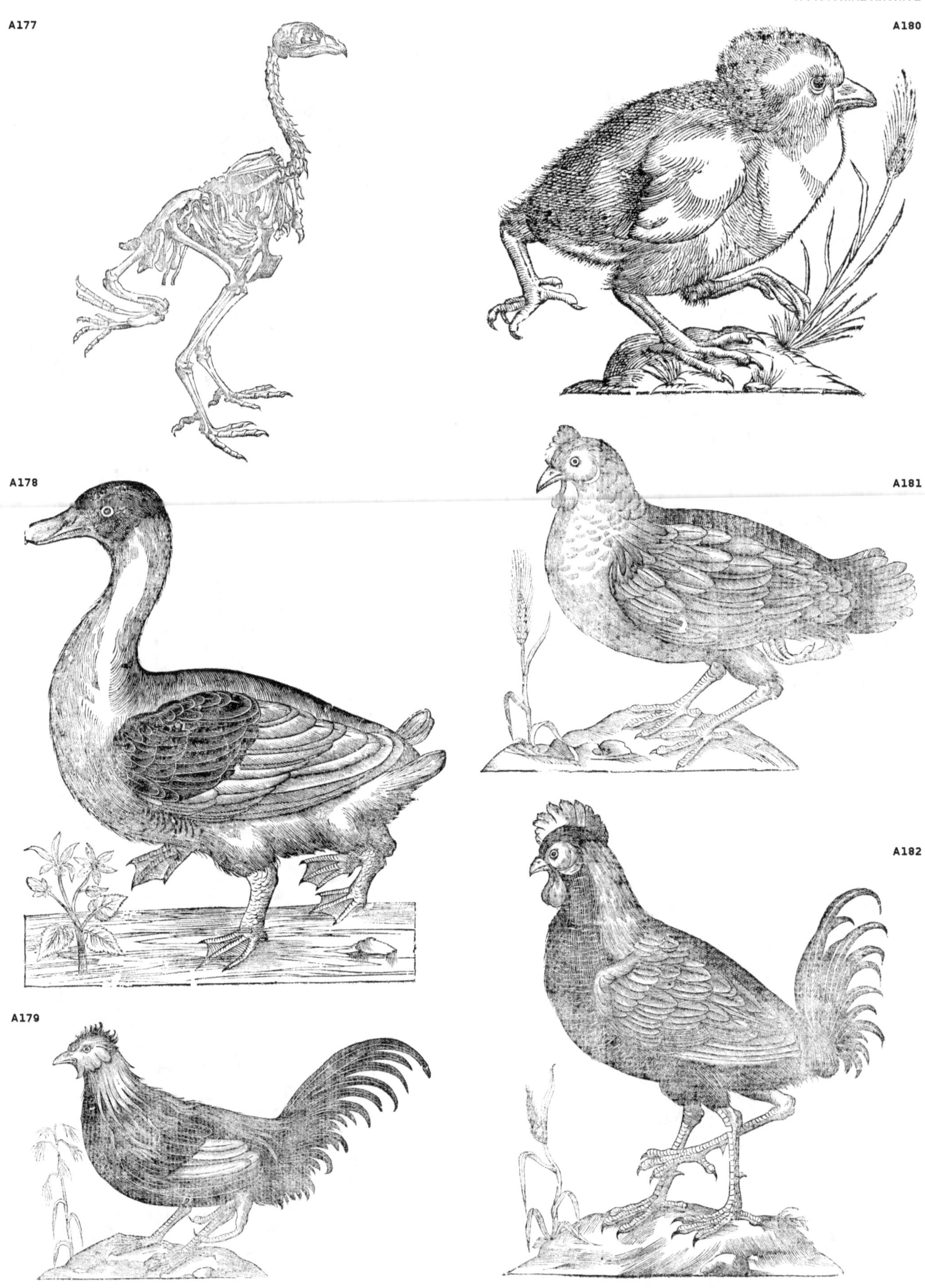

A183

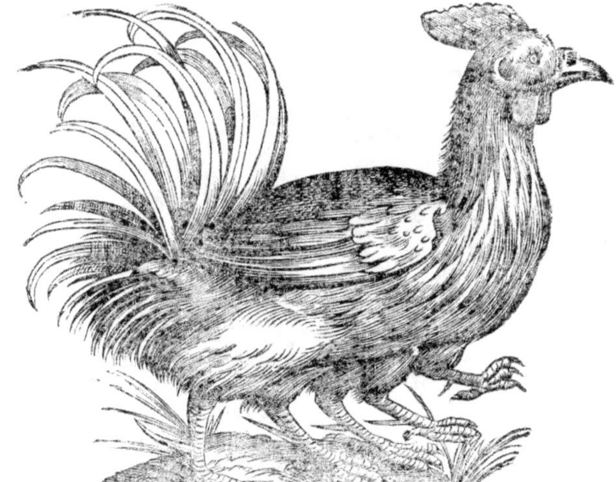

A186

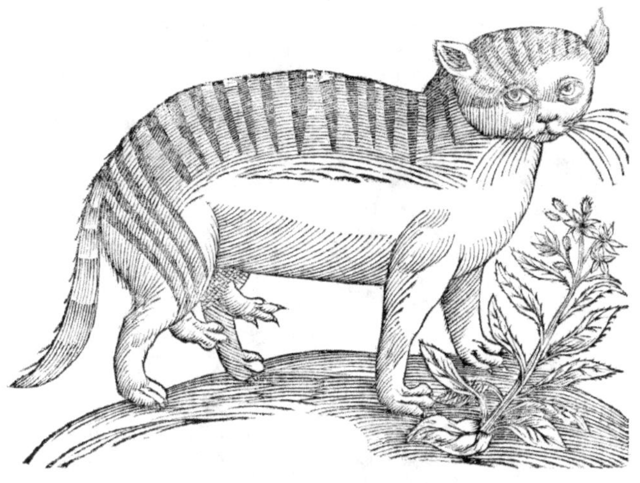

A184

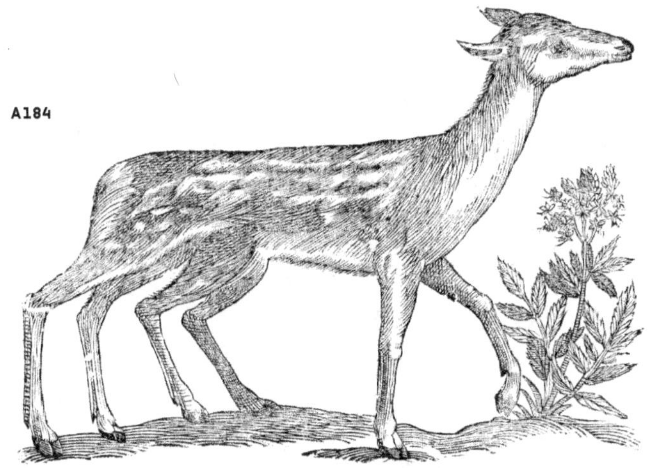

A187

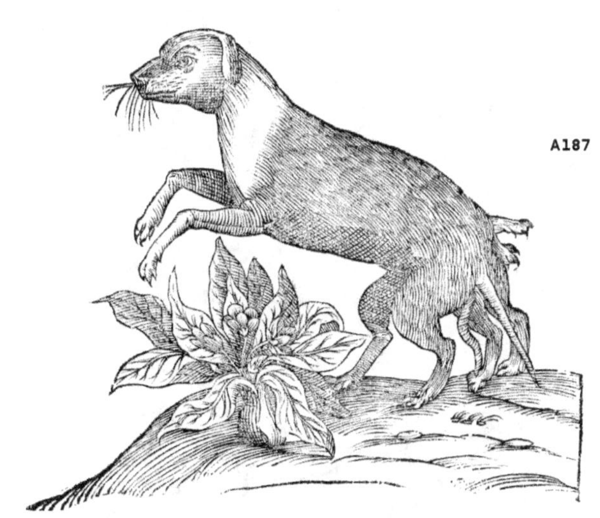

A185

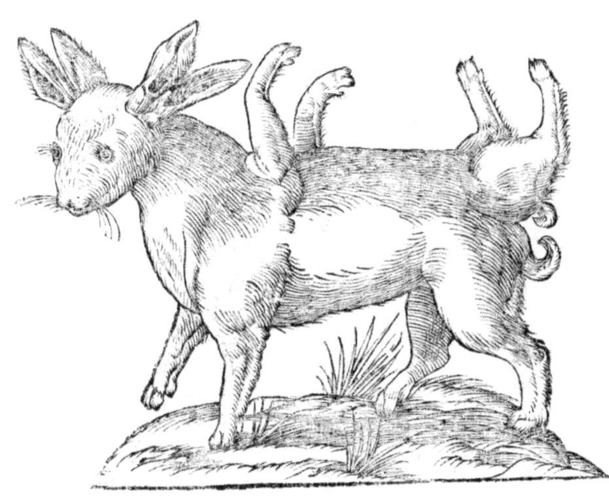

A188

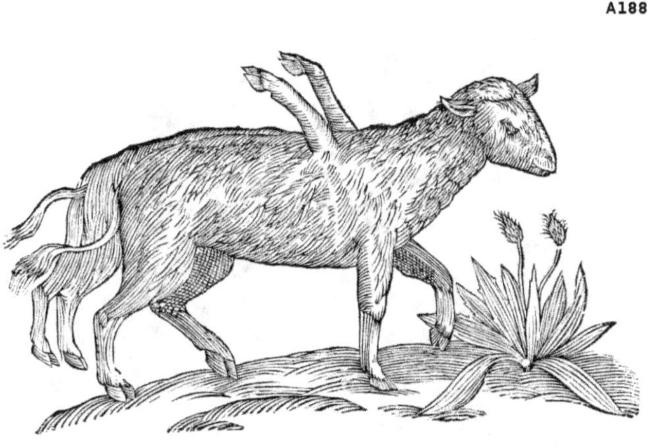

A189

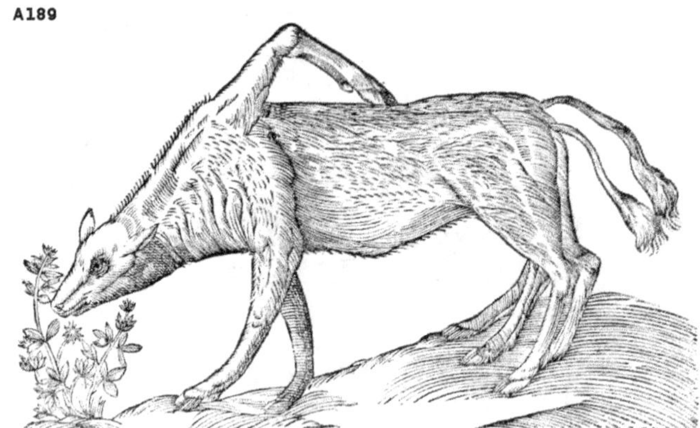

A193

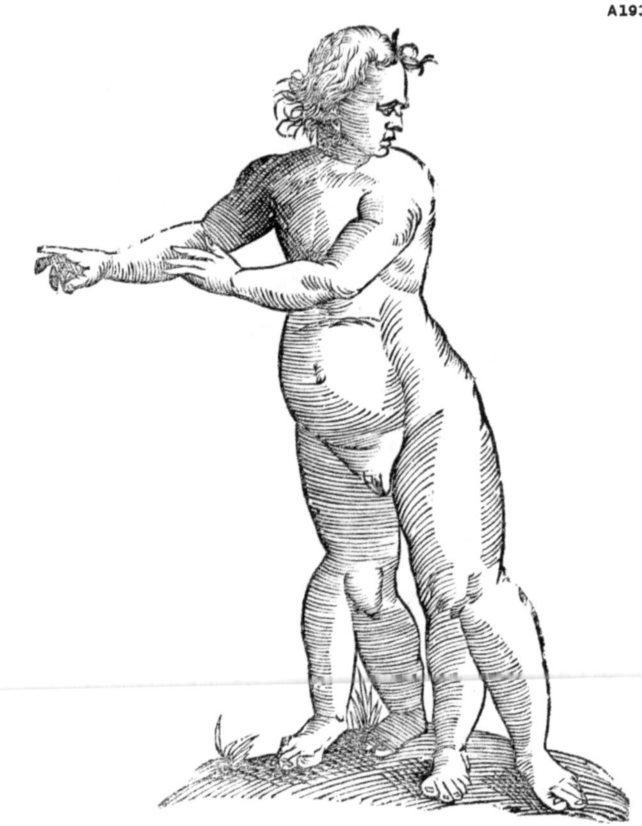

A190

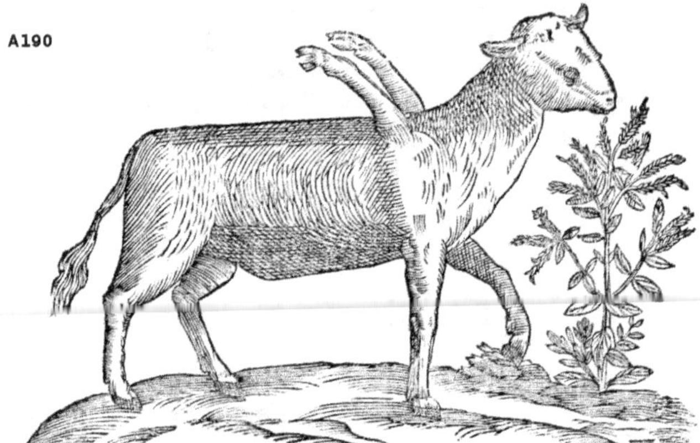

A191

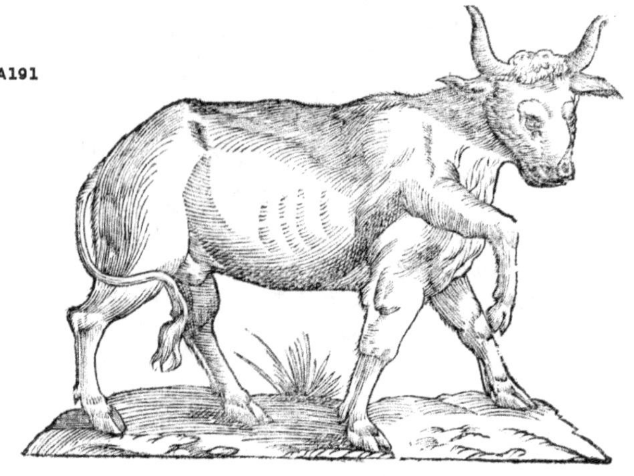

A194

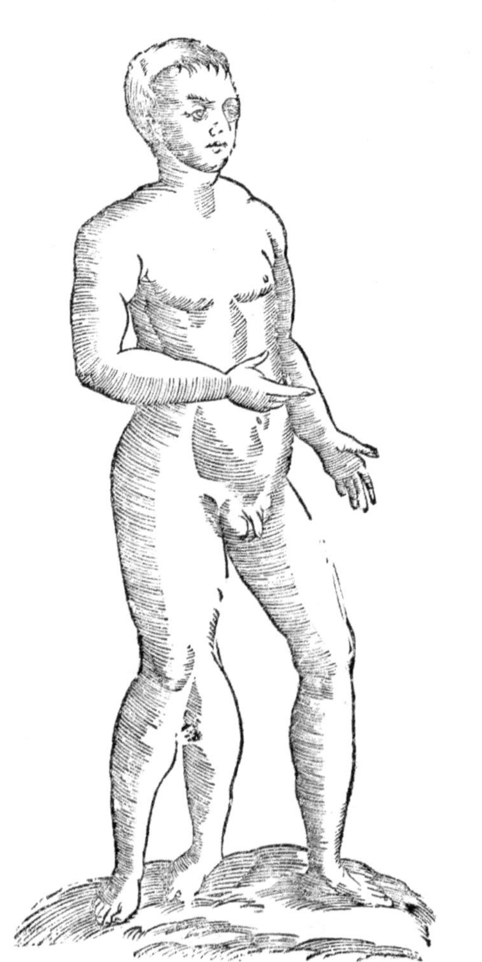

A192

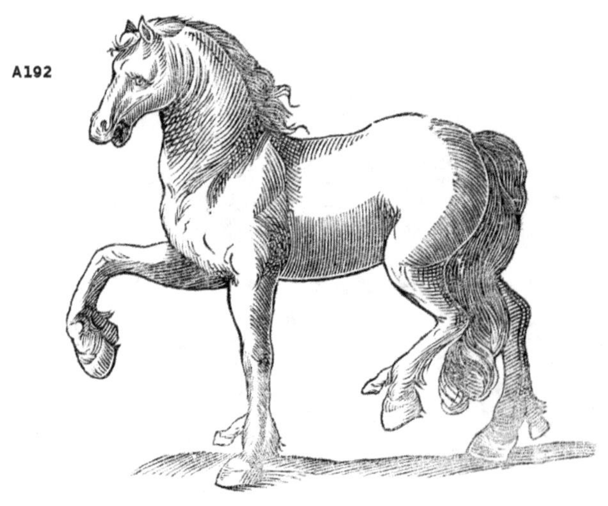

A195

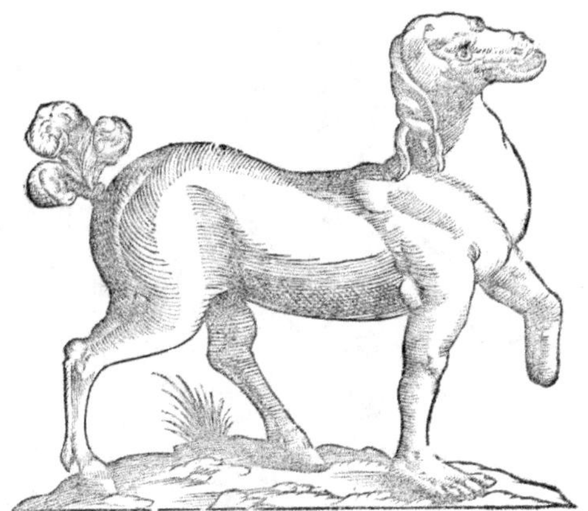

A198

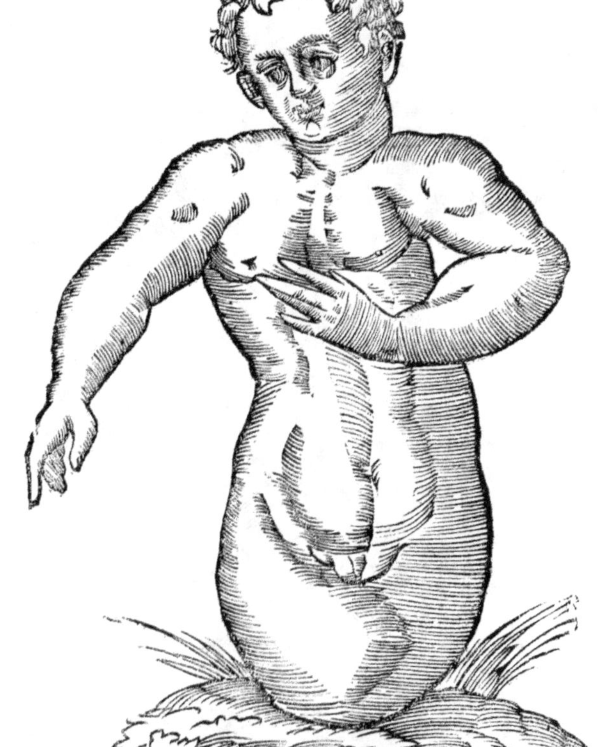

A196

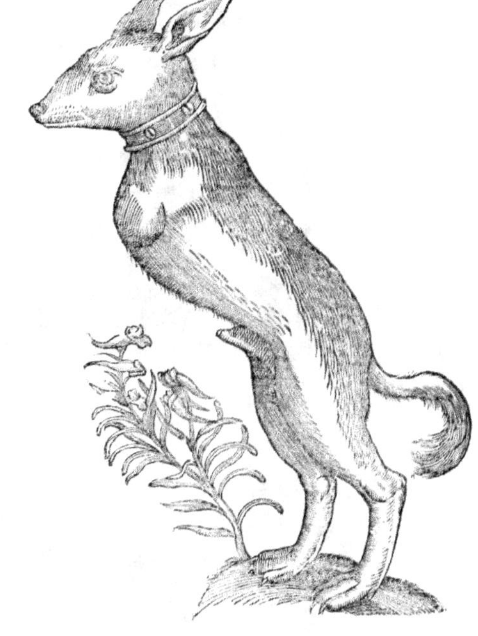

A197

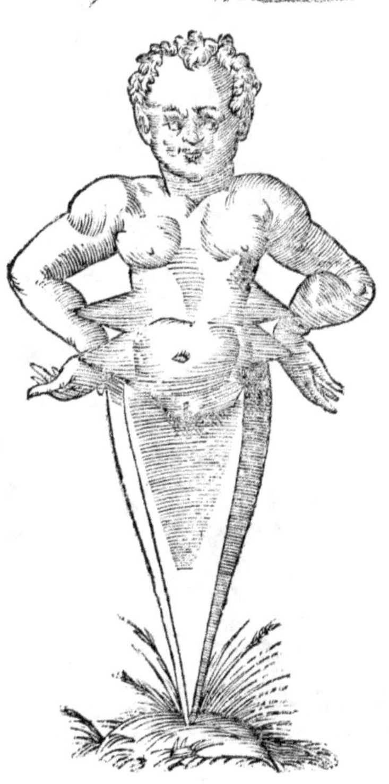

A199

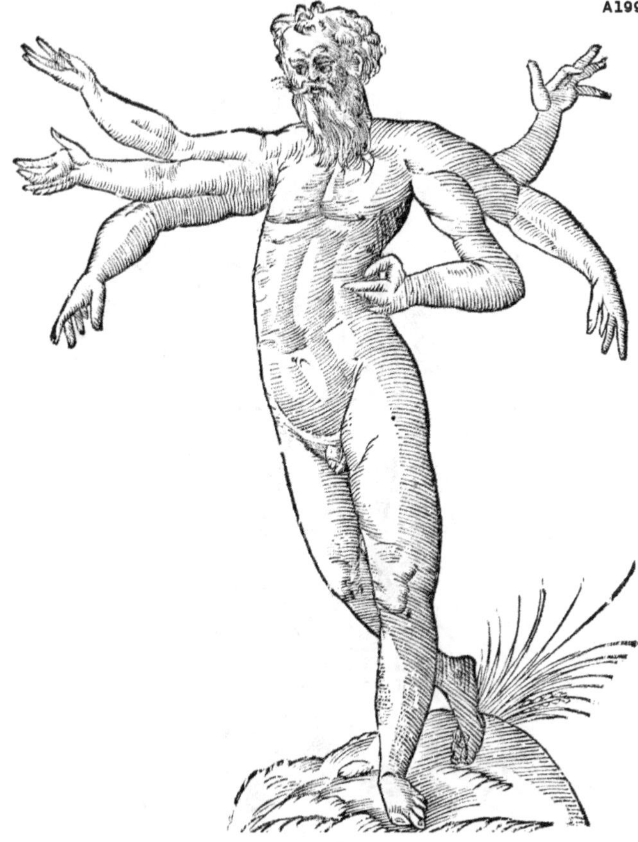

A200

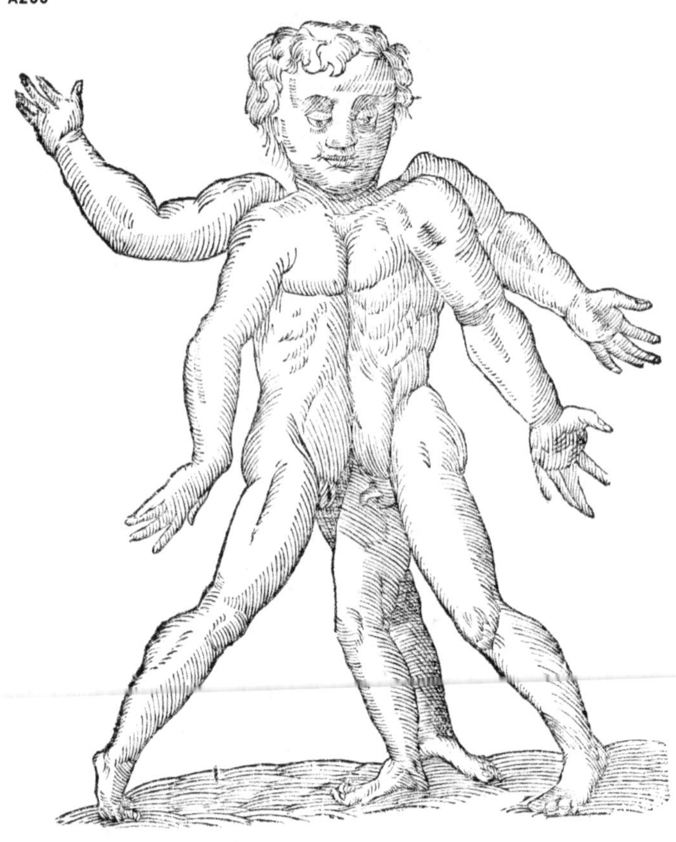

A202

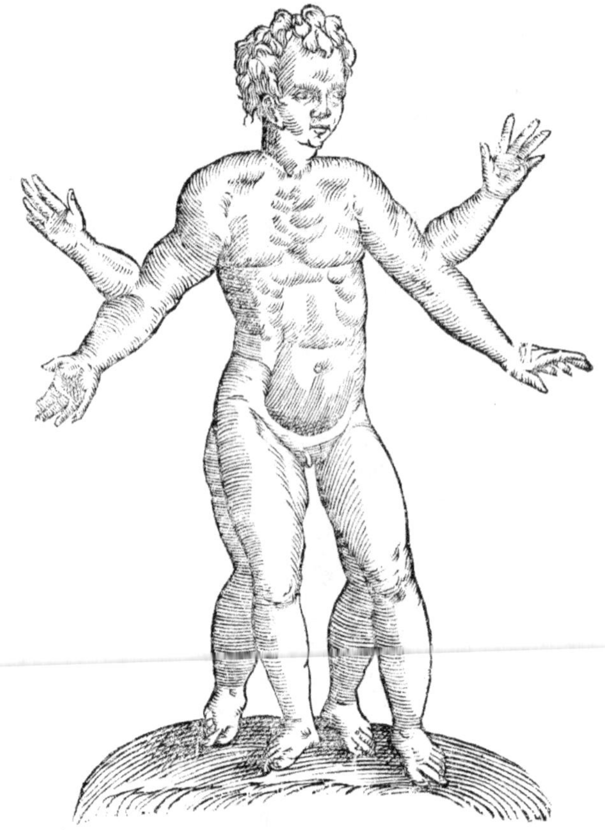

A201

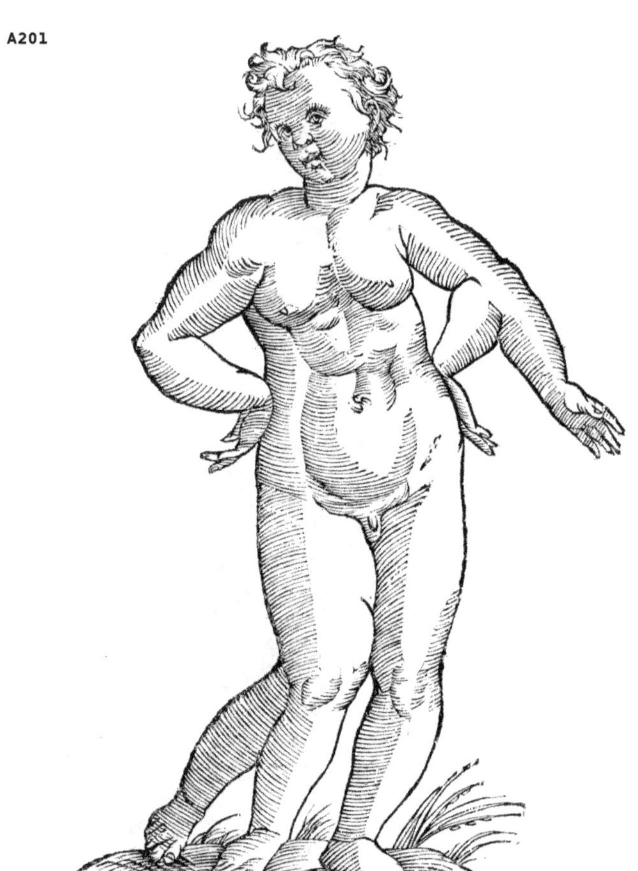

A203

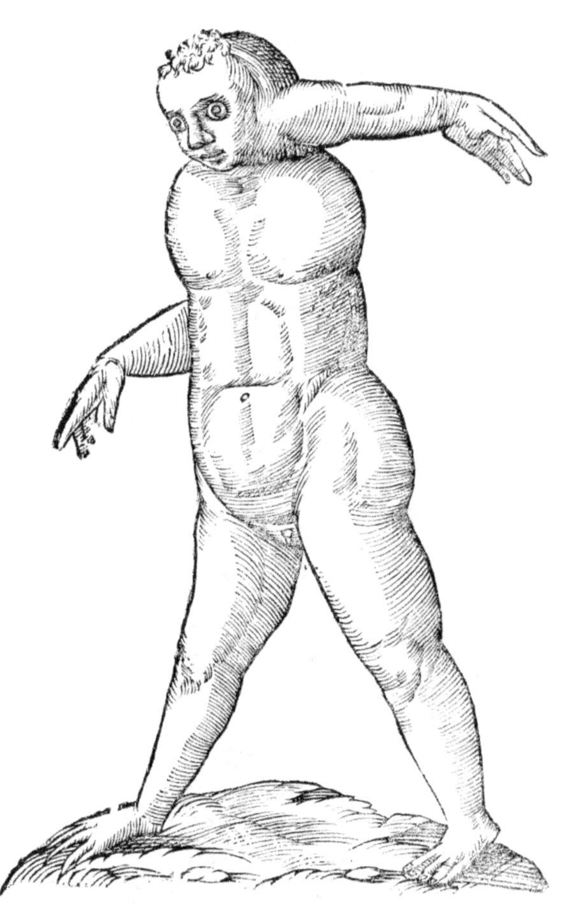

A204

A205

A206

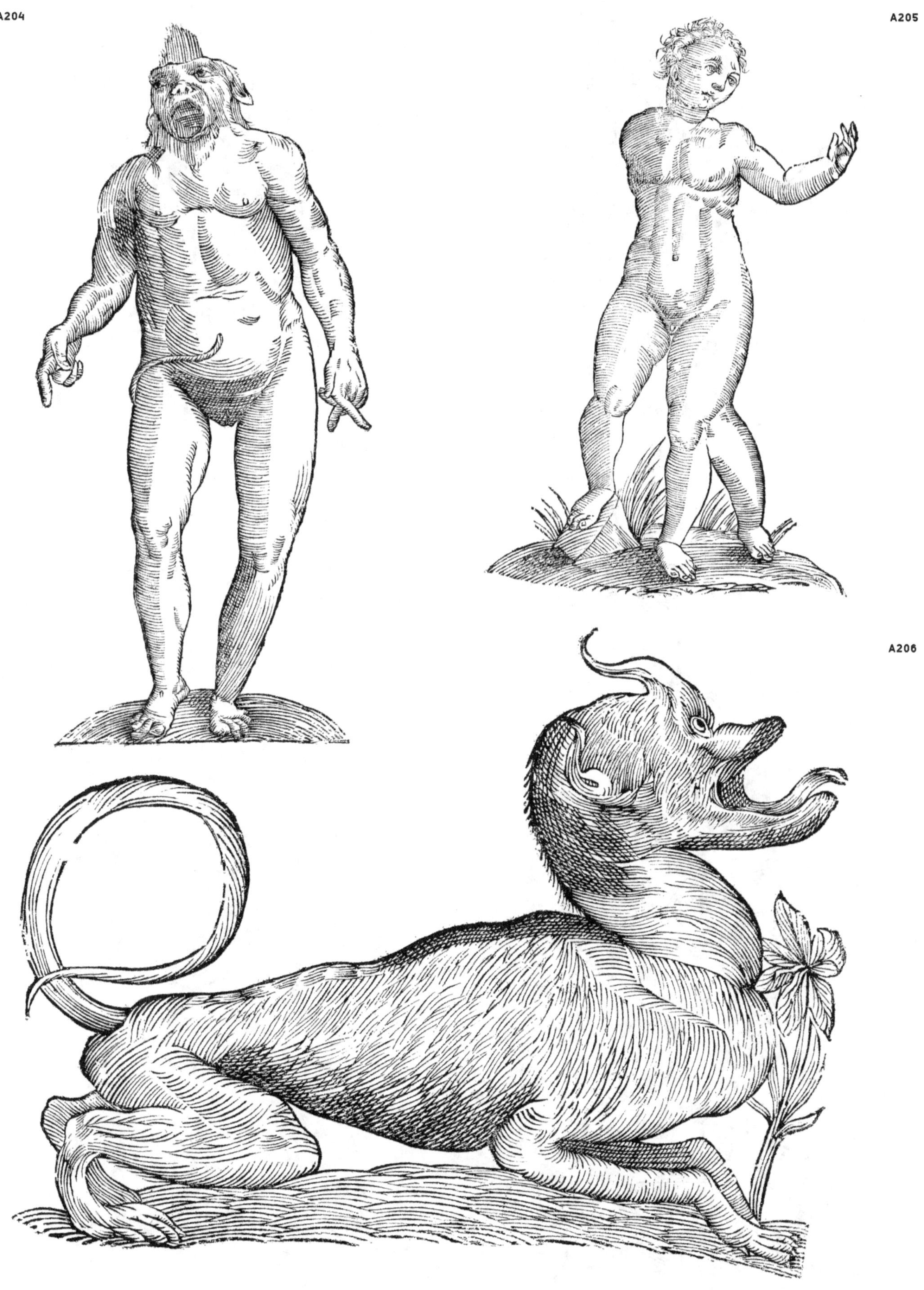

A207

A209

A208

A210

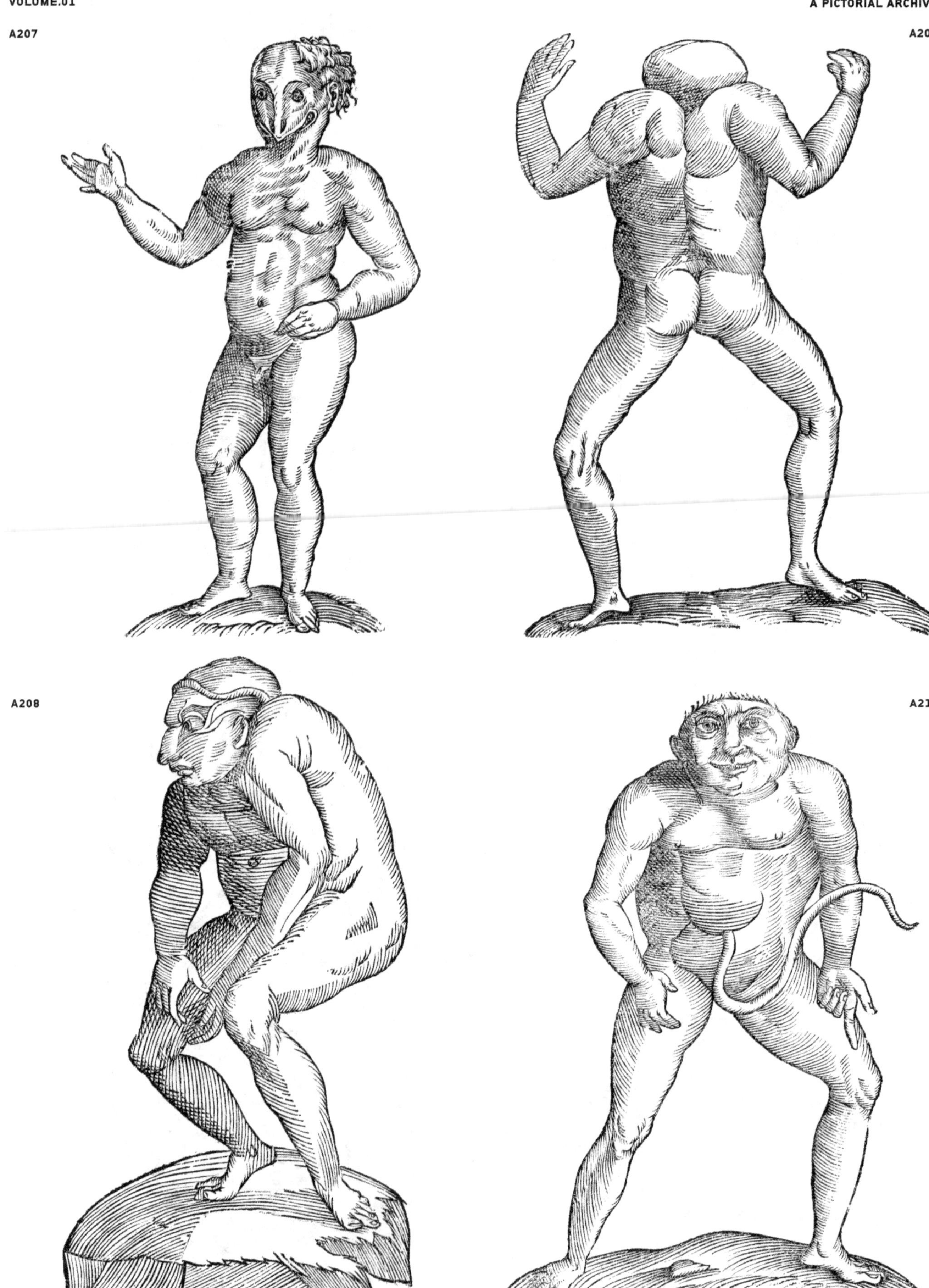

A211

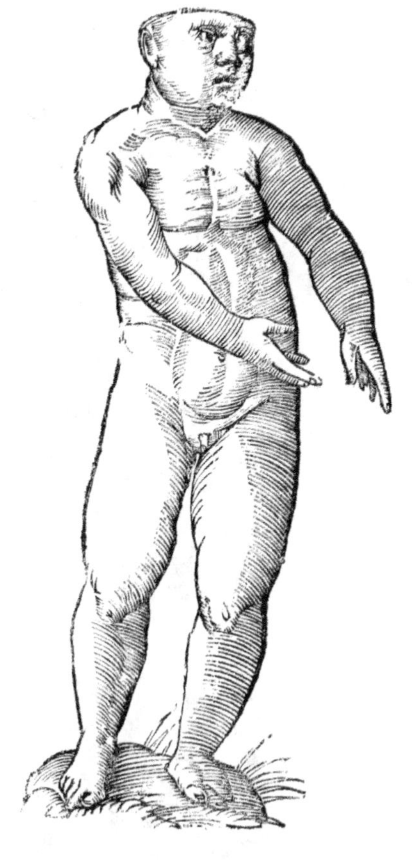

A213

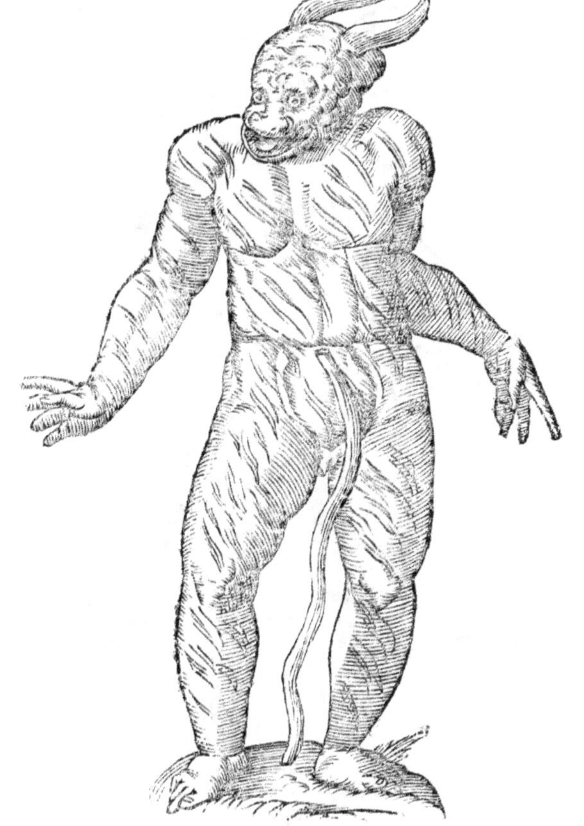

A212

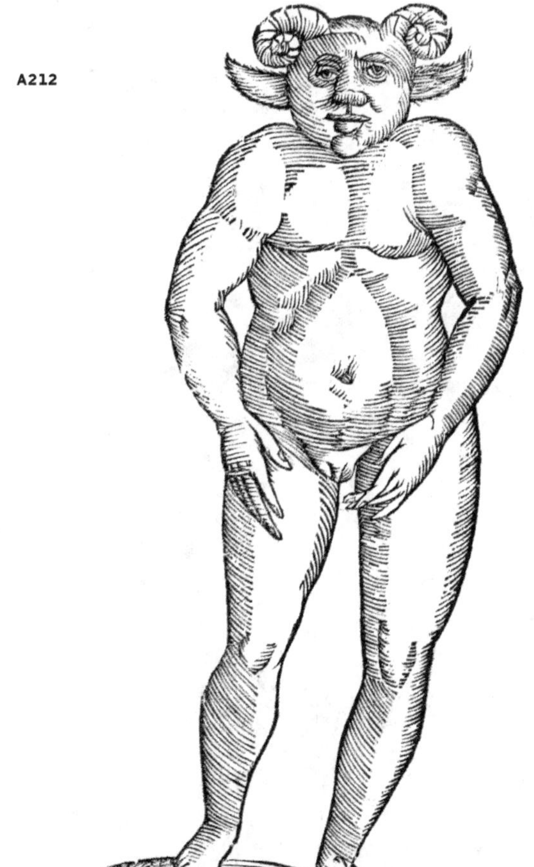

A214

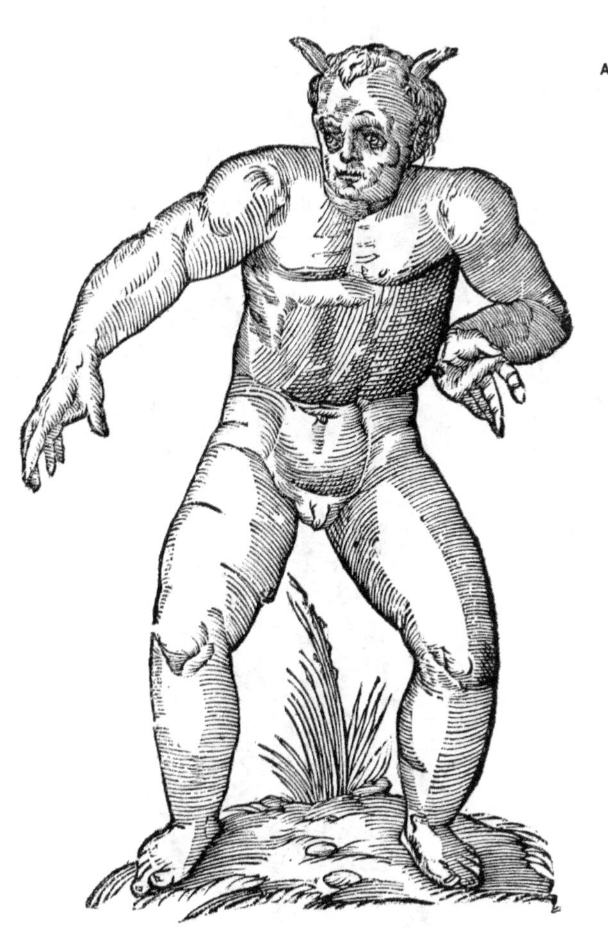

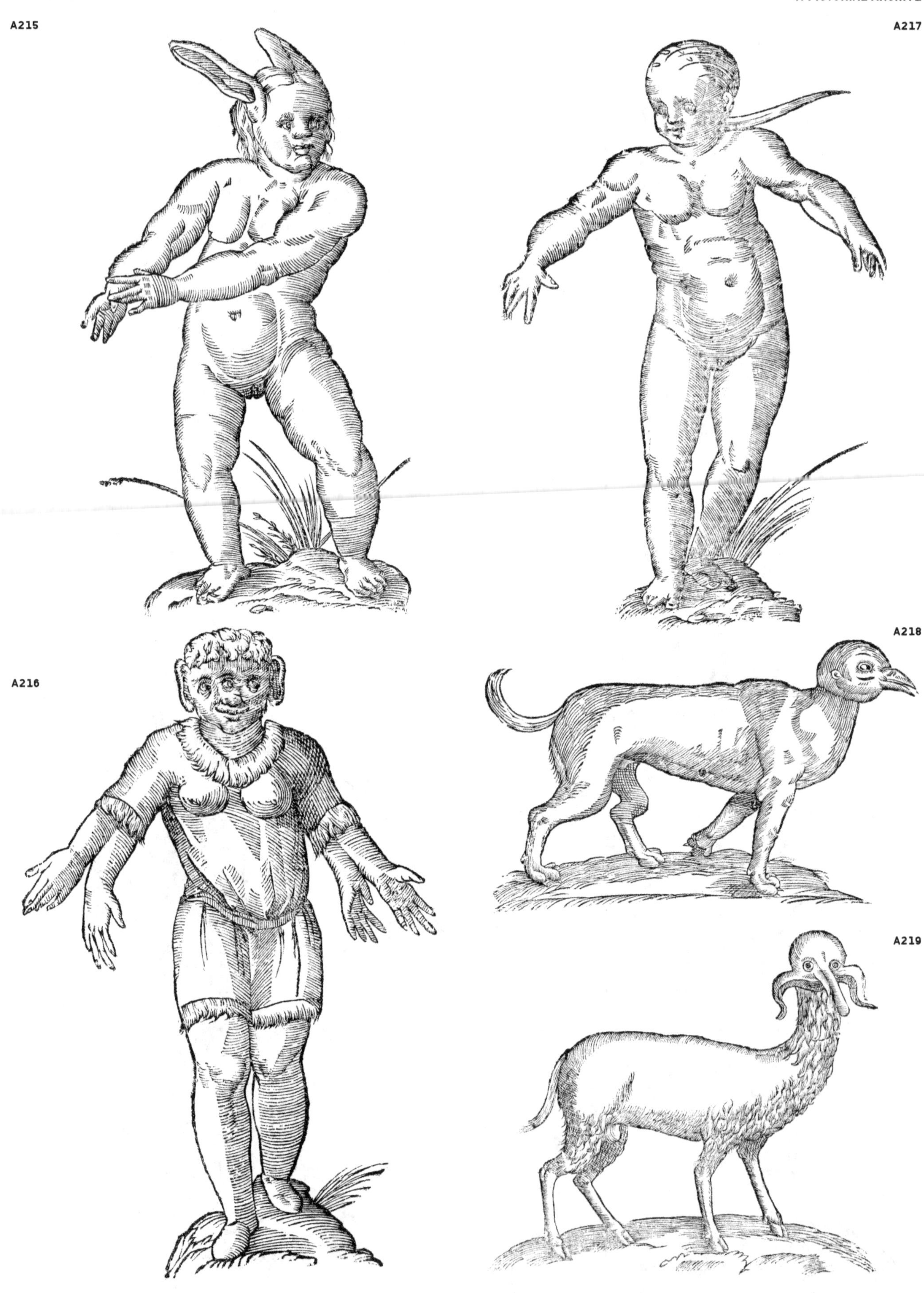
A215
A217
A216
A218
A219

A220

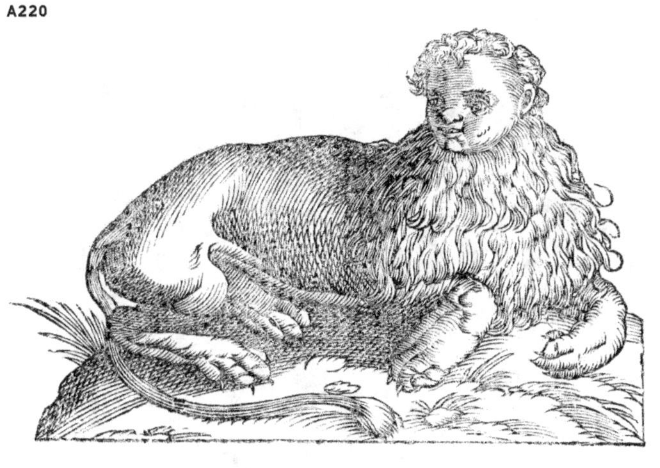

A224

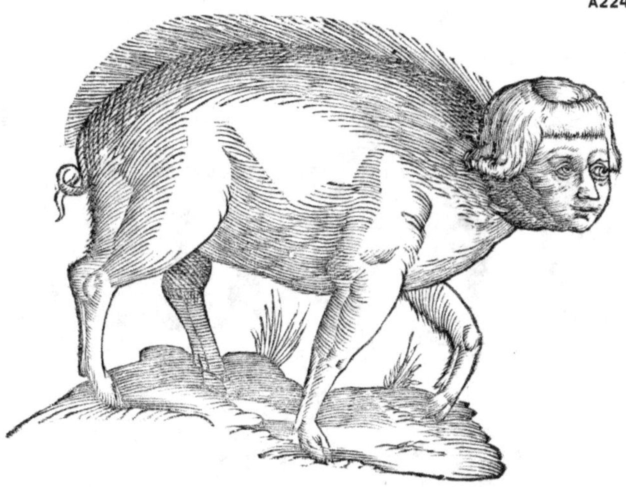

A221

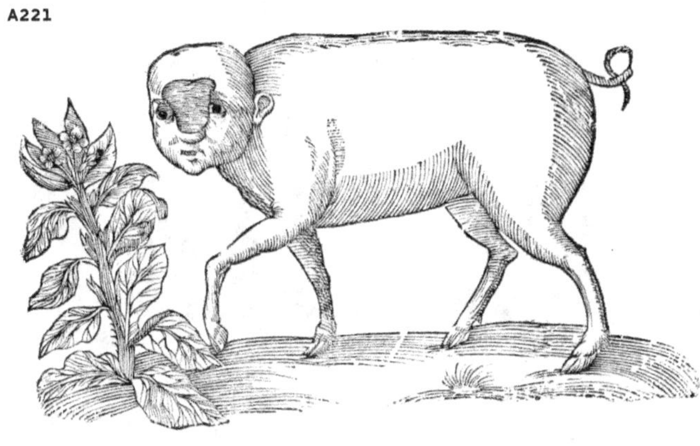

A225

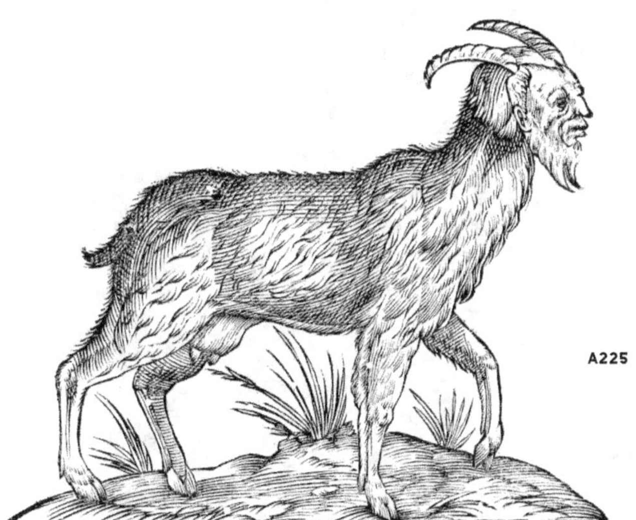

A222

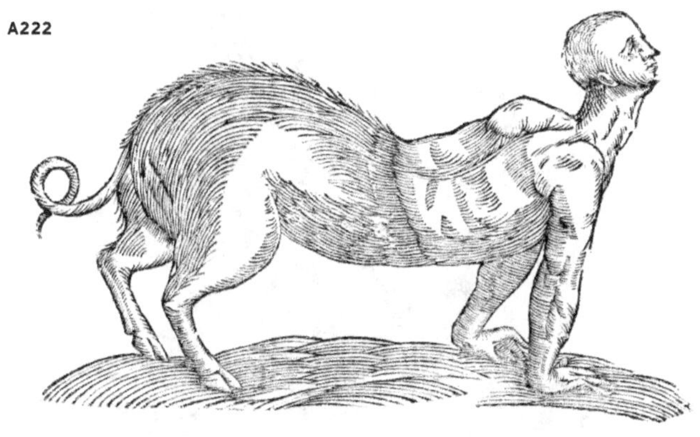

A223

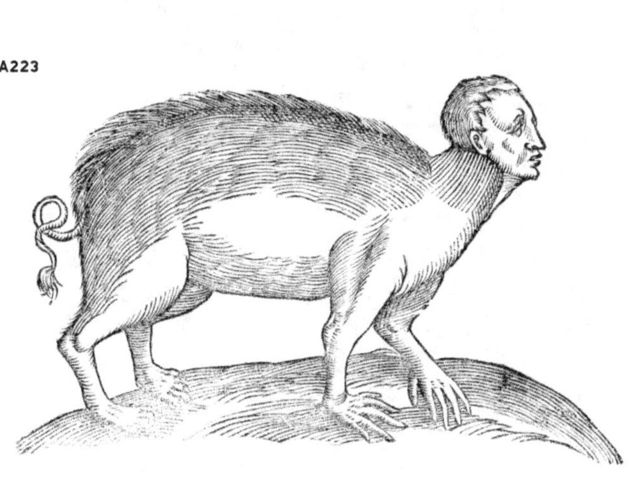

A226

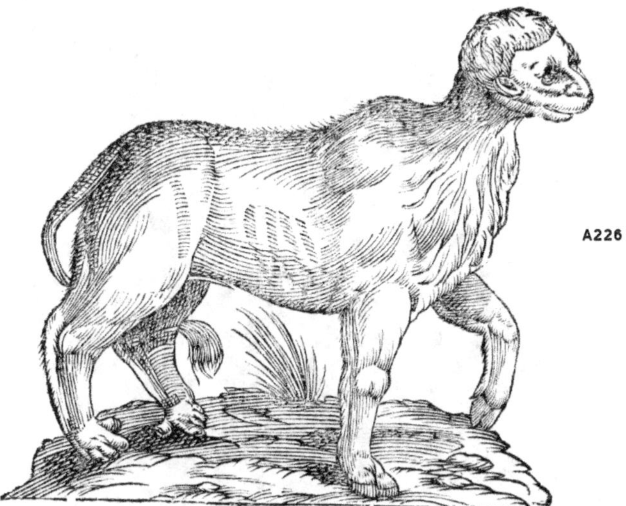

A227

A230

A228

A229

A231

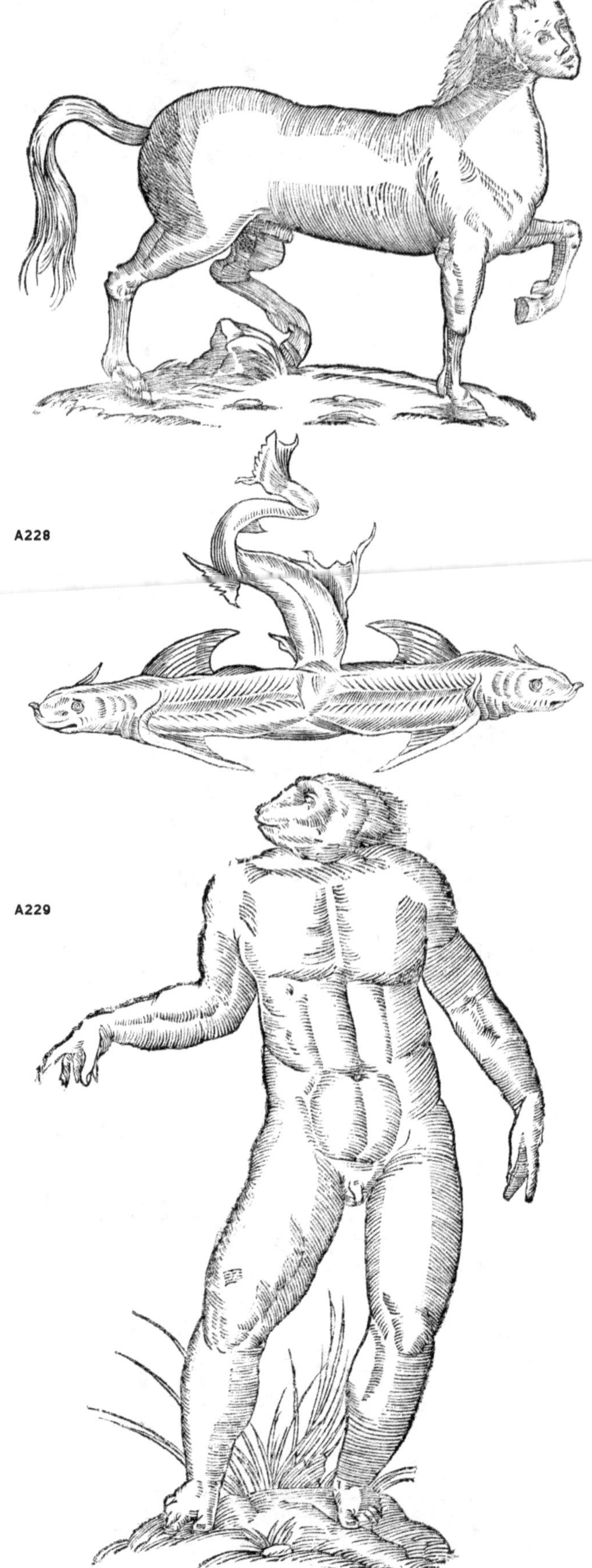

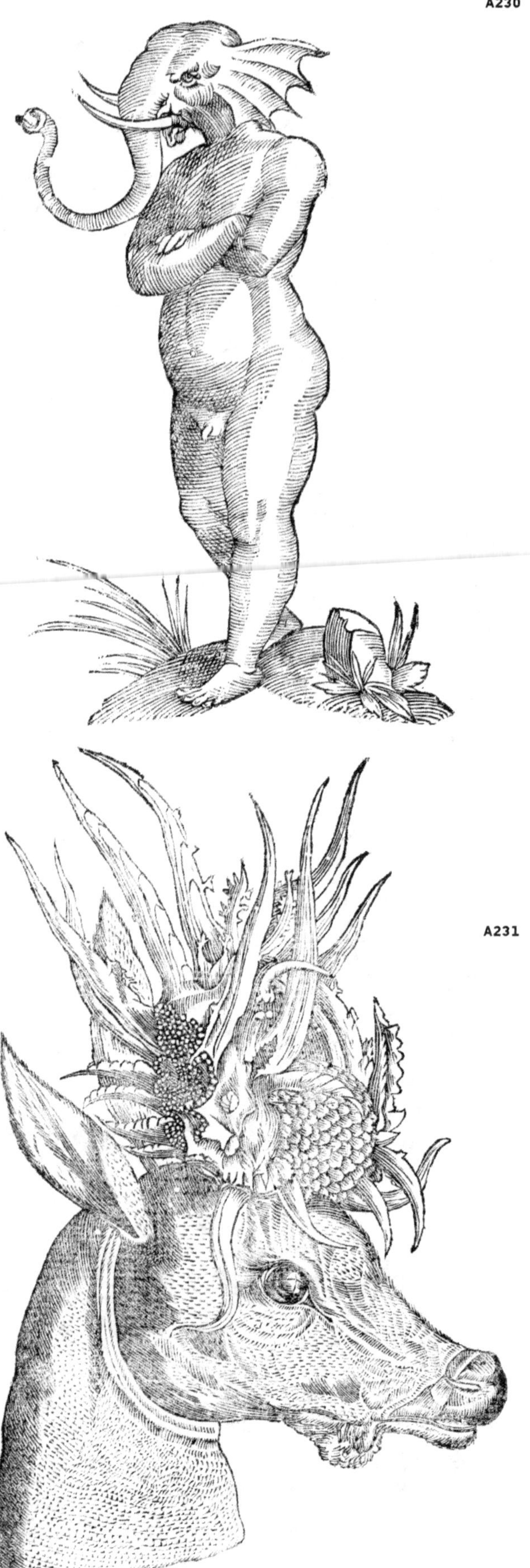

A232

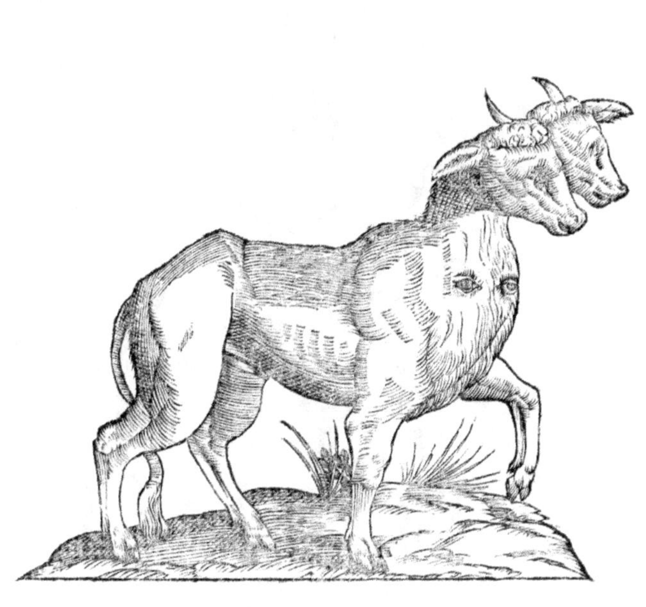

A235

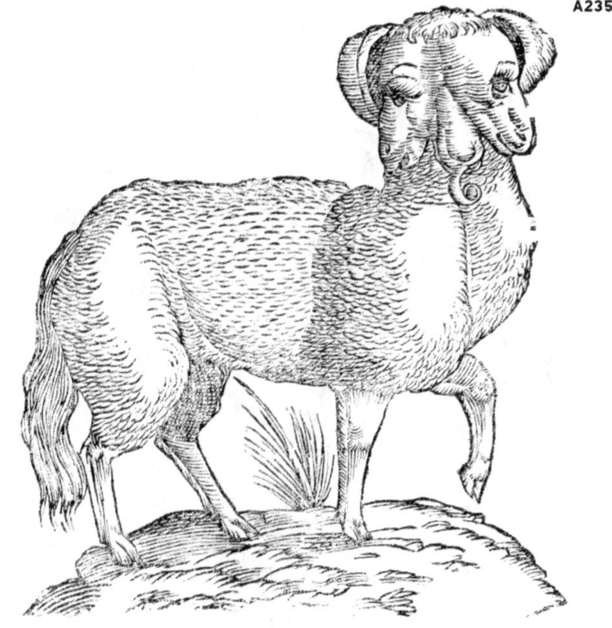

A233

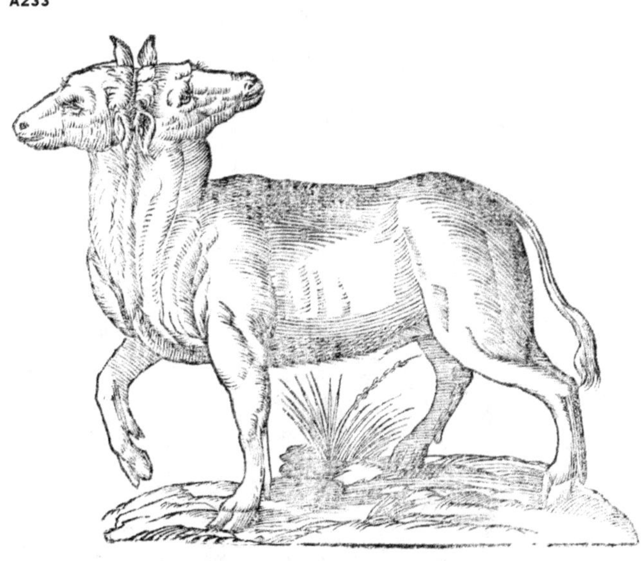

A236

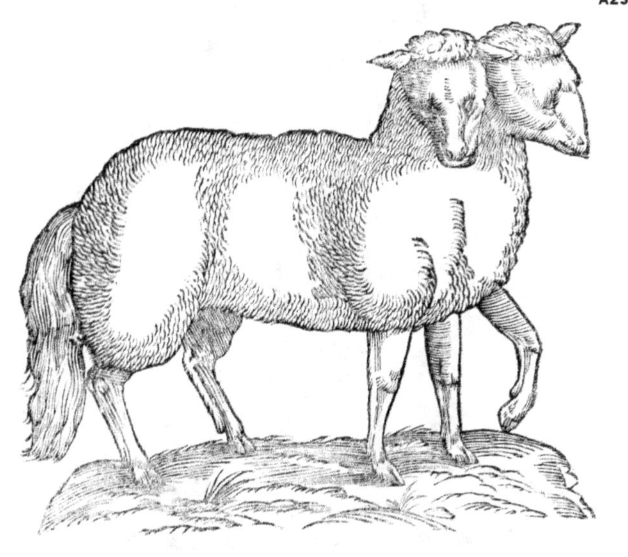

A234

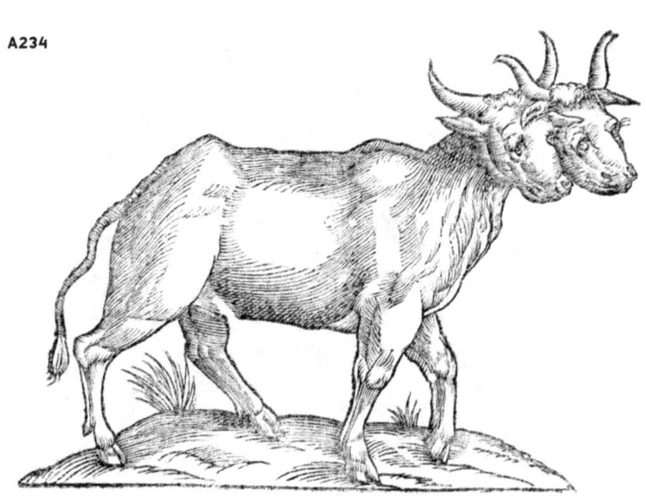

A237

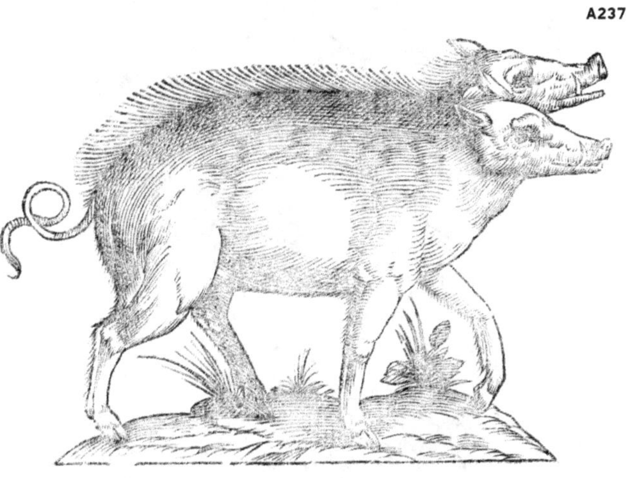

A239   A241

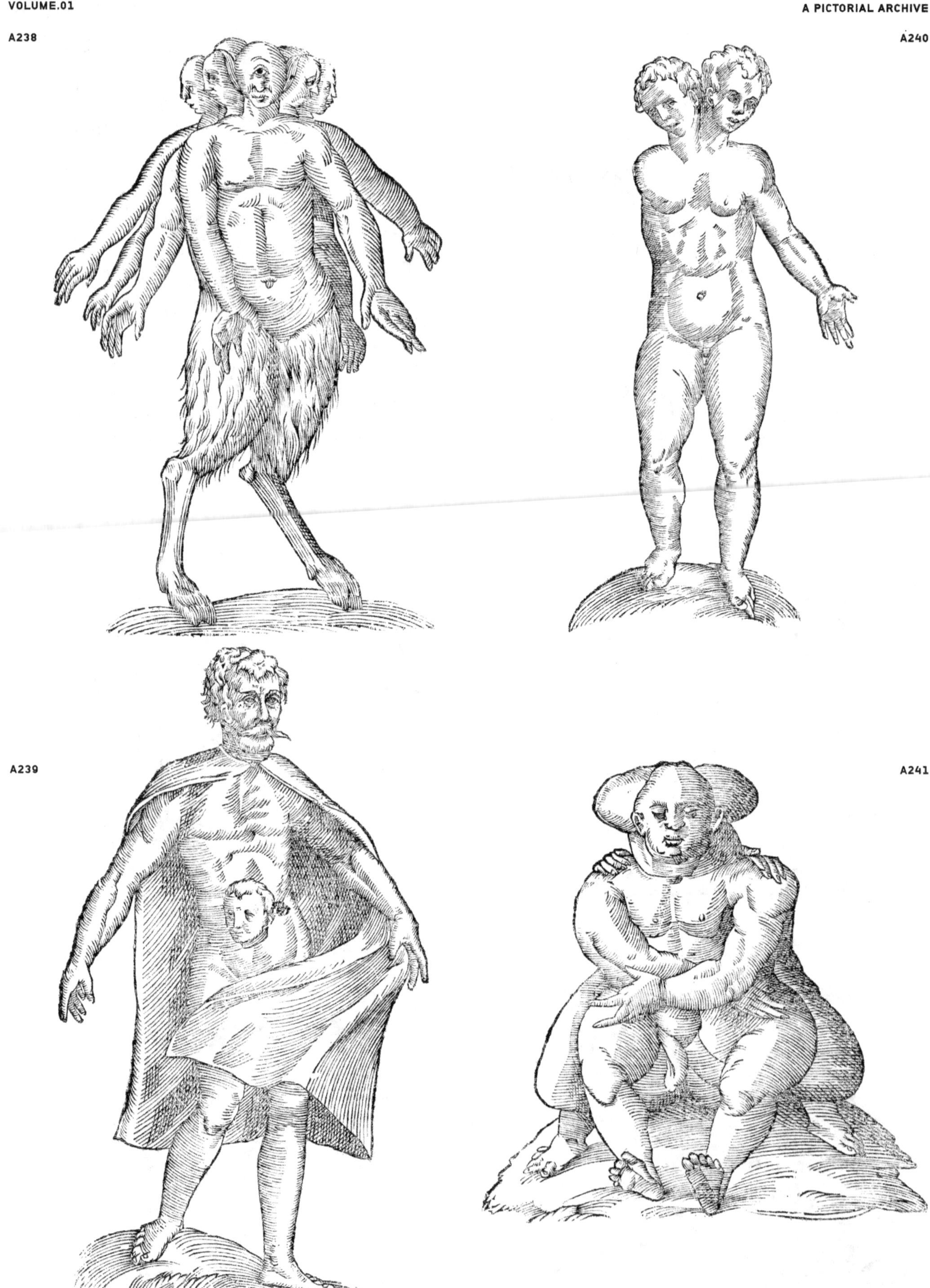

A242

A244

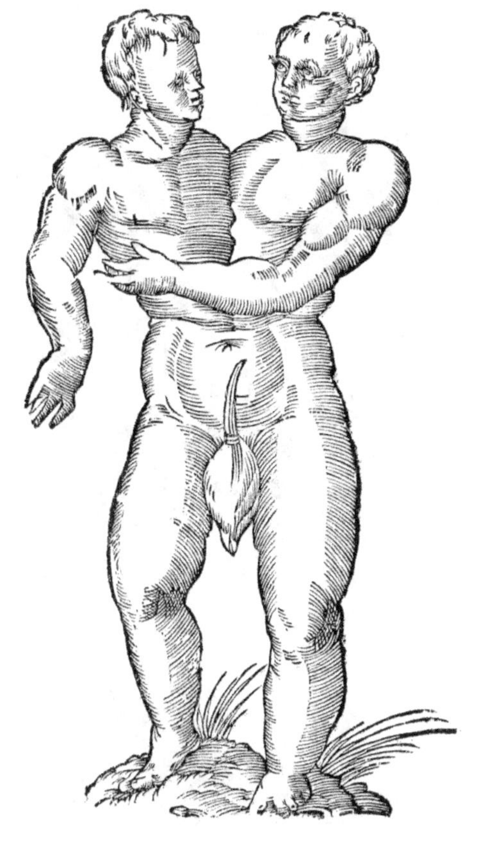

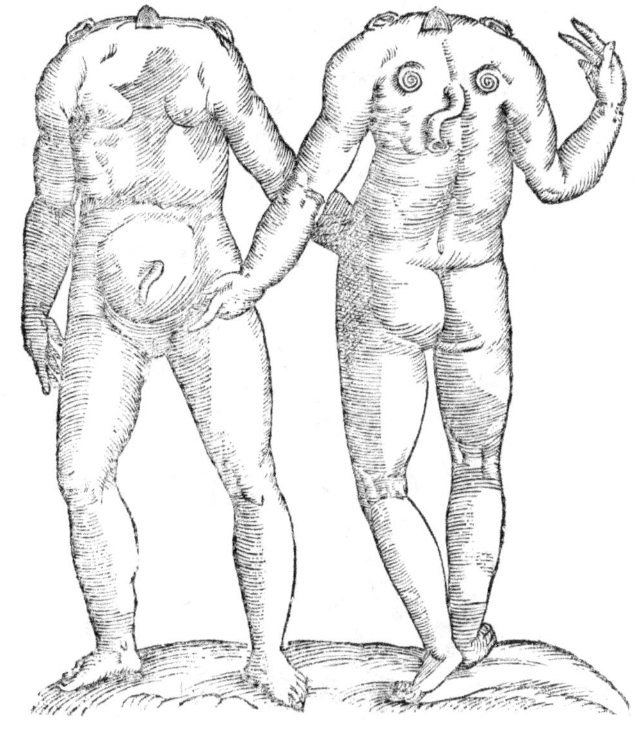

A243

A245

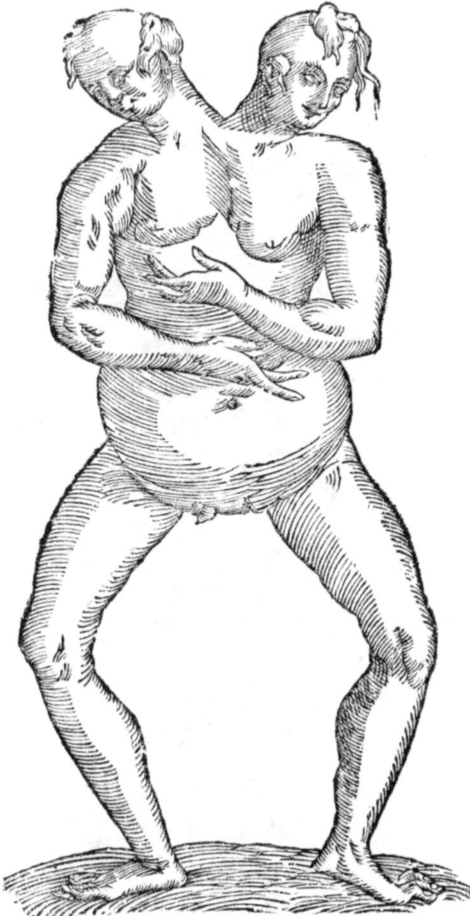

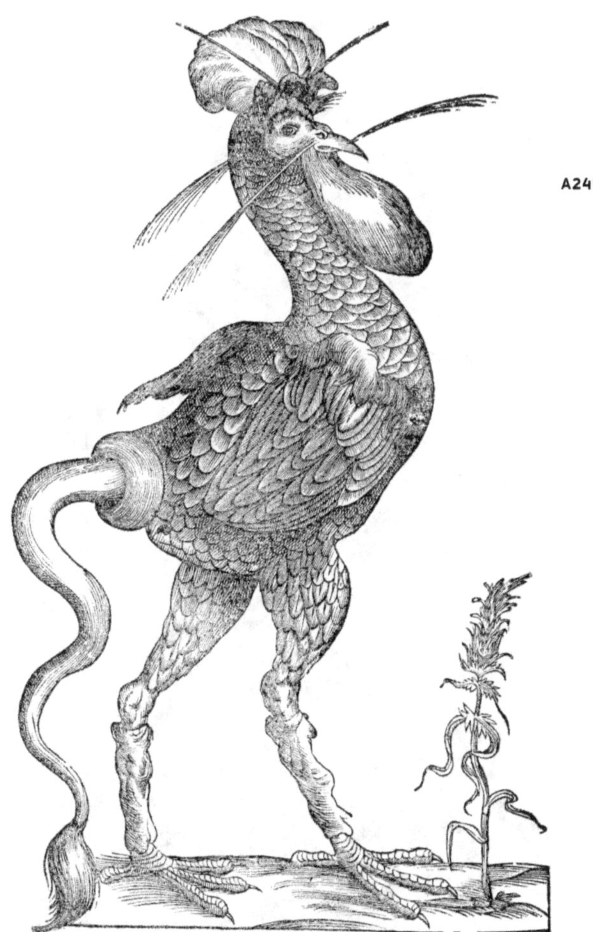

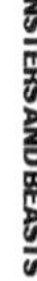

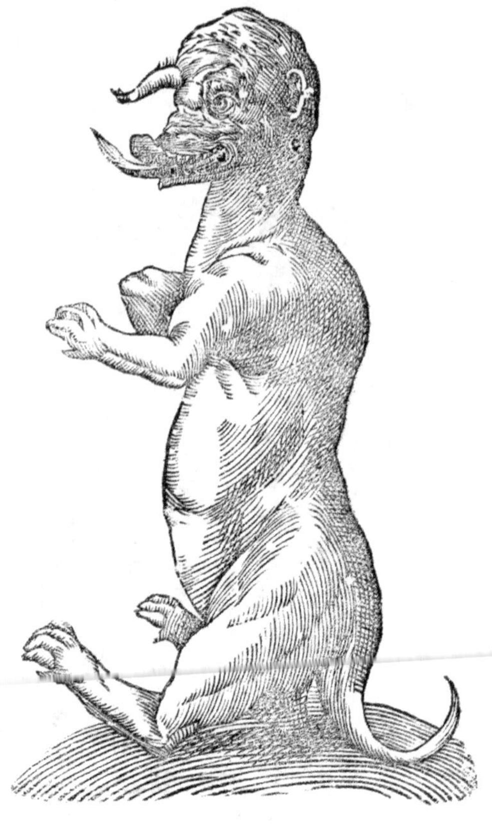

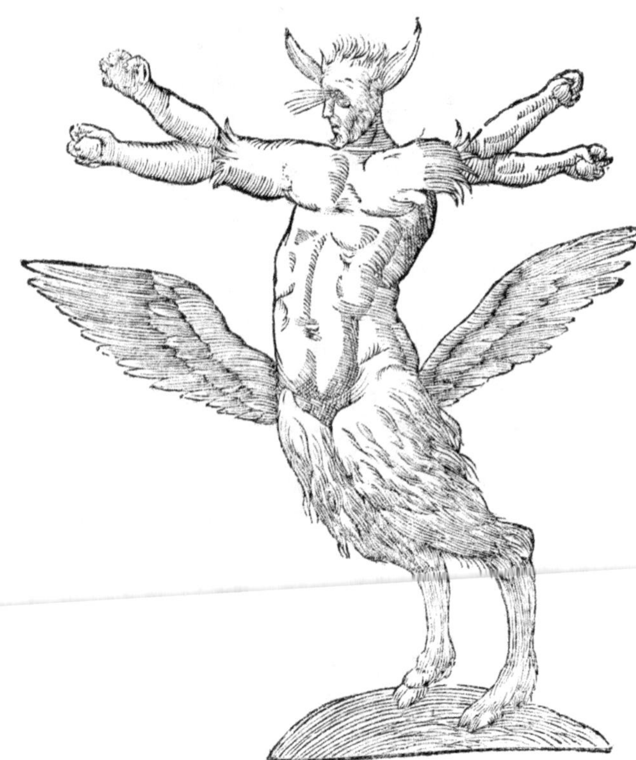

A247

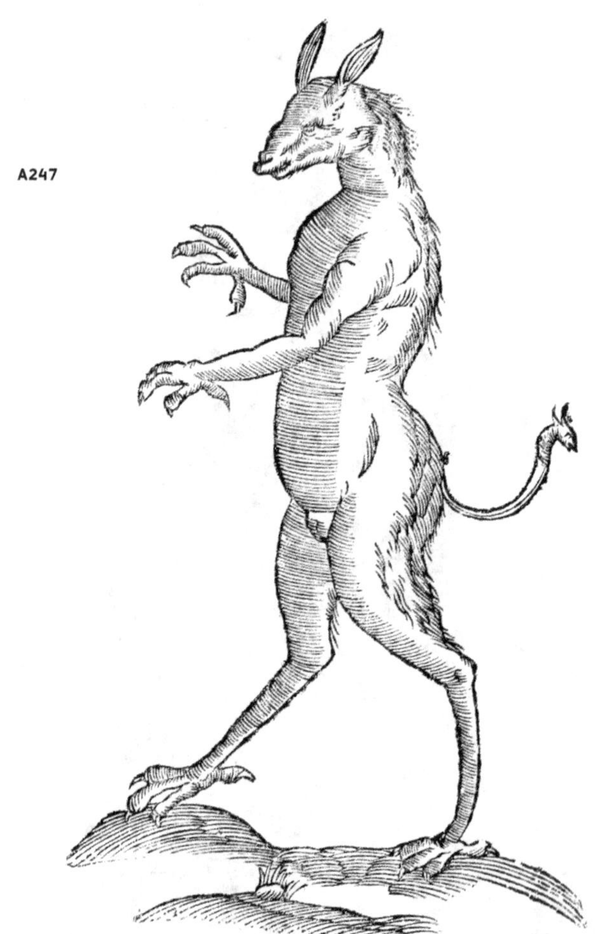

A249

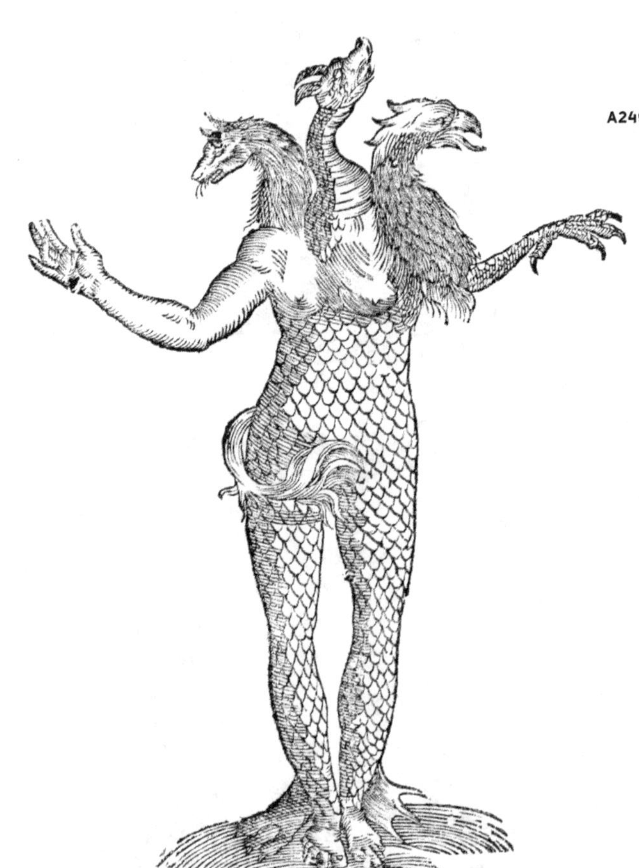

A250

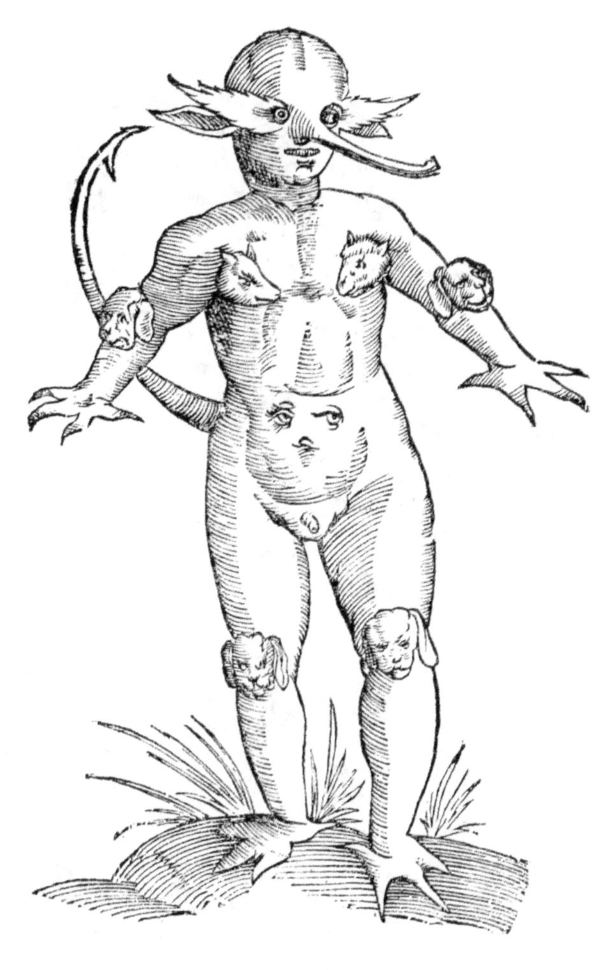

A251

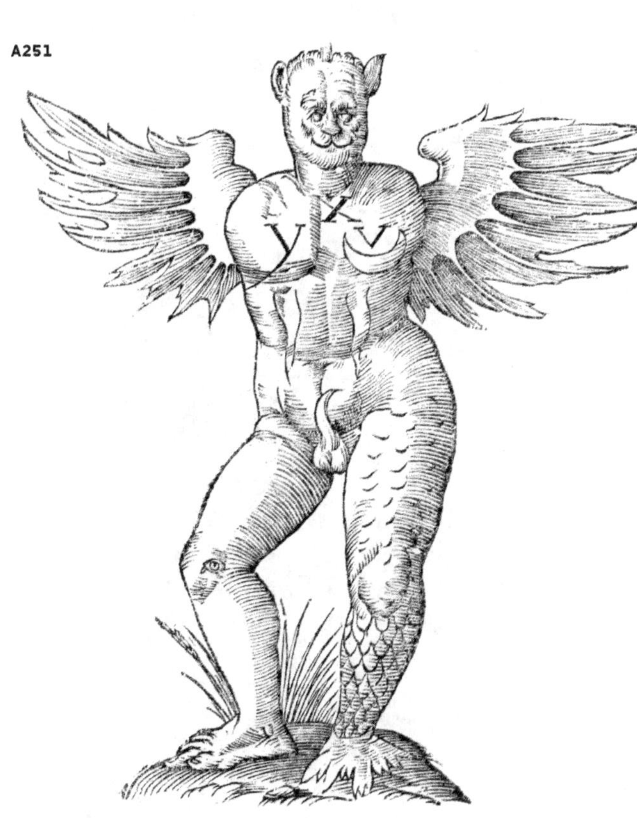

A252

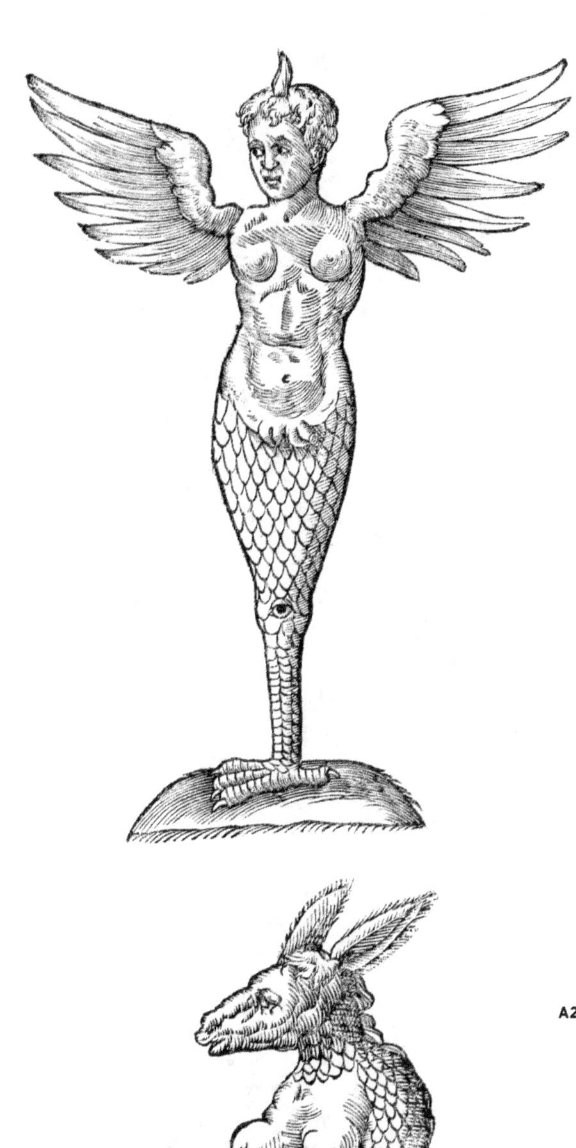

A253

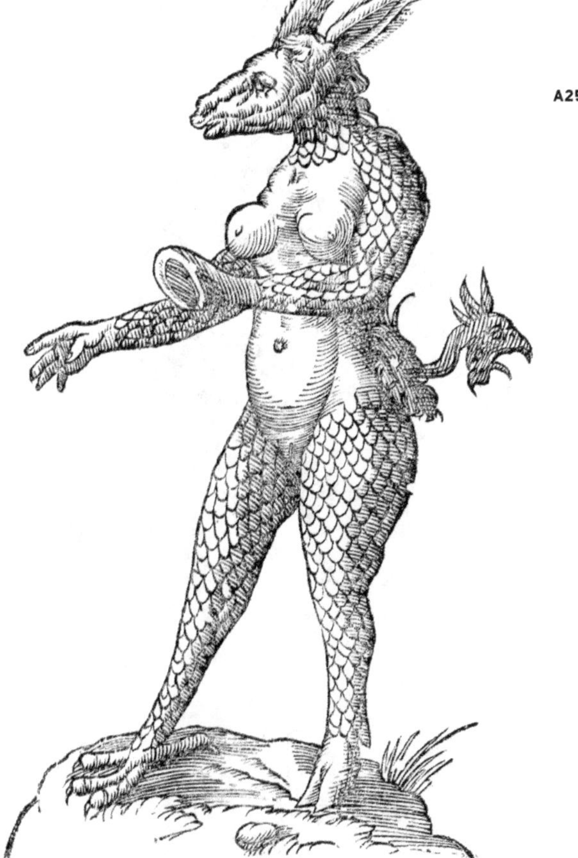

A254

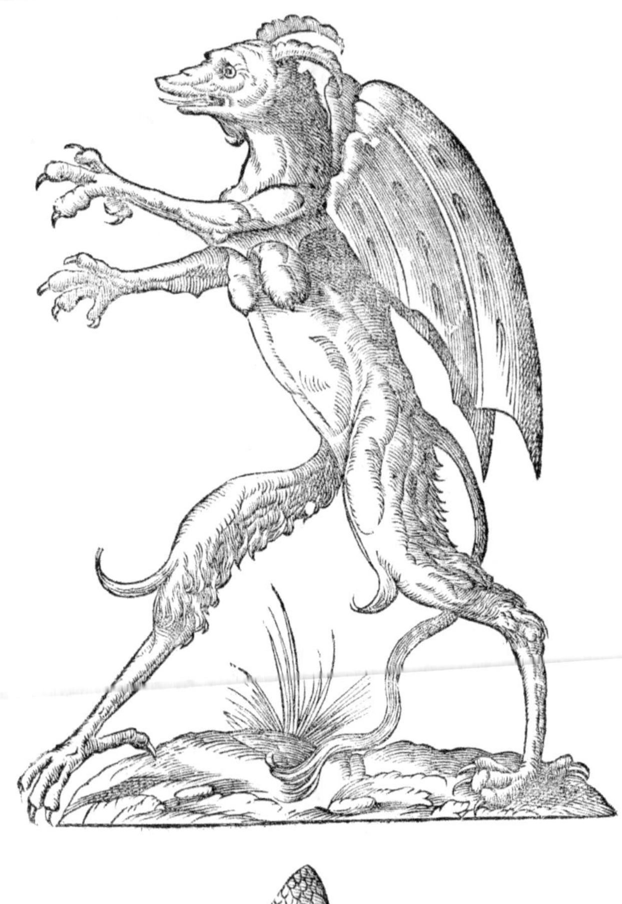

A256

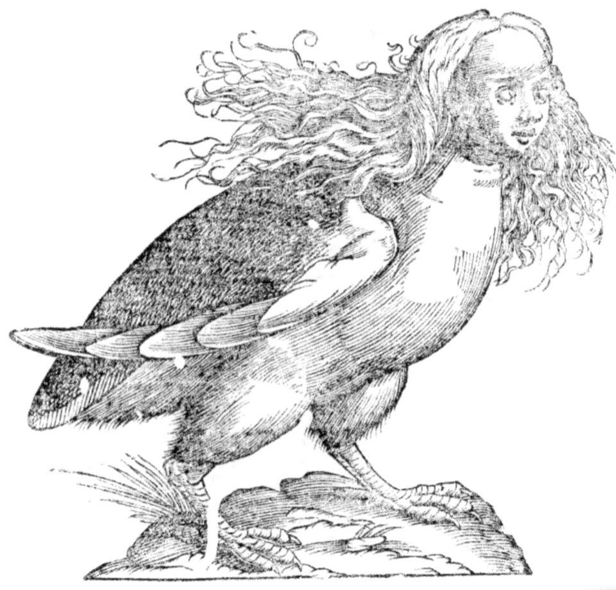

A257

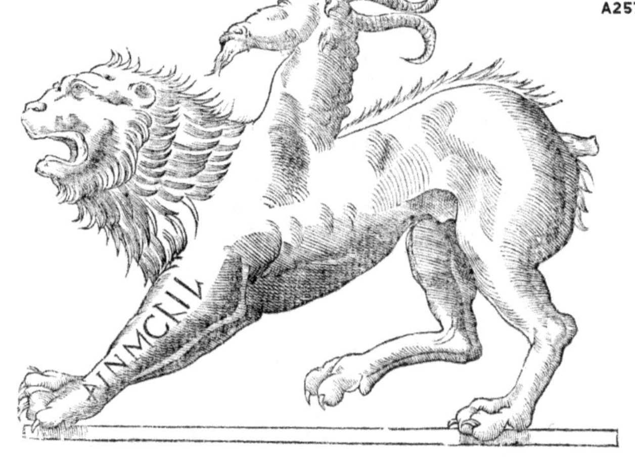

A255

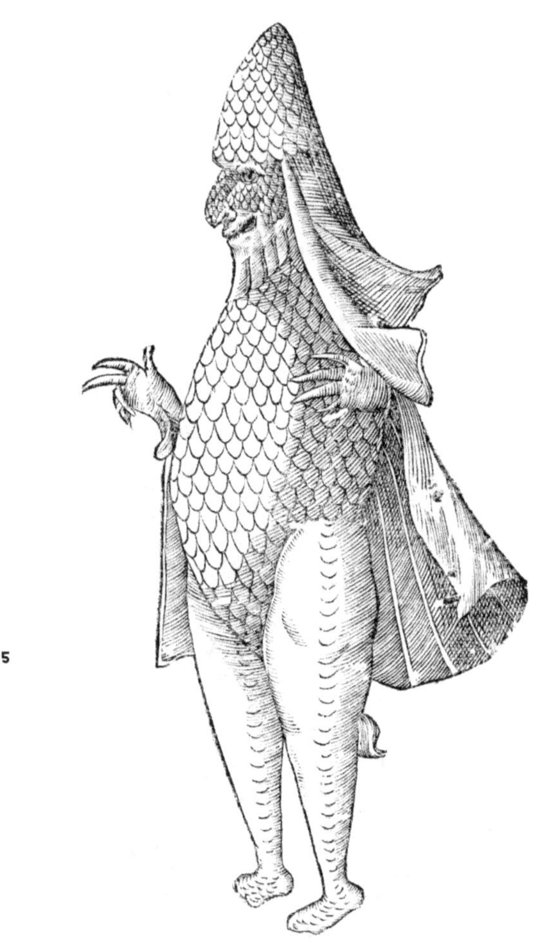

A258

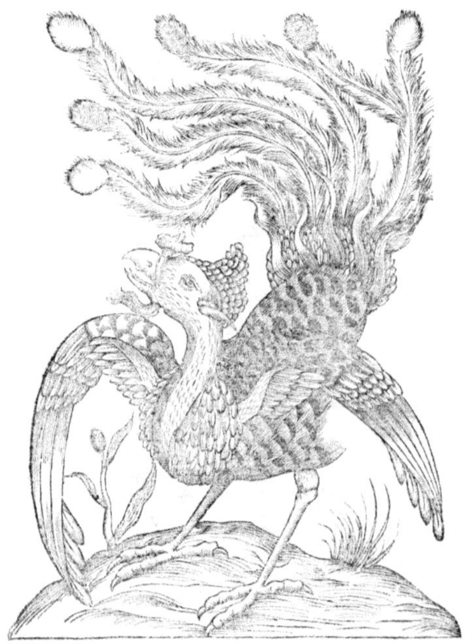

A220

A259

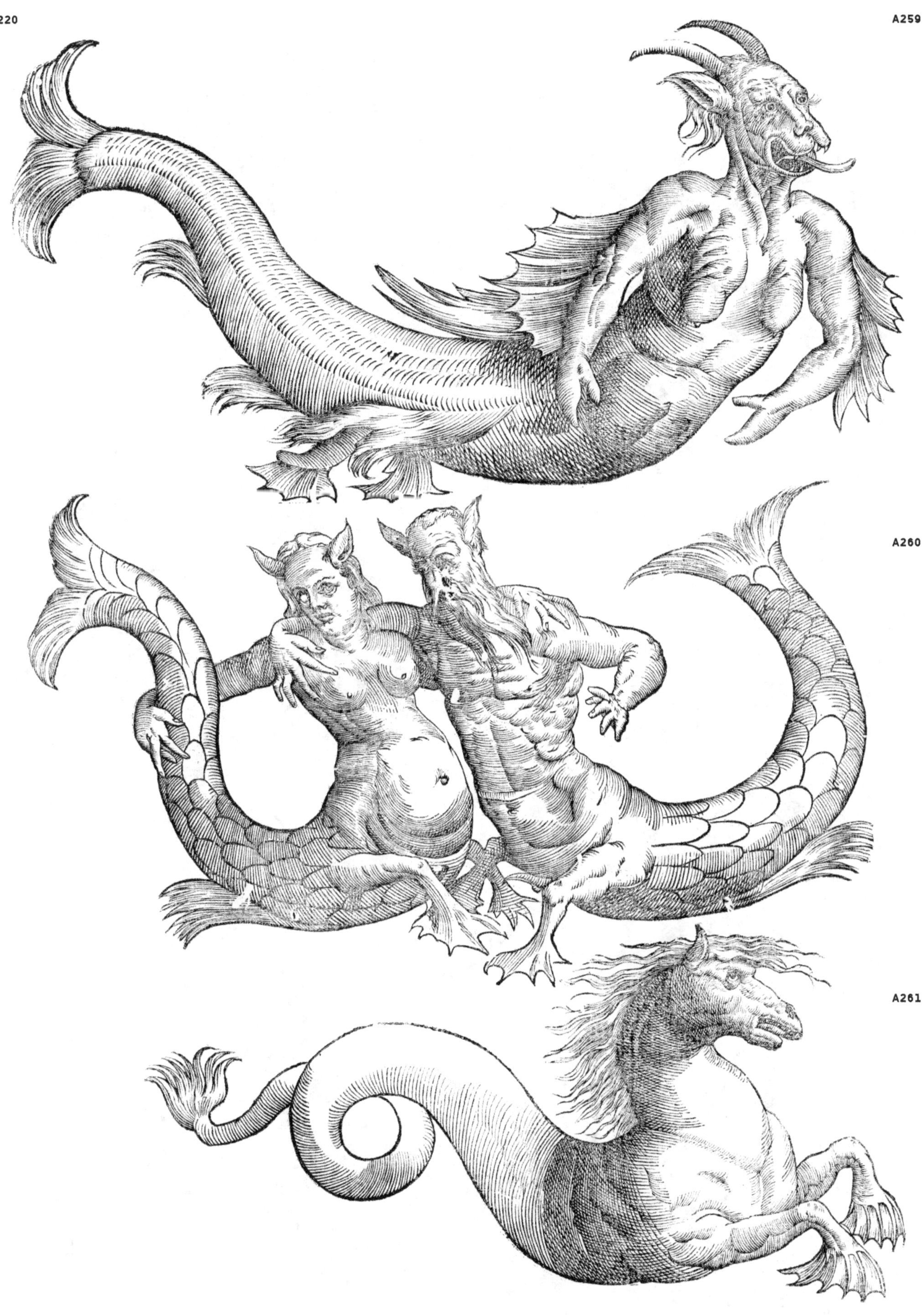

A260

A261

A262

A263

A264

A265

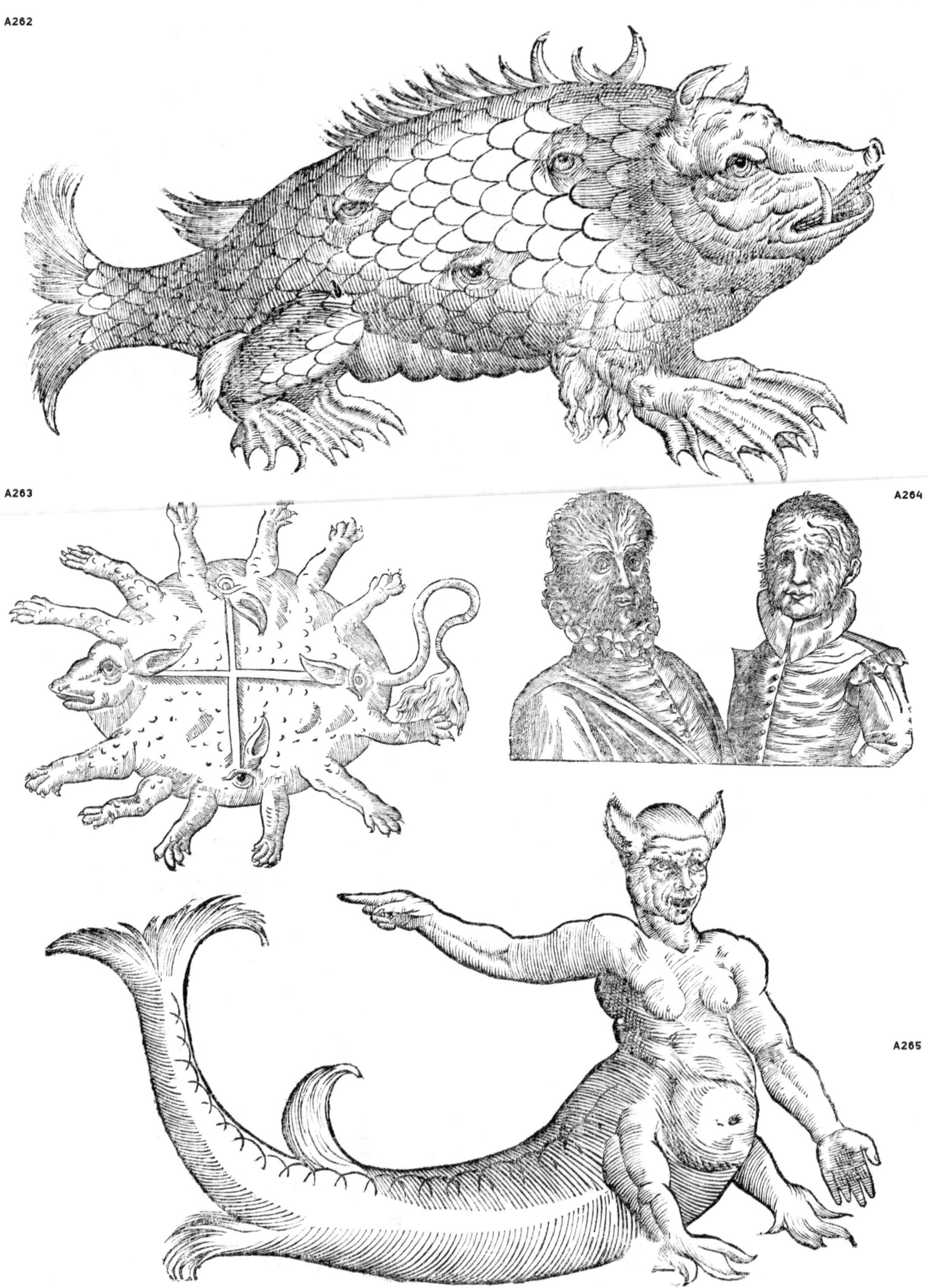

A266

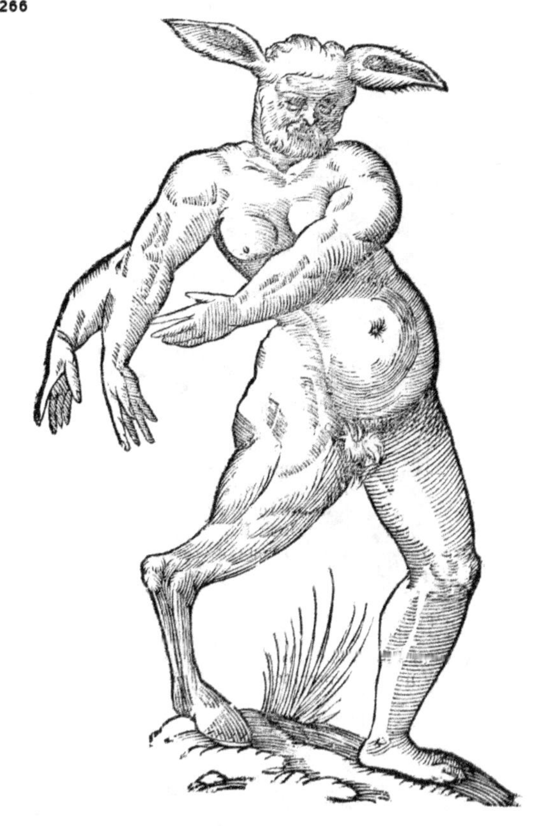

A268

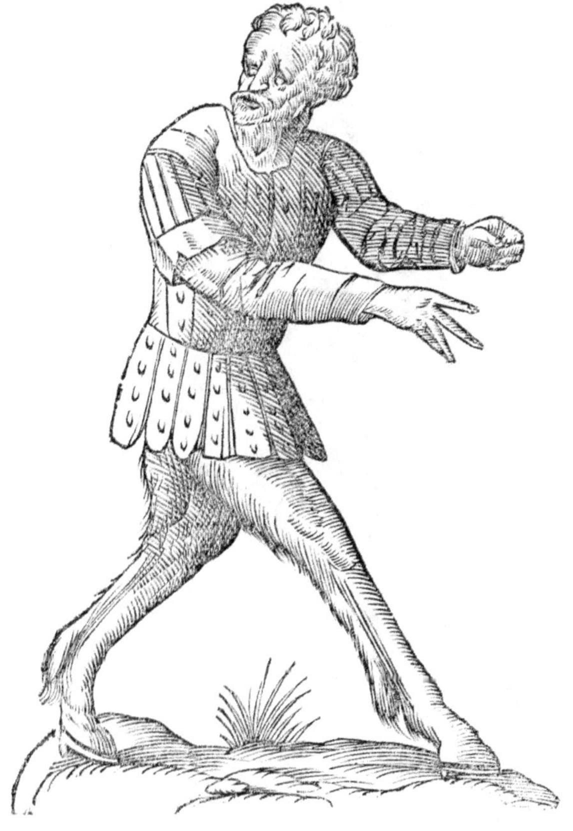

A267

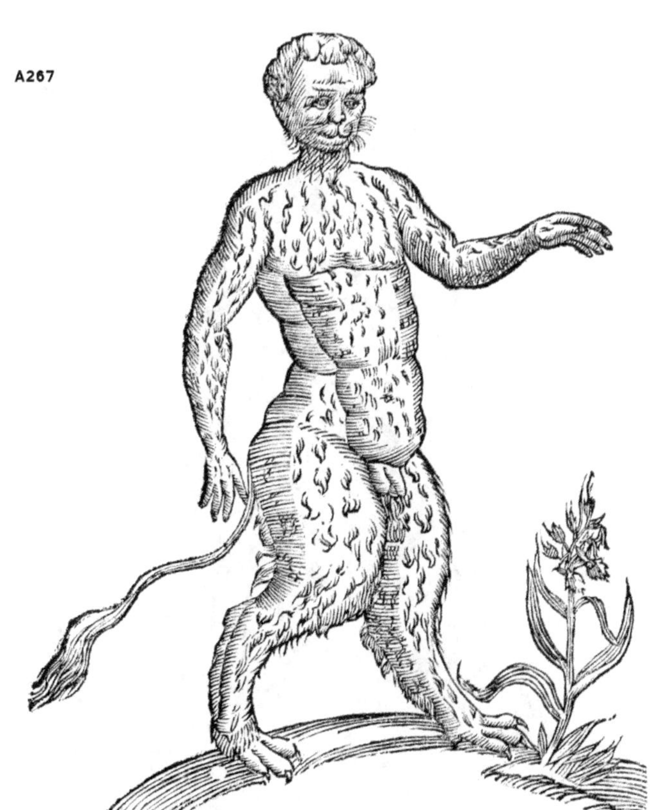

A269

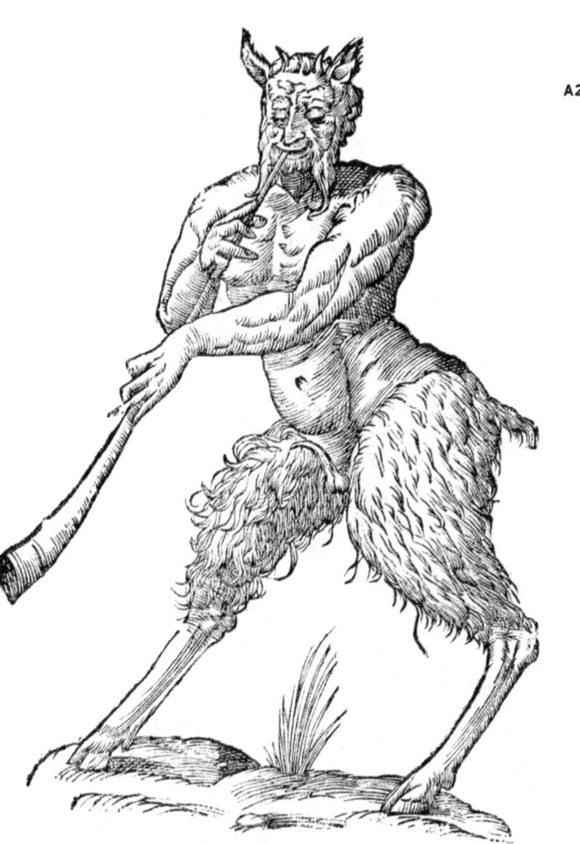

A270

A272

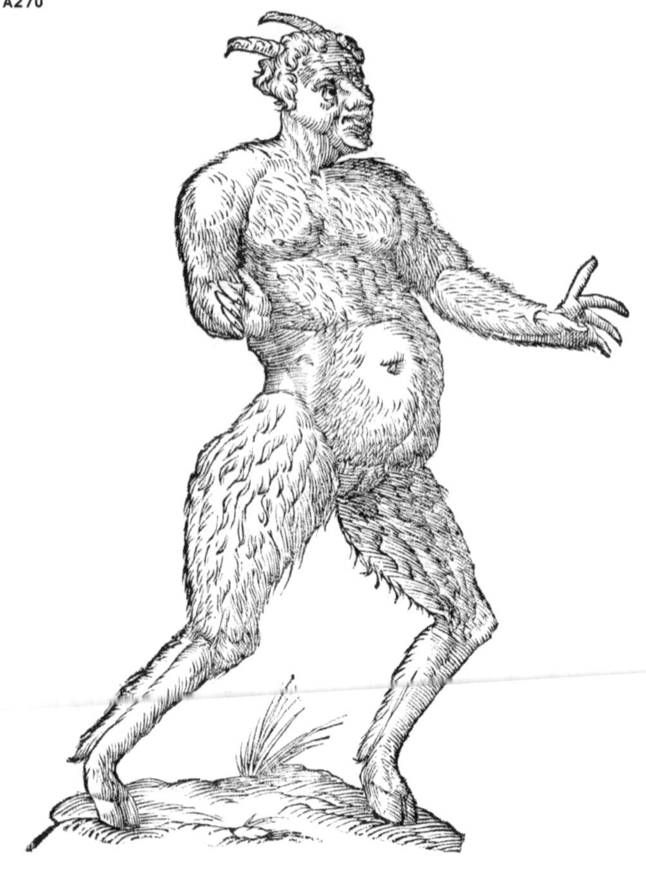

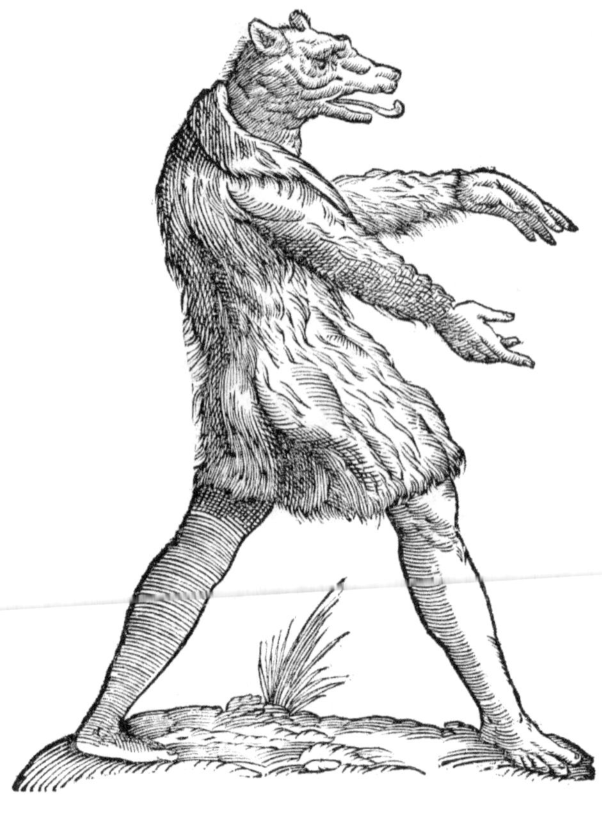

A271

A273

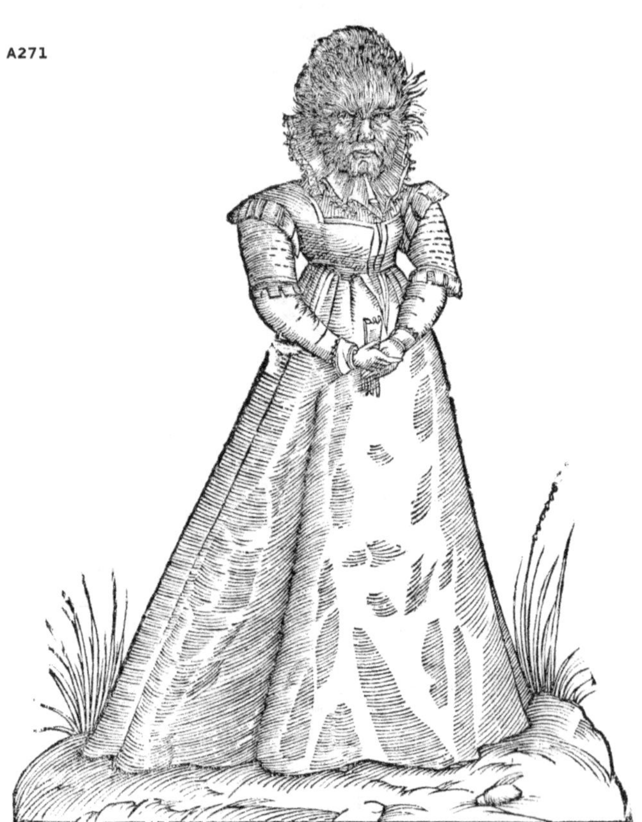

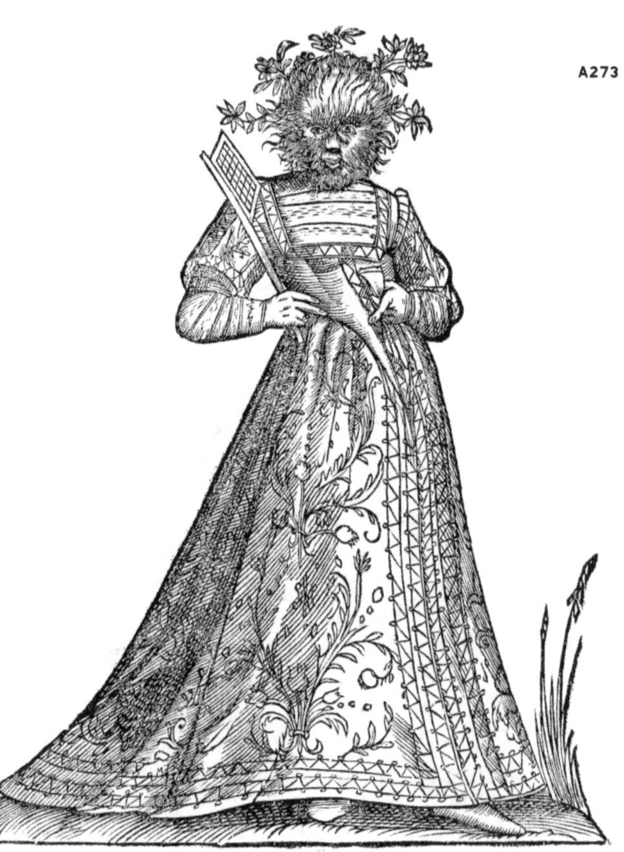

A274

A276

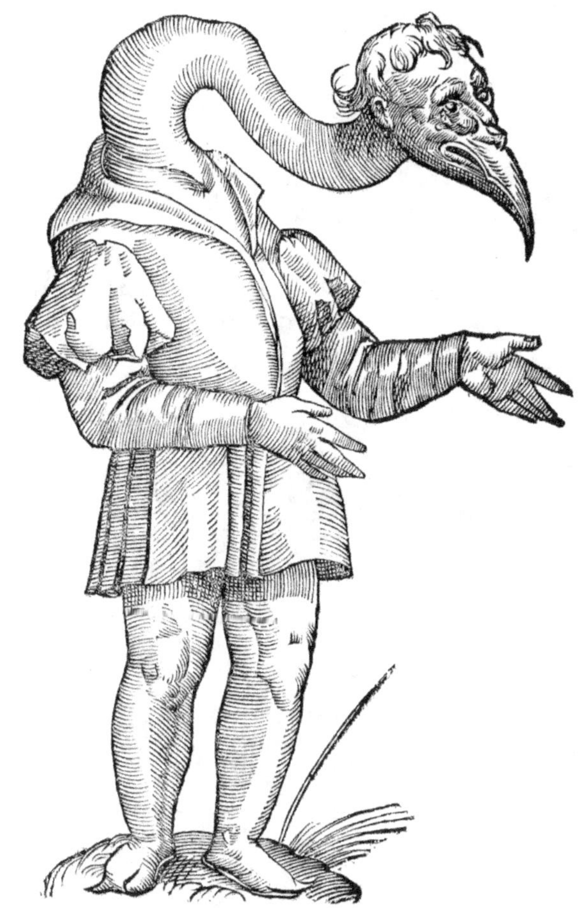

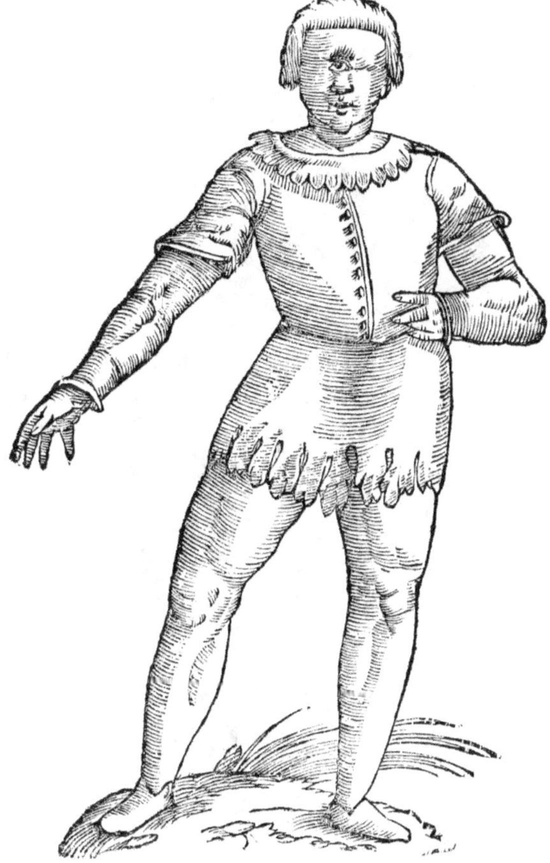

A275

A277

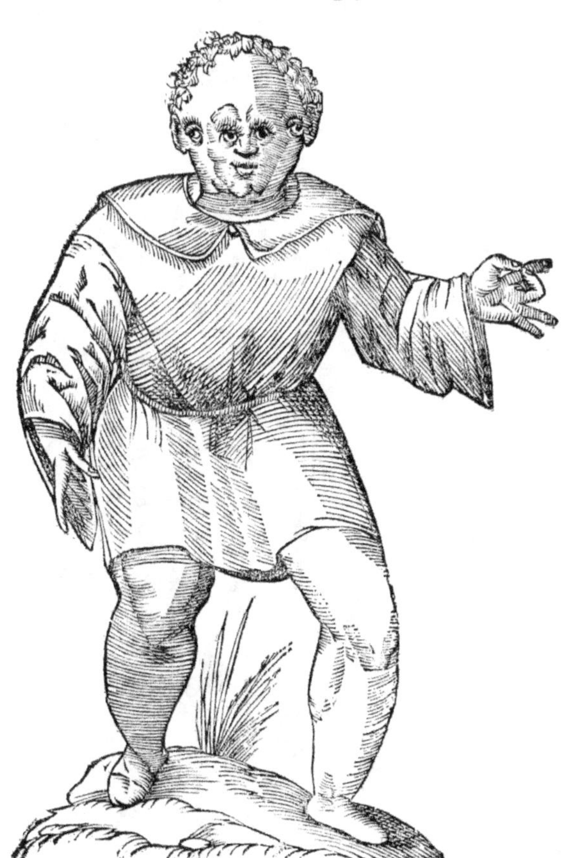

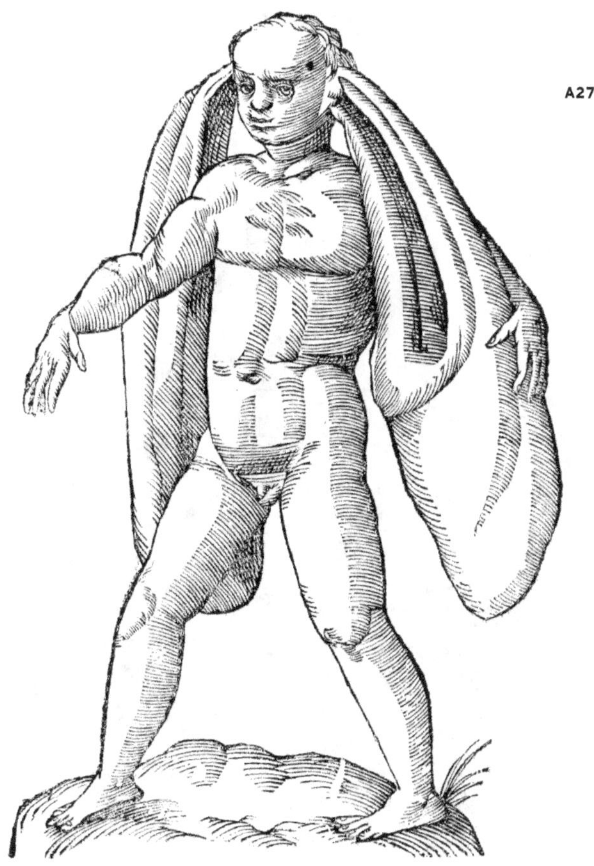

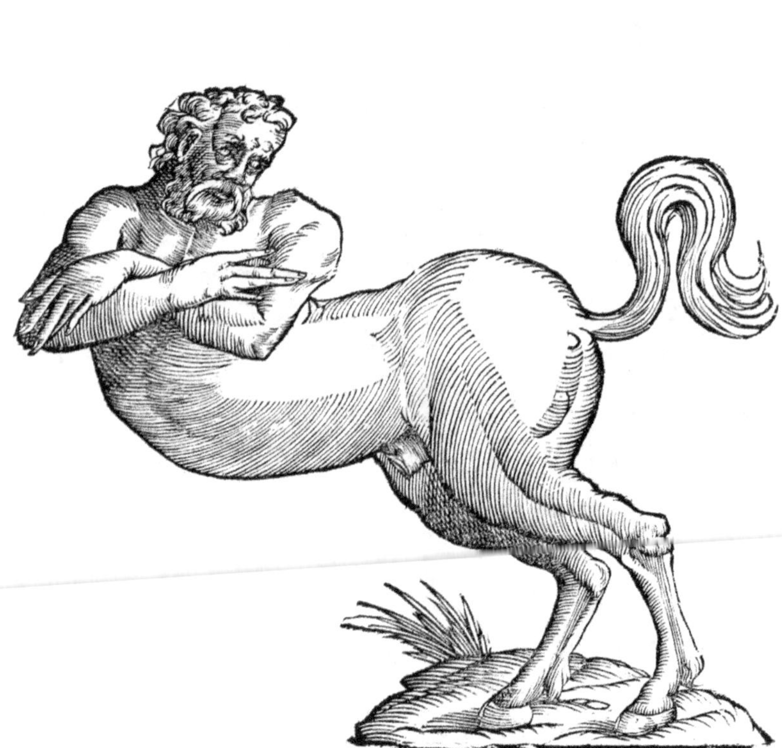

A279

A281

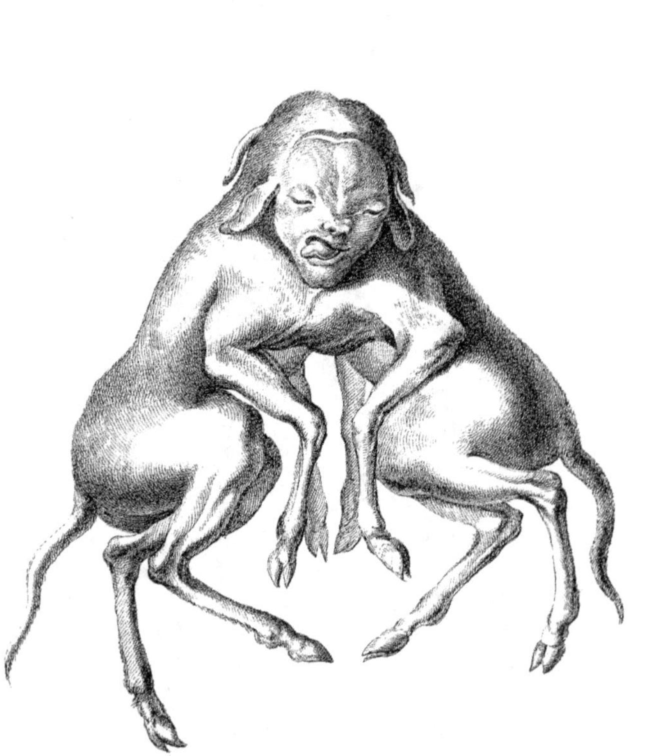

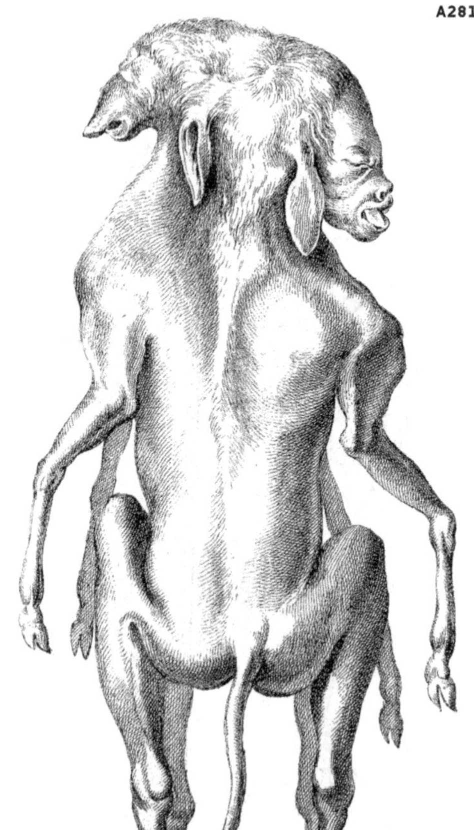

A282

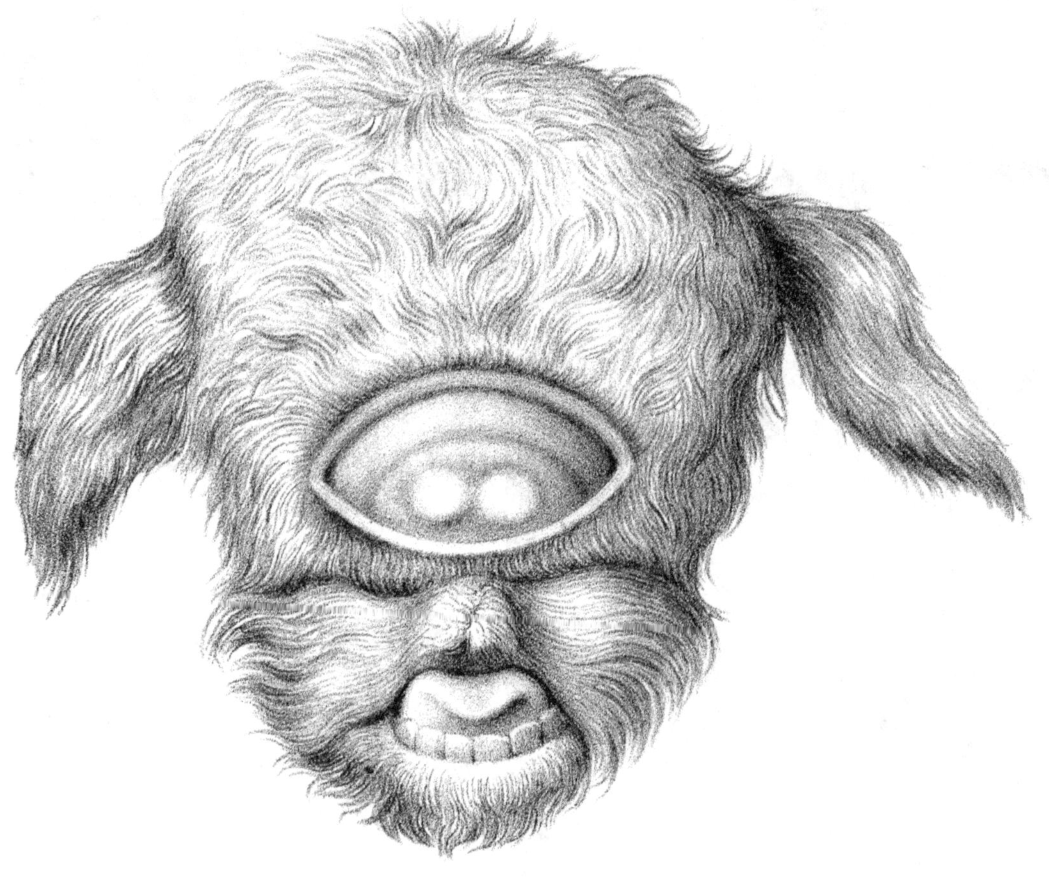

A283

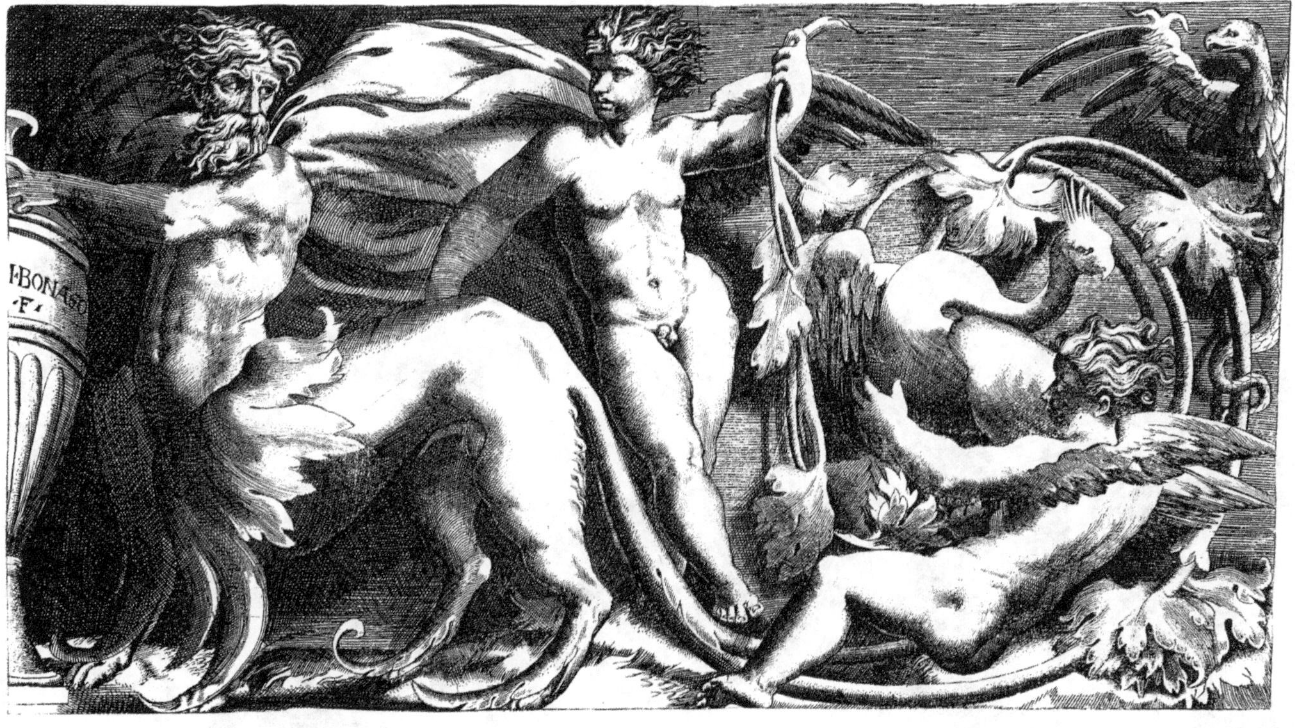

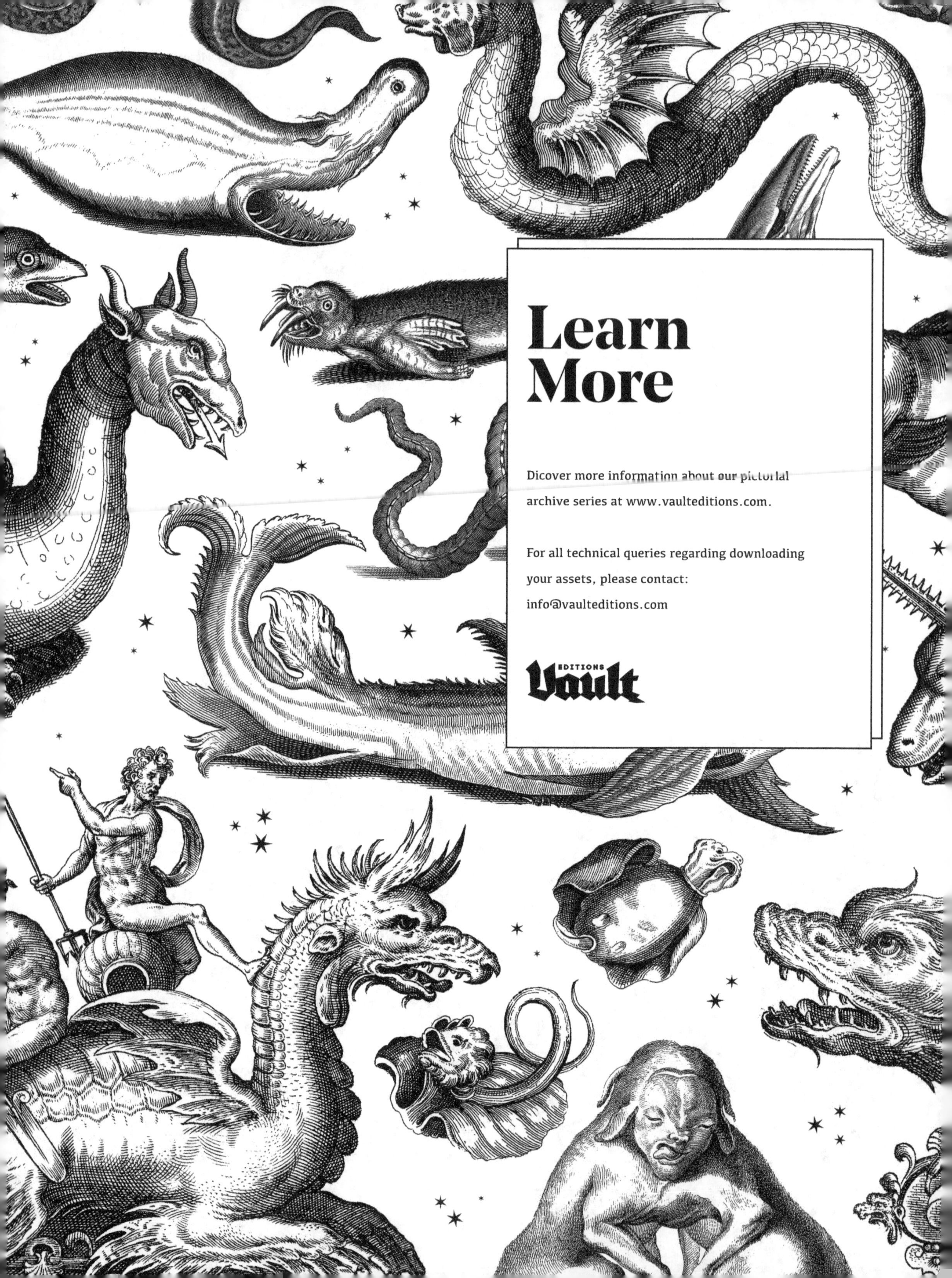
Learn
More

Dicover more information about our pictorial
archive series at www.vaulteditions.com.

For all technical queries regarding downloading
your assets, please contact:
info@vaulteditions.com

EDITIONS
Vault